PAUL KOCKELMAN

THE
CHICKEN
AND THE
QUETZAL

INCOMMENSURATE
ONTOLOGIES
AND PORTABLE VALUES
IN GUATEMALA'S
CLOUD FOREST

Duke University Press   Durham and London   2016

Printed in the United States of America on acid-free paper ∞
Designed by Heather Hensley
Typeset in Warnock Pro by Tseng Information Systems, Inc.

Library of Congress Cataloging-in-Publication Data
Kockelman, Paul, author.
The chicken and the quetzal : incommensurate ontologies
and portable values in Guatemala's cloud forest /
Paul Kockelman.
pages   cm
Includes bibliographical references and index.
ISBN 978-0-8223-6056-8 (hardcover : alk. paper)
ISBN 978-0-8223-6072-8 (pbk. : alk. paper)
ISBN 978-0-8223-7459-6 (e-book)
1. Culture and tourism—Social aspects—Guatemala.
2. Non-governmental organizations—Guatemala.
3. Kekchi Indians—Social life and customs. I. Title.
G155.G9K63 2016
306.4′81909728151—dc23
2015026282

Cover art: Quetzel: David Tipling / Alamy; rooster:
Radius Images / Alamy; background image:
Susan E. Degginger / Alamy.

For Mia, Zeno, and Lara

CONTENTS

ACKNOWLEDGMENTS

I first began working with speakers of Q'eqchi' in 1996, focusing my early efforts on the collection and use of a tree sap (*copal*) by recent immigrants to the tropical lowlands of northern Guatemala, who were making a living in and around the Biosphera Maya. This early research led to a three-year graduate research fellowship from the Environmental Protection Agency (1997–2000) for a project entitled "Commons Management among the Q'eqchi'-Maya," with a particular focus on the cognitive and political ecology of tropical rain forests in relation to migration and dispossession. This fellowship paid for most of graduate school at the University of Chicago and, with its generous research funds, almost all my early fieldwork. (That said, I actually applied for the fellowship while I was a student at the University of Michigan, having just taken an inspiring core course in cultural anthropology that was team-taught by Tom Fricke and Roy Rappaport, and where I was supported by a grant from the National Science Foundation, under the auspices of the Culture and Cognition program.) So thank you EPA, NSF, and UMich.

At the University of Chicago I was steeped not just in linguistic anthropology (taking classes with Norman McQuown, Bill Hanks, and Paul Friedrich, and having as my advisors John Lucy and Michael Silverstein), but also in "political economy" in a variety of manifestations. In part, this was because the first courses I took were with John Kelly and Moishe Postone, with their often maximally complementary concerns; and, in part, this was because there was no escaping the ideas and energies of Terrance Turner, Nancy Munn, Marshall Sahlins, and Jean and John Comaroff. And finally, during this phase of my training, a number of close friends—Mike Cepek, Jessica Jerome, Anya Bernstein, and Stephen Scott—contributed heavily to my early intellectual development, partly through a series of jointly undertaken conference panels (on indigenous intellectual property, Gramsci, value, and commensuration), and our conversations at and around these. This mishmash of teachers, friends, and influences led to a 2002 dissertation composed of two (only seemingly) irreconcilable halves, as evident in the title: "Minding Language and Measuring Labor: Stance and Subjectivity under Neoliberal Globalization." In short, thanks to a whole lot of people are in order—with special thanks to John Lucy, Beth Povinelli, and Michael Silverstein, who, during the writing of my dissertation, were particularly generous with their time and helpful with their suggestions.

On the way to writing this book I received a lot of good advice and inspiration from a number of places—but perhaps most notably John Haviland and Asif Agha, Judy Maxwell and Robert Hamrick, Paul Manning and Miyako Inoue, Gustave Peebles and Chris Ball, Joe Hankins and Rihan Yen, Laura Ahearn and Bruce Mannheim, Ben Smith and Zoe Crossland, Jim Wilce and Jessie Shipley, Tanya Luhrmann and Jane Guyer, Susan Gal and David Pedersen, Brian Larkin and Antina von Schnitzler, Walter Little and Joe Errington, Katie Stewart and John Hartigan, Tony Webster and Elizabeth Keating, Andrea Ballestero and Stephen Langdon, Drew Gilbert and Laura Kunreuther, Richard Parmentier and Vincent Colapietro, Paige West and Angie Heo, Danny Law and Sergio Romero, David Tavarez and Eben Kirksey, Paja Faudree and Gary Tomlinson. And since 2007, I have been in extended discussion with Julia Elyachar about many of the key themes in this book. Without her ideas, advice, and encouragement, I don't think it ever would have gotten written. The writings of Bill Maurer have also proved invaluable, as has his specific feedback on many parts of this monograph. And long conversations with Nick Enfield about interaction and distributed agency, language structure and cultural systems, and meaning and relationality also found their way into this monograph. Thank you.

In regard to Project Eco-Quetzal, David Unger was incredibly generous with his time and resources early on. And friends, coworkers, and interlocutors in the villages of Chicacnab, San Lucas, and Corozal and in the towns of Cobán, Chamelco, and Carchá were essential to this project; particular thanks to Flora, Alejandro, Gregorio, Elvira, Alberto, Angelina, Gregoria, Efraín, Maynor, Ermelina, and the families Yat Xol, Car Tun, and Pop Pop.

I want to thank the editors and staff of the journals *Public Culture*, *Language in Society*, and the *Journal of the Royal Anthropological Institute* for allowing me to incorporate parts of the following three articles into this book (which were radically transformed in content and style, as particular sections of chapters 1, 3, and 4): "A Mayan Ontology of Poultry: Selfhood, Affect, Animals, and Ethnography," *Language in Society* 40, no. 4 (2011): 427–54; "Number, Unit, and Utility in a Mayan Community: The Relation between Use-Value, Labor-Power, and Personhood," *Journal of the Royal Anthropological Institute* 13, no. 2 (2007): 401–17; "Enclosure and Disclosure," *Public Culture* 19, no. 2 (2007): 303–5.

And finally, I want to thank my editor Gisela Fosado at Duke University Press. Along with two reviewers, her suggestions were instrumental in transforming this monograph.

Introduction

A Strange Form of Sovereignty

In 1537, after the Spanish crown had failed to conquer the indigenous peoples living in what is now Alta Verapaz, Guatemala,
the Dominican Friar Bartolomé de Las Casas was permitted to
"pacify" the area through religious methods. As he seemed—
or at least claimed—to have succeeded, the name of the region
was changed from Tezulutlan (a Nahuatl word, meaning "Land
of War'") to Verapaz (a Spanish word, meaning "True Peace").
The governor of Guatemala granted the Dominicans full control
over the area—banning secular immigration, removing remaining military colonies, and nullifying previous land grants. For
almost three hundred years, it remained an apparently isolated
enclave, somewhat protected by the paternalism of the church,
at least in comparison to other parts of Guatemala. This isolation ended abruptly in the late 1800s, with the advent of coffee
growing, liberal reforms, and the immigration of Europeans. Divested of their land, and forced to work on coffee plantations,
indigenous speakers of Q'eqchi' began migrating north. Within
the last fifty years, this migration intensified, fueled by the civil
war that ravaged the countryside, with the Q'eqchi' fleeing not
only scarce resources and labor quotas, but also government
forces and paramilitary. In this way, the last century has seen the
Q'eqchi' population spread from Alta Verapaz, to the Petén, and

finally to Belize, Mexico, and the United States. Indeed, not just the second largest of some thirty Mayan languages (with upward of one million speakers), Q'eqchi' now has the largest percentage of monolinguals, and the fastest growing and geographically most extensive population of any ethnic group in Guatemala.[1]

Peace accords were signed in 1996, bringing to a ceremonial end a civil war that lasted almost forty years, claimed upward of 200,000 lives, upended communities and institutions throughout the country, and culminated in charges of genocide against one of its former heads of state. In the war's aftermath, hundreds of nongovernmental organizations were established, attempting to meet the often stated challenges of post–civil war society. These included overpopulation, deforestation, illiteracy, illness, poverty, damaged infrastructure, nonexistent democracy, and—as evinced in an explosion of vigilante justice in rural villages—a growing sense not only of state illegitimacy but of state impotence.

One of these organizations was Proyecto Eco-Quetzal (PEQ), which was founded in 1990 by German ecologists with the goal of protecting the numerous bird species that reside in Guatemala's remaining cloud forests. PEQ grew and diversified considerably over the years, its stated goals coming to include the promotion of alternative crafts, biomonitoring, intensive farming, soil conservation, sustainable development, disaster preparedness, literacy, health care, and conflict resolution. In other words, as it expanded and transformed, its functions extended into domains the state could not reach—a sphere that continually seemed to grow rather than shrink.

At the center of PEQ's interventions was the village of Chicacnab, itself located outside of Coban, the capital of Alta Verapaz. Given its relatively high altitude and remote location, and as per the NGO's initial goals, this village was surrounded by cloud forest. The cloud forest provided the perfect environment for a high density of endangered avifauna—in particular, the resplendent quetzal (*Pharomachrus mocinno*), which is also the national bird of Guatemala, the name of its currency, and an important figure in Mayan histories of the conquest.

Approximately eighty families lived in Chicacnab in 2000, each with an average number of six children, amounting to a total population of around six hundred people. Although some men, who had served time in the army or worked as itinerant traders, spoke fluent Spanish, the majority of villagers were monolingual speakers of Q'eqchi'. While all villagers engaged in corn-based or milpa agriculture, very few had enough land to meet all their subsistence needs. Most men in the village thus engaged in seasonal labor on plantations (often up to five months a year). Women dedicated their time to poultry husbandry. And many families engaged in itinerant trade (women weaving baskets and textiles for the men to sell).

To preserve the cloud forest that surrounded this community, and to protect it from "slash-and-burn" agriculture, Proyecto Eco-Quetzal initiated an ecotourism project. Its goal was to provide alternative sources of income to community members. In its efforts to promote global biodiversity and protect local key species, the main strategy of this NGO was to add value to local products (by marketing them internationally) and to add value-creating ability to local villagers (by educating and training them to recognize and produce such value), so that community members would be motivated in a way that was beneficial for both themselves and the cloud forest. In short, while the NGO began with the goal of protecting birds, it ended up not just creating new kinds of values, but creating new kinds of evaluating agents.

This book is about the relationship between meaning, measurement, materiality, and money. It develops an analytic framework for understanding the entanglement of what at first appear to be distinct values—use value (function), exchange value (price), semantic value (meaning), and deontic value (morality). It foregrounds the relation between enclosure and disclosure, showing the ways in which processes that create, interpret, and reveal values are concomitant with processes that capture, carry, and reify them. It examines the conditions and consequences of making valued entities and evaluating agents seem relatively portable, in the sense of being widely applicable, contextually independent, and scale-free. This analytic lens is used to offer a cultural history of a Mayan village in the early twenty-first century—a community surrounded by vigilante violence and opened to ecotourists, situated at the end of civil war and the onset of neoliberal reforms, and standing at the edge of the Guatemalan state and the center of a strange form of sovereignty.

Enclosure and Disclosure

In certain historical and ethnographic contexts, scholars such as Marx (1967) and Evans-Pritchard (1940) used what at first appeared to be simple objects to disclose ensembles of meaningful relations: the commodity in modern capitalist society, or cattle among the Nuer. Around such "objects"—understood as ensembles of social relations, semiotic practices, and material processes—these scholars elucidated modes of perceiving and acting, thinking and feeling, categorizing and evaluating. Indeed, so extensive was the reach of such objects that the ensembles they disclosed constituted the grounds of collective existence insofar as they mediated space and time, substance and form, quality and quantity, ontology and cosmology. Moreover, in the hands of these devoted scholars, such relational ensembles were epistemologically immanent, that is, simultaneously objects to be interpreted and methods of interpretation. Finally, at least in the work of Marx, such modes of *disclosure*—such techniques of revealing, opening, unfolding, and elucidating—were tightly coupled with modes of knowledge and power. To paraphrase Francis Bacon, and taking the term *nature* to include "second nature" (and "*n*th-natures" more generally), if the task of knowledge is to find for a given nature the source of its coming-to-be, the task of power is to superinduce on a given body a new nature (Bacon [1620] 2000: 102; Kockelman 2012b).

Ethnography—and critical theory more generally—is not only a mode of disclosure but also a mode of enclosure. Enclosure has many interrelated meanings, but prototypically involves processes of objectification, formatting, stabilization, dispossession, and containment. For example, there are enclosures in the everyday sense: not only zoos, cages, museums, and jails, but also biological reserves, clean rooms, and chicken coops (Bacon [1627] 2002). There is enclosure as aestheticization: to give intelligibility, form, and permanence to things that are otherwise distant, murky, and fleeting (Bakhtin 1990). There is enclosure as *bios*: biography as a kind of interpretive frame that gives a human life meaning, coherence, and closure (Arendt 1998). There is enclosure in the sense of physical objectivity: being continuously present to the senses, surrounded by a medium, detachable from context, and transportable across contexts (Gibson 1986). There is enclosure as the extension of a network: creating the conditions for scientific objects to reproduce their effects outside the laboratory (Latour 1988). There is enclosure as *interresement*: incorporating and regimenting possible relations among agents, and thus the identities of agents, through definitions and interventions that problematize them in particular ways (Callon 1986). There is enclosure in the sense of scientific objectivity: a form of knowledge that is spatially and temporally portable, so far as it holds good independently of the process of its production (Porter 1995). There is enclosure as articulation: conferring propositional content on an experience, and hence the possibility of truth value, by means of making an assertion. There is enclosure as deontization: the process of creating, articulating, rationalizing, and enforcing norms, and thereby constituting laws (Maine [1866] 2002). There is enclosure as entextualization (Silverstein and Urban 1996): the process of making multiple signs cohere as "text," and thereby seem amenable to cross contextual interpretation. There is enclosure as commodification: on the one hand, the conditions by which something is alienated, unitized, quantified, standardized, and priced; and on the other hand, the conditions by which something is produced, circulated, and consumed. Following Whorf (1956), there is the enclosure of formless substances with substanceless forms, as evinced in any set of measures: for example, pats of butter, bolts of cloth, square meters of space, hours of time, and bricks of gold. There is enclosure as productive labor: making products that last beyond the production process itself, such that they may be more widely circulated, and ultimately more highly valued, before being consumed (Smith [1776] 1976). There is polis-ization (Fustel de Coulanges [1873] 1955): the art of making a wall, be it symbolic or material, that encloses a body politic, such that values on the inside of the wall, in confrontation with those on the outside, seem relatively shared—a language, a morality, an economy, a technology, a system of weights and measures, a structure of feelings, a sovereignty. And finally, following scholars like Marx, Polanyi, and Foucault, there is the historical phenomenon of enclosure: on the one hand, that process whereby common lands were turned into private property, and peasants became proletariat; and on the other hand, that process whereby such doubly "freed" persons—from both masters and means of production—were brought into disciplinary institutions, from the workhouse to the asylum.

Crucially, there are also the limit figures that seem to escape from, or at least reside at the edges of, such enclosures (Kockelman 2013b, 2015). This book is, in part, about such figures—perhaps best understood as figurations (Deleuze 2003).

With all these processes (and potentials) in mind, two overarching claims of this book are as follows: Various modes of enclosure are both the condition and consequence of disclosure. That is, knowledge of and power over (and profit from) any given domain is both facilitated by, and productive of, various forms of enclosure. And, in this vein, anthropology has a relatively precarious position: on the one hand, it seeks to interpret local modes of enclosure and disclosure; and, on the other hand, its interpretations at once enclose and disclose.

The Portability of Value

Most of the things that surround us may be interpreted in a variety of ways and thereby construed in terms of different kinds of value. For example (and to radically simplify for the sake of explication), this assemblage of metal, plastic, and ink that I hold in my hand can be wielded as an instrument (used to write a letter). It can be exchanged as a commodity (sold for $5). And it can be represented with an utterance (referred to as a "pen"). Loosely speaking, it is simultaneously caught up in use value (function), exchange value (price), truth value (semantic meaning), and many other kinds of value besides. One contribution of this book is to argue that such seemingly distinct kinds of value are best understood from a common theoretical framework. This aspect of the book thereby stands at the intersection of studies of material culture, political economy, and linguistic anthropology.

Evaluated things are bound to evaluating people. Whoever wields, exchanges, and refers can be framed as an agent (e.g., capable of flexibly wielding means toward ends). They can be framed as a subject (e.g., capable of holding mental states and expressing speech acts). They can be framed as a self (e.g., capable of being the means and ends of their own actions, or the object of their own private and public representations). And they can be framed as a person (e.g., capable of bearing sociopolitical rights and responsibilities). Loosely speaking, they are simultaneously a locus of causation, representation, reflexivity, and accountability (Kockelman 2013a). Another contribution of this book is to show concretely how such value-oriented capacities are themselves both mediated by, and mediating of, ontologies, infrastructure, and interaction.

As shown in the previous section, hand in hand with the disclosure of value is the enclosure of value. For example, for people to attain power over, gain knowledge about, or profit from a given practice may involve aestheticization as much as objectification, commoditization as much as entextualization, *interresement* as much as dispossession. That is, processes that create, interpret, and reveal value are concomitant with processes that capture, carry, and reify value. A third contribution of this book is to analyze the conflicts and contradictions that arise when evaluating people and evaluated things are subject to processes of enclosure and disclosure. This aspect of the book develops a relatively open-ended and multidimensional framework to characterize a series of complex, interrelated processes that are usually lumped together, if not elided altogether, under rubrics such as "quantification," "objectification," "commensuration," and "abstraction" (themselves often taken to be the essential quality of some "modern condition"). In particular, it examines the conditions and consequences of making value (and thus both valued entities and evaluating agents) seem relatively *portable* (Kockelman and Bernstein 2013), in the sense of being widely applicable, contextually independent, or scale-free.

More carefully, portability might be best understood as a way of characterizing the degree to which the meaningfulness and means-ends-fullness of a medium is, *or at least seems to be*, applicable to many contents and applicable in many contexts (at various degrees of scale). For example, and in a relatively abstract sense, the different and diverse forms of enclosure detailed above all contribute to the relative portability of a given medium. Crucially, to be applicable in many contexts does not so much mean that a medium is independent of context, but rather that the context the medium is dependent on can be recovered from the medium, transported with it, or established wherever it is found. Relatedly, to be applicable to many contents does not so much mean that a medium is preternaturally primed for the contents of any domain it should encounter, but rather that it has the capacity to assimilate such contents to itself, or accommodate itself to such contents, on the fly or after the fact. Such a focus is inherently reflexive, as the conceptual framing I develop in this book is designed to be relatively portable—simultaneously able to do justice to the vicissitudes of village life and the analytic categories of a particular kind of critical ethnography.

Summary of Chapters

This monograph tells a small story of a village and an NGO, the microhistory of each around the turn of the century, and the ethnographic details of their encounter. While speakers of Q'eqchi' are the most obvious protagonists, the NGO and ecotourists, biologists and anthropologists, cloud forests and conservation movements, and even chickens and quetzals, also play large roles. In telling this ethnographic story, I also attempt to tell a small analytic story—about meaning and value, quality and quantity, materiality and objectivity, utility and modality, commensuration and governance, ephemerality and portability, and ontologies in transformation.

Chapters 1 and 4 concern the relation between the village and the NGO, with a particular focus on the genealogy of the project's various interventions and the impact of ecotourism on village institutions. Chapters 2 and 3 treat the logic and history of village-specific practices that played a key role in mediating this village-NGO relation: poultry husbandry as an understudied mode of production and reproduction, and replacement and grading as poorly understood modes of replenishment and measurement. Such chapters thereby offer a sociocultural history of the semiotic entanglement of actors evaluating (ostensibly) overlapping worlds by (seemingly) incommensurate ontologies.

In chapter 1, "NGOs, Ecotourists and Endangered Avifauna," I detail the history of the NGO's interventions in the village of Chicacnab, paying particular attention to its fostering of the ecotourism project as a means to promote conservation of the cloud forest. I foreground the tense relation between immaterial labor (qua commodified interactions between villagers and tourists), intersubjective intentions (qua shared goals underlying joint activities), and incommensurable values (qua disparate evaluative standards grounding practical reasoning). The first part of this chapter discusses the rationale of the NGO's attempts to govern the behavior of villagers, while simultaneously detailing the range of its interventions, for example, biomonitoring and disaster preparedness, candle making and organic agriculture, language teaching and environmental awareness, traditional crafts and ecotourism. Building on this analysis, the second part of the chapter turns from the strategic and practical impulse of the project's interventions to the limits of its achievement. By way of an ethnographic description of a group of ecotourists, and the day-to-day workings of the NGO itself, I show the discrepancy and overlap between the project's portrayal of a standardized ecotour and ecotourists' actual experiences, demonstrating how different kinds of values (such as morality and money) and distinct forms of personhood (such as villagers and tourists) were and were not made commensurate. Later chapters will systematically detail the effects such an impulse had on village social relations.

In chapter 2, "A Mayan Ontology of Poultry," I focus on women's care for chickens, and the key role animal husbandry plays in the domestic mode of production. In some sense, this chapter takes what at first seems to be the most portable of animals and shows its radical rootedness in a particular cultural history. It is ethnographically organized around various frames on, or local figurations of, the relation between women and chickens, the relation between chickens and other species, and the relation between Q'eqchi'-speaking women and other identities. It offers one way of analyzing some of the myriad semiotic and social relations underlying the entangling of various "life frames" and "frames of life" (Kockelman 1999a, 1999b, 2005, 2011). The first part is the most stereotypically linguistic and symbolic. It details a variety of frames, ranging from lexical taxonomies surrounding domestic animals, to ontological qualities related to *not* being a mammal and *not* having a self that are revealed in the context of discursive disruptions. The second part is the most stereotypically economic and material. It focuses on social relations mediated by the reproduction, distribution, and consumption of chickens. And the third part is the most stereotypically psychological and subject centered. It focuses on a cluster of frames, ranging from modes of action emergent in situations of disruption, such as the attack of a chicken hawk, to local forms of illness and the relation between pregnant women and brooding hens. I analyze these frames in terms of three key themes: *ontology* (what kinds of entities there are in the world), *affect* (cognitive and corporeal attunements to such entities), and *selfhood* (relatively reflexive centers of attunement). Broadly speaking, I argue that these three themes are empirically, methodologically, and theoretically inseparable—each must be simultaneously attended to if one is to understand the others.

In chapter 3, "From Reciprocation to Replacement," rather than asking how two use values can have the same exchange value, a central concern of philosophers from Aristotle through Marx, I ask how two distinct entities can have the same use value (and what we might usefully mean by this term in the first place). Among the Q'eqchi' Maya, replacement (*eeqaj*) refers to activities as disparate as house-building, civil-religious elections, vengeance, loans, illness cures, adultery, namesakes, and resource-replenishment. Such practices involve the substitution of one entity for another entity, insofar as these entities have shared properties, and insofar as they hold a role in an obligatory position. For example, one man may substitute his labor for another man's labor insofar as men have similar degrees of strength and skill, and insofar as a position in a labor pool must be filled. Concomitant with this analysis of replacement, I foreground practices of grading (such as "this bag is very heavy") in comparison to practices of quantification (such as "this bag weighs fifty pounds"). I show the importance of grading to all things anthropological, focusing on the social relations, cultural values, and historical processes that get expressed and elaborated through such practices. Through the lens of grading, I analyze replacement as a process whereby substances get utilized, unitized, and numericalized, or qualified and quantified more generally. And I theorize this local articulation of use value in terms of labor power (or *potentia*, more generally) and personhood (as a particular *kinding* of human potentia). Finally, and perhaps most generally, I show how *quantia* are prior to *qualia*.

Chapter 4, "From Measurement to Meaning," uses the institution of replacement (as it plays out in the context of labor pooling and house building) as a lens to examine long-term transformations in social relations brought on by the NGO's ecotourism project. I analyze what happens to local values when there are pressures for people, objects, and activities to change from being equivalent (via the local system of replacement) to being commensurate (via the money-making opportunities initiated by ecotourism). And I track how local ontologies, and the values embedded therein, enable and constrain the recoding of such values and the rechanneling of such pressures. I argue that this pressure to move from equivalency to commensurability was facilitated by the NGO's interventions, which helped to produce not only "irreplaceable" persons (via the new modes of immaterial labor in which only certain villagers were capacitated to engage), but also signs of these persons' nonreplaceability (via the awards and certificates villagers were given and the new and highly visible houses in which they were encouraged to live). I argue that the project's strategies and techniques inadvertently resonated with this system of replacement, rather than displaced it. That is, whereas replacement was once a condition for local values (constituting, as it were, the systematic provisioning of social life), irreplaceability (as opposed to commensurability per se) became, for those villagers implicated in the ecotourism project, a value in itself.

As will become clear, across these chapters, I focus on the conditions for, and ramifications of, successful and unsuccessful *transformations*, a deliberately wide notion that includes more stereotypic processes (such as "translation" and "transaction") as distinct species. That is, I focus on how, why, and to what effect different actors made or broke, or failed to make and break, various kinds of *equivalences*—practical, conceptual, monetary, and moral (among many others).

In the conclusion, "Paths, Portability, and Parasites," I take up such issues at length, theorizing a variety of tightly coupled frames of equivalence—or modes of transformation—whereby two entities (qualia, events, individuals, processes, etc.) that are otherwise differentially positioned, may be connected by a kind of path, or "third." I review the wide range of paths that are detailed in this monograph, such as codes and channels, functions and algorithms, norms and laws, virtues and force fields, aesthetic compositions and material productions, identities and types, metaphors and markets, theories and habits, inter alia. And I review the even wider range of ways such paths could parasitically go awry, arguing that the "functioning" of such paths is best understood in terms of their capacity to fail (Kockelman 2010a). To do this, I focus on the ways such paths were created, distributed, and regimented during my fieldwork, constituting interactions as much as institutions, imaginaries as much as infrastructures, as instigated by the NGO as much as by villagers. By pointing back to each of the foregoing chapters, and by synthesizing the various senses of value, ontology, portability, and equivalence that have been deployed along the way, this chapter acts as a summary as much as an extension of the entire book. Phrased another way, the conclusion reflexively reframes an ensemble of empirically motivated interpretive conclusions in relatively portable terms, such that they may be understood as applying to a much wider range of contents, as applicable in a much wider range of contexts. More intrepid readers are welcome to read it now if they wish.

CHAPTER 1

NGOs, Ecotourists, and Endangered Avifauna

IMMATERIAL LABOR, INCOMMENSURATE VALUES,
AND INTERSUBJECTIVE INTENTIONS

Early Scientific Expedition

In the spring of 1989, ten German ecologists traveled to Guatemala to evaluate the extent and condition of cloud forest—the ecological home of the resplendent quetzal. Their endeavor was sponsored by the Landesbund für Vogelschutz, an organization dedicated to protecting the endangered avifauna of Germany and the world. Using satellite photos, they located all the regions in Guatemala where cloud forest still remained, an area approximately nineteen hundred square kilometers in size. Under the assumption that cloud forest requires a minimum annual rainfall of 2,000 mm, and a minimum altitude of 1,500 m, they inferred that this area constituted a mere fraction of Guatemala's original fifty-two hundred square kilometers of cloud forest. Using old maps of Guatemala, they determined that most of this destruction happened within the last thirty-six years (a period relatively coterminous with the civil war). Destroyed, they hypothesized, were first those areas of cloud forest that were lowest in elevation and closest to roads. If conditions remained the same, they predicted that by 2020 all of Guatemala's remaining cloud forest would be gone.[1]

The ecologists decided to limit their conservation efforts to the Sierras, or mountainous regions, of Caquipek, Yalijux, and

Guaxac in the Department of Alta Verapaz, an area approximately 270 square kilometers in size, wherein lived some six thousand people in thirty-four different communities. They gave two reasons for their decision. First, its population density of quetzals was the right size for a conservation effort to be fruitful. Any lower a density, and a population of birds would not be able to reproduce itself, no matter how otherwise favorable the environment. And second, the cloud forest in this area was in immediate danger because of the clearing of forest by indigenous peoples. Indeed, the ecologists called this region "one of the most seriously endangered (*amenazadas*) areas in Guatemala owing to the high density of indians (*indios*) that live in the region." In other words, this area became the focus of the ecologists' attention owing to its high density of both endangered birds and endangering people.

As the ecologists then saw it, a simple strategy would underlie their future conservation efforts: "to incite a co-existence between the indians and the forest" (*incitar una coexistencia entre los indios y el bosque*). Such an incitation would require a number of interventions, such as terracing and reforesting, eliciting grants from private organizations, and petitioning the government for environment-friendly laws. Most important, they thought, indigenous people should be integrated into the interventions. For example, they suggested that "Indians be paid for their work in the region, ranging from the construction and maintenance of infrastructure to the constant patrolling of the area." Last, they issued a warning aimed at Guatemalan national pride: insofar as Guatemala was known as the "Land of Forest" (*Tierra del Bosque*), and insofar as the quetzal was the national bird, with the loss of its cloud forest and quetzals, Guatemala was "losing an important part of its identity."

Let me summarize the logic of these ecologists' projected interventions. The quetzal bird was the main value in need of protection, and the cloud forest was its necessary habitat. The indigenous people, with their "slash-and-burn" agriculture, were the main agents in the destruction of the cloud forest. The indigenous people should play a key role in stopping this destruction; and they could play such a role if they were offered economic incentives. Only in this way could "coexistence" of birds and people be "incited."

Under this logic, economic and political conditions underlying the indigenous destruction of the cloud forest were elided. No mention was made of Guatemala's historical, sociological, or political conditions or history.[2] The ultimate value of the ecologists was biodiversity conservation; in other words, these interventions were not humanitarian in the strict sense. That is, while the indigenous populations played a necessary role as a means to the end of biodiversity, they were not an end in themselves. Last, it is important to note that the ecologists presupposed two distinct modes of personhood. Indigenous people could be most effectively moved to action by appealing to their instrumental values (cash payment). But funding agencies and national organizations could be most effectively moved to action by appealing to their ethical values (loss of national identity or biodiversity).[3] That is to say, each of these groups of actors was understood to be best motivated by different evaluative standards (Kockelman 2010c). The strategies and tensions underlying the ecologists' interventions were in place from the very beginning, as clear in their initial plans.

At this time, however, the ecologists still emphasized the importance of securing state-level support. Over the next ten years, as their efforts ultimately became institutionalized as the NGO Proyecto Eco-Quetzal, their appeals to the Guatemalan state would diminish, and their dependence on international funding would increase. For example, ten years later, in a grant sent to the Global Environmental Fund (GEF 2000), Proyecto Eco-Quetzal had a more developed understanding of the cause of deforestation. While they still blamed unsustainable agricultural practices (and the frequent resettlement that soil loss required), they also blamed the state and the market. They argued that deforestation was caused in part by a lack of awareness and coordination on an institutional level (in particular, the forest lacked a protected status). And they argued that villagers lacked both knowledge (and thus needed technical assistance in the sustainable use of biodiversity) and incentive (and thus needed marketable products—such as candles and ecotourism—as alternative resources).

Nonetheless, their main strategy of "inciting coexistence" by means of instrumental interventions, or incentivizing, remained in place throughout. They wanted to "manage the selected sites with the participation of local people and institutions in accordance with local biophysical, cultural, and social realities." And, to do this, they would have to "provide incentives to land owners to encourage them to conserve or sustainably use their forests." Finally, noting that the quetzal was a unique species, they argued for the "global significance of local biodiversity." While still appealing to the instrumental incentives required to get the indigenous population to change their behavior, they had moved from a national idiom of identity to a global idiom of biodiversity as an existential value that would appeal to transnational funding agencies.

This chapter examines the history of this NGO's interventions in the village of Chicacnab, paying particular attention to its fostering of an ecotourism program as a means to promote conservation of the cloud forest. Broadly speaking, and in conjunction with chapter 4, I focus on a particular intervention: the project's capacitation of villagers to engage in novel social relations and semiotic practices, such as the hosting and guiding of ecotourists, as a means to make commensurate disparate ontological domains: not just instrumental and ethical values, or "money" and "morality," but also villagers and tourists, and people and birds—and so various life forms and forms of life.[4] In particular, the impulse, if not achievement, of the project's intervention was to coordinate villagers' and tourists' actions (and thereby turn them into "interactions"), calibrate these modes of coordination with cash (by articulating, instilling, measuring, standardizing, and pricing them), and thereby conduct villagers' local economic actions toward seemingly global ethical ends.

The next three sections describe the range of the NGO's interventions, focusing on the history of its ecotourism program, and the logic underlying its strategies.[5] And the last five sections turn from the strategic and practical impulse of the NGO's interventions to the limits of its achievement. By way of a detailed description of how ecotourists were primed for their experience in the village, and an ethnographic description of a group of ecotourists, it shows the discrepancy and overlap between the NGO's portrayal of a standardized ecotour and ecotourists' actual experiences. In some sense, then, this chapter takes what is ostensibly the most portable of institutions (the NGO) and shows its radical rootedness (and fruitedness) in a particular context. I conclude by theorizing some of the key features of so-called immaterial labor, loosely understood as commoditized interactions linking villagers and tourists in novel social relations and semiotic practices. It will constitute our first analytic foray into seemingly incommensurable values.

This chapter is constructed in terms of the categories and values of the NGO and ecotourists. In some sense, it is a view of the village, and the villagers, from where Proyecto Eco-Quetzal stood. Indeed, even the category of immaterial labor itself, and the way evaluation and commensuration are initially to be understood, sticks close to the NGO's categories, commitments, and conduct (and hence its "worldview" or "cosmology" so to speak, as fluid and messy as it often was). Later chapters will offer other perspectives on, and describe other agencies in, these same entanglings of the village and NGO, focusing on the categories, commitments, and conduct of the Q'eqchi' speakers themselves, both as they unfolded ethnographically and as they transformed historically.

Other Interventions as an NGO

In 1990, following the initial scientific expedition, David Unger, one of the original ten ecologists, founded Proyecto Quetzal with the help of GEO Tropical Rainforest of Hamburg, Germany. In 1994, this organization was renamed Proyecto Eco-Quetzal (PEQ) and came under the executive direction of the Biosphere and Sustainable Agricultural Development Association (BIDAS), in Cobán, Guatemala. The association was established as an environmental nonprofit organization under Guatemalan law in November 1993 (PC 1997b). The association never had another project. Its only reason for existence was to give Guatemalan institutional legitimacy to what was originally a German organization, and what came to coordinate a variety of complex and changing transnational funding sources and affiliations. Under the national umbrella of BIDAS, and under the personal direction of David Unger, PEQ engaged in a wide range of interventions throughout the 1990s—ranging from sustainable agriculture and medicinal plants, to women's development centers and environmental education.

Beginning in 1992, for example, with the help of UNICEF (the international children's rights and emergency relief organization) and CONALFA (Guatemala's national literacy committee), PEQ provided teachers for fourteen schools in the Sierras. More than four hundred students between the ages of six and twelve were taught to read and write in both Spanish and Q'eqchi', and received basic mathematics training and environmental education. Despite the scope and success of this intervention, the schools had to close down in 1998 because no politician would approve their renewal, and because many other NGOs became involved with schools at the end of the civil war. Owing to this, members of PEQ thought it would be better to focus their efforts on conservation (PC 1997b).

By the mid-1990s, PEQ had established four women's development centers in the Sierras. These centers were designed to provide skills training to Q'eqchi' and Pocomchi women in the production of internationally marketable crafts of local origin. Among these crafts were *tejidos*, or woven fabrics, made using either the traditional backstrap loom or a larger foot-pedaled loom. The fabrics were then embroidered to make *huipiles* (blouses), curtains, placemats, and other decorative household items. Other marketable products included baskets, rope bags, baked goods, and hammocks (PC 1997a). As will be discussed in chapter 4, these activities often generated intrahousehold tensions; for example, older women went out for daylong training sessions, while their daughters and daughters-in-law had to take over these women's usual household chores in addition to their own.

In 1998, in the realm of sustainable agriculture, PEQ began a long-term, intervillage intervention called the "corn revolution." This intervention was designed to involve farmers in the conservation of soil by making better use of land already under cultivation. It entailed a commitment not to burn the land before planting (i.e., using fallow land rather than recently burned forest), growing on contours, using natural soil enhancers (compost), and planting live barriers to minimize soil erosion. During the first year of this intervention, PEQ reported that such methods yielded 12 percent more corn than fields planted in the traditional way. Despite this initial success, however, PEQ noted that this was a difficult intervention for a number of reasons. For example, maize agriculture was a "holy tradition"; the soil of the Sierras was very poor; and local technology was rudimentary. To minimize these problems, PEQ offered various incentives to farmers to make them try the new methods. For example, participants could purchase seed potatoes, fruit trees, and potentially a cow on a loan basis. And PEQ promised to make up any difference in yields. After the first season, however, the project noted that such incentives were barbed; in particular, having to collect loaned money and having the promised cows not arrive strained relations, causing many participants to drop out. Such drop-outs were referred to by PEQ as "defectors" (NFWF 1999).

In 1999, PEQ instituted a *finquita*, or "small plantation," program. In this intervention, farmers were trained to make their own tree nurseries, whose fruit could then be harvested and sold. Unlike the corn revolution program, which was designed to minimize the impact of subsistence agriculture on cloud forest, the finquita program was designed to offer a cash-based mode of production in place of subsistence agriculture. In comparison to the corn revolution, the finquita project was a huge success. Three times as much fruit as corn was harvestable in the same size plot. Unfortunately, as a consequence of good harvests, local markets became clogged with fruit. By 2000, PEQ was investigating better ways to market the fruit—such as turning it into jam to be sold internationally (NFWF 2000).

Perhaps the most economically successful intervention of the NGO was candle making, which was set up by two Australian volunteers in 1998 (PC 1999). Q'eqchi' farmers neighboring the cloud forest collected seeds of the arrayán tree (*Mirica cerifera*) and sold an extracted wax to PEQ's business (NFWF 2000). The language of this intervention echoed PEQ's original philosophy that the Q'eqchi' were instrumentally motivated and tourists were ethically motivated. For example, signs on the candles read, "This income is also good for the cloud forests. With an outside income Q'eqchi' people are less inclined to slash and burn the forest to grow crops. Thus destruction of forest habitat is prevented." And, in advertising these candles to buyers, signs said that the candles were natural rather than synthetic, and made by women rather than men. For example, "This arrayán candle was handmade by Q'eqchi' women of the Guatemala cloud forests." While the Q'eqchi' were portrayed as motivated by income, the consumers of the Q'eqchi's handicrafts were presumed to be motivated not only by cloud forest conservation, but also by natural products and women's rights.

Last, PEQ took on biomonitoring. In 1998, several German doctoral candidates in ecology began to document endangered birds in the cloud forest of the Sierras. Such documentation of endangered species not only increased funding possibilities; it also provided a way to assess changes in the size and health of the cloud forest as a function of the NGO's conservation efforts (PC 1999). Density of birds would serve as an index of habitat size, hunting pressure, forest degradation, and climatic change (NFWF 1999). To actually track such changes in density, PEQ began training local men to monitor the populations. Unlike other interventions, this one had a particular logic of individualization and conversion. For example, PEQ wrote, "Individuals that are notorious hunters will be employed as biomonitoring agents and thus be converted into conservationists" (GEF 2000). This intervention also had a strategic circularity; it simultaneously monitored indices of the success or failure of PEQ's own programs—changes in populations whose size or number its own interventions were designed to increase. Notice, then, an interesting trajectory: while PEQ first began to focus on a relatively general form of intervention (education), it subsequently turned to a relatively specific and self-referential form of intervention—biomonitoring. Along with this trajectory, PEQ moved from interacting with entire villages to interacting with particular people, such that its interventions came to target and address not only nondescript "indios" but also nameable "notorious individuals." Finally, notice the religious idiom of "conversion," echoing the efforts of Las Casas, and the Dominicans, some five hundred years before.

From this ensemble of interrelated interventions may be drawn a number of points. The scope of the NGO's interventions was very large, touching on many aspects of Q'eqchi' life, for example, subsistence- and cash-based agriculture, traditional and novel forms of crafts, standard and environmental education, and candle making and biomonitoring. The logic of these interventions was in each case the same, to add value to local products (by marketing them nationally and internationally) and to add value-producing ability to local villagers (by educating and training them to recognize and create such value). And the project's ethos was ecological rather than humanitarian; such valuable products and abilities would then be vied for by the instrumentally driven Q'eqchi', thereby promoting—at one degree of remove—a relatively existential or ethical value, that is, conservation of biodiversity. In sum, politics was reduced to management, and morality to money, by fostering market-based behavior as the pervasive form of social conduct.[6]

Early Days of Ecotourism

Before 1968, what is now Chicacnab was owned by the landlord of Finca Santa Teresa. Q'eqchi' speakers who lived in the village of Popobaj (located to the south and at a lower altitude than Chicacnab) were permitted to plant and harvest their maize in this area in exchange for two weeks of labor per month on the finca, a kind of plantation (Secaira 1992: 20). In 1968, a group of villagers formed a land acquisition committee, and purchased fifteen caballerías (678 ha) of land from the finca owner for forty-two thousand quetzals (or US$4,200 at the time). While this land was legally owned by the entire community, it was divided among the original thirty-three villagers in relation to the size of each of their original contributions. Despite joint ownership, there were radically different levels of control; some villagers controlled as much as forty-five ha (one caballería), while others controlled as little as 4.5 ha (one hundred cuerdas, or 6.5 manzanas). From the time of purchase on, villagers began to build their houses where before there had only been cloud forest interspersed with milpa parcels (Secaira 1992: 20). According to the school's census (Secaira 1992: 21, 52), between 1968 and 1991 the population of Chicacnab more than doubled, rising from thirty-three families (and 175 people) to seventy-four families (and 392 people). And by 1992, half of the land originally purchased had been cleared of cloud forest (Secaira 1992).

By 1992, PEQ was sending extensionists to Chicacnab, and other villages in the Sierras, to promote soil conservation practices and environmental education (Secaira 1992: 29–30). In addition, villagers could tune into a weekly program that contained conservationist ideas promoted by PEQ (Secaira 1992). At this time, PEQ already had plans to provide economic opportunities for the villagers, most of which turned on making and marketing traditional crafts. And the NGO even had plans for an ecotourism program. As one ecologist, sponsored by PEQ, suggested in 1992, "Certainly, the magnificent scenery of [Chicacnab] offers ample potential for tourism, and hopefully, [tourism] may offer opportunities for local villagers to provide some paid services, such as food, shelter and guidance" (Secaira 1992: 30).

While PEQ facilitated some ecotourism in the Sierras as early as 1991, tourists began visiting Chicacnab only in 1993, and even then in very limited numbers. For example, in 1996 only twenty-two tourists visited the village; and this was a larger number than any of the three previous years. In addition to such a small number of tourists, there were also no standards for tourism per se. For example, in its early years, PEQ would alert the villagers that tourists were coming by sending a message over public radio. A guide would then come down the mountain and meet the tourists in Caquipek—the nearest bus-accessible village (PC 1997b). Aside from these agreed-on modes of communication and coordination, however, once tourists were in the village, there were no formal guidelines for what they should expect in the way of room, board, or guidance.

Nonetheless, given the positive reception and relative informality of these early visits, PEQ asked the Peace Corps to send two volunteers to assess, formalize, and expand the ecotourism program. Between February 1997 and February 1999, two such volunteers—one in charge of small businesses, and the other in charge of environmental management—engaged in the evaluation, planning, implementation, and promotion of ecotourism. By 1997, PEQ had begun to focus on a single village, ecotourism had become its key intervention, and the American Peace Corps had joined forces with a transnational NGO dedicated to environmentalism. By June 1999, PEQ could boast that over 336 tourists from twenty-one countries had visited Chicacnab since the program's inception (NFWF 1999).

Beautiful Simplicity

In May 1997, the Peace Corps volunteers could say that their objective, like that of the NGO itself, was to identify new sources of income for locals that were not based in agriculture, and thereby provide an economic justification for the preservation of the cloud forest. They thought that ecotourism provided a perfect means to do this. For example, in a slide show about the project presented around this time, the volunteers said, "It is our hope that tourists' income will serve as an incentive to preserve the forest and its endangered flora and fauna, as a valuable resource." In addition to this emphasis on new forms of non-agriculture-based income as a means to promote conservation, the volunteers also emphasized that the program would "provide visitors with the opportunity to explore the cloud forest, and experience the Q'eqchi family life" (PC 1997a). In short, tourist income (to be earned) would serve as the key incentive for the Q'eqchi'; and village life and environs (to be explored and experienced) would serve as the key incentive for tourists.

Relatedly, the volunteers characterized the logic of such interventions as *beautiful* and *simple*, thereby initiating an aesthetics of environmental intervention. For example, they said, "The beauty of the Program of Low Impact Tourism is that everything done for the tourists is of direct, continuing benefit to the family as well. PEQ is needed to bring in the tourists, arrange for their visit, and be ready to respond in case of emergency. The community is doing the rest." Similarly, they reported that the "participating families are enthusiastic, and for the first time they acknowledge an economic advantage in not cutting forest. It's an economic decision; tourists pay to see the cloud forest, and they will not come if the forest is gone. Simple" (PC 1997a). As advertised to funding agencies and tourists, the aesthetics of beautiful simplicity underlying this intervention turned on not only maximum local participation and minimal external intervention, but also transparent logic and self-reinforcing effects.

Ecotourism in Alta Verapaz

While its ancient Mayan temples and vibrant indigenous cultures have always been the main attraction for tourists visiting Guatemala, by the late 1990s there were a large number of official ecotourism sites along with various degrees of promotion. For example, in the national airport and at information booths throughout the country, tourists could receive copies of the *Mosaic of Guatemala*, a state-financed magazine, dedicated to promoting "sustainable tourism programs in rural communities, along with the conservation of natural resources and archaeological sites" (2001). This magazine provided an overview of various places of interest to ecotourists, including ecological reserves, waterfalls and lakes, lowland rainforests, and highland cloud forests—in particular, the village of Chicacnab, as a tourist destination made possible by the NGO's efforts. It was sponsored by PROGUAT (a branch of the Guatemalan Ministry of Economy), focused on "attracting private investment in various sectors of the country." To give the reader a sense of the style and priorities of this magazine, its introduction listed a code of conduct whose first rule was to "walk quietly when in the forest and speak in hushed tones." And the conclusion of this introduction ended with the injunction "remember that your visit here generates life, as well as development."

Having no large-scale archaeological sites, Alta Verapaz, one of Guatemala's twenty-three departments, was never known as a tourist attraction. And guide books routinely mentioned its overcast skies and incessant rain, as well as its lack of bars and Spanish schools. Before the project, when tourists did come to Alta Verapaz, it was usually only for a weekend trip to see Semuc Champey, a natural rock formation along the Cahabón river, and the caves of Lanquín, "where indigenous tribes used to make their sacrifices and the walls are black with smoke" (Williams 2001: 90). During the late 1990s, however, its popularity as a tourist destination grew, due in part to its self-portrayal as "the green heart of Guatemala" during a boom in ecotourism throughout the country. And, indeed, in 2000 there were many more ecological activities that one could undertake there. For example, a poster found throughout tourist spots in Guatemala advertised the mixture of cultural and ecological riches that could be found in Alta Verapaz: the natural waterfalls and rivers; the flora and fauna; the rich customs of the indigenous populations; and the arts and crafts. And there was an ecotourism fair each year, where one could participate in conferences and classes about environmental education, in addition to experiencing local food, cultural, ecology, and art. At the first such fair (1999), credit was given to Proyecto Eco-Quetzal for having initiated the ecotourism movement in the Verapaces.

In Cobán, the capital of Alta Verapaz, there was a well-run hostel frequented by tourists and local elites. It was owned by an American woman (married to a Guatemalan man) who had come to Guatemala twenty years before as a Peace Corps Volunteer. There were also two Internet cafés with slow phone lines and high prices. One could take a coffee-tasting tour at Finca Santa Margarita, originally owned by W. E. Dieseldorff (circa 1888). There, for $4, "our expert coffee taster, Mr. Romeo Agusto Yat Xol, will teach you to 'taste' coffee" (from its promotional flier). In nearby Chamelco, there was Don Jeronimo's, described by the owner as a "cottage sanctuary in the magical rainforests of the Kekchi Indians." For US$25 a day, one could get "three scrumptious meals (vegetarian)," as well as the opportunity to "hike the power mountains, spelunk in spooky caves, idly inner tube down the sweet river, swim, and play in the sun." Locally, the owner was often referred to as that "crazy gringo with rubber boots." Given such a venue, most tourists who came to Cobán did so only for a weekend venture; they stayed in the hostel, visited the river and caves, spent a night in Chicacnab, got a coffee, checked their e-mail, and then traveled back to more tourist-friendly sites like Antigua and Lake Atitlan.

Environs and Employees of the Ecotourism Project

Project Eco-Quetzal's offices were housed in a relatively simple building a block off of the main road into town, but about a mile away from the town center. Inside the building was a covered courtyard, a small patch of grass and trees, a house with five or six little offices and a tourist-orientation room, and a ramshackle room where candle making and other hands-on projects took place. The front door was usually left open, and tourists could wander into the orientation room, where they would be met by a project member. In this room were six comfortable chairs where tourists could spend their mornings before a trip, exchanging names, nationalities, experiences, and plans, while being primed for their upcoming experience by project members.

Inside the orientation room were pictures, maps, and lists documenting the NGO's many interventions: a map of Cobán, with tourist spots pointed out; a regional map explaining how to get to Chicacnab; and a map showing the vegetation around Chicacnab, with a legend showing how much cloud forest remained (as of 1991), and how much had existed before. On a dividing screen there was a calendar with the names of project members, and descriptions of their work schedules for the upcoming months. There was a photomontage of a school, an earlier focus of the NGO's interventions, with pictures taken by the children themselves. There was a layout of arrayán candles, showing the production process through which they were made, along with an array of differently shaped, colored, and sized candles for sale. In one corner of the room was a large book written by an American ethnobotanist containing forty pages of dried, and rapidly disintegrating, plants to be found around Chicacnab. Inside, it listed common names, Q'eqchi' names, taxonomic placement, and reported uses. Last were PEQ T-shirts pinned to the wall. In addition to having a picture of a male quetzal against the background of a tree, these shirts had the words, "Ecoquetzal, Cobán. Save the Quetzal!"

As of 2000, eight people worked in the project's office. Ana, the receptionist, was born in Cobán and spoke Spanish and Q'eqchi' fluently. She was called PEQ's *alma*, or "soul," by the other members. Pablo, the accountant, was a Spanish-speaking Ladino from Guatemala with whom villagers communicated by walkie-talkie. Perhaps as a function of such radio-mediated interactions with them, they all spoke of him as "angry" or *josq'*—and I would certainly have called him "gruff" (but a good guy). Elinor was the latest Peace Corps volunteer to be in charge of the ecotourism project. She had majored in anthropology at the University of Wisconsin but was planning a career in the nonprofit sector. Deborah was from Guatemala and had spent ten years in Boston. Fluent in English and Spanish, she also spoke highly serviceable Q'eqchi' (one grandparent on each side was a native speaker of Q'eqchi'). Humberto, relatively new to the project, was an energetic Guatemalan man with a cell phone and a baseball cap. He was in charge of the sustainable agriculture programs. Quite friendly, he bristled only if you mistook him for a speaker of Q'eqchi'. Diego, a Q'eqchi'-speaking man who lived in Cobán, acted as an agricultural extensionist to outlying villages. And last among these, Alberto was the main liaison between the village and the project. He spoke fluent Spanish and Q'eqchi', and was used as a translator at village meetings. In addition to this core group, any number of other people could be found in the project's office. There might be Q'eqchi'-speaking men in the adjacent building making candles. There might be eco-guides from Chicacnab who had stopped in to pick up tourists or relay information. There might be assorted ecologists entering fieldwork data into laptops in cramped offices. And there might be the occasional gringo volunteers, who helped out with odd projects and tended to abuse their e-mail privileges. A common refrain among people working in the offices was that they visited the village far too infrequently.

Last, there was David, the German ecologist who had started the NGO ten years before. He was a tall, gaunt man, with sandy-blond hair, muscled arms, and a sun-beaten face. He and his wife, a Ladina from Cobán, had a one-year-old son, and another child on the way. He said that his children were going to learn Spanish, German, and Q'eqchi' (if they could get a local woman to help look after them). He was still in the midst of his doctoral dissertation, an attempt to infer a set of laws that would explain the color of birds as a function of camouflage strategy, mate attraction, color band width, and so on. Having been working on it for more than a decade, he was less and less sure each year that he would ever finish. He was amiable, soft-spoken, and generous. Quite open to my writing about the project, he introduced me to everyone working there and told them that I would be hanging out and pestering them with questions. And he gave me full access to all of the project's documents. When I first began working in Chicacnab, villagers always wanted to know whether he had sanctioned my stay there, saying that my being there was all right with them if it was all right with him. And many times it was reported favorably that he had said, *tinkamq arin Guatemala*, or "I will die here in Guatemala." His legitimacy with villagers was thus very high, based partially on his long-term commitment to the village and his serious attempts to learn and speak the Q'eqchi' language. Project members were quite admiring as well. Though when I was praising the project to one volunteer, she agreed with me, but then talked about the need to keep the project small, saying that David was extending himself too much. And other volunteers sometimes characterized him as a poet rather than a bureaucrat, saying that he enjoyed beginning projects more than continuing them. In short, while there was some ambivalence toward David by members of the project, it was directed only at his suitability for bureaucracy—not his sincerity, dedication, or fairness.

Amid the general hubbub of the office—David on the phone checking computer prices; project members discussing their work in Spanish, German, and English; shy guides from Chicacnab sitting together speaking Q'eqchi' quietly; Ana or Elinor going back and forth to sign tourists in, collect their money, or explain what an ecotour would be like; and newly introduced tourists discussing their experiences and plans—an otherwise unengaged tourist might sit back and flip through a large binder that sat on a desk in the middle of the orientation room. In this binder were beautiful pictures of village life along with a sort of "guided tour," in question-answer fashion, of what awaited a tourist in the village. Insofar as this was a common genre whose descriptions were articulated in a variety of forms (ensuring that a tourist would at one point or another have come across them), it is worth quoting at length. Not so much a description of what a tourist will experience, it was a projection of what a tourist could experience if the project's attempts at standardization were successful. As a kind of wishful catechism of the ecotourism experience, it may speak for itself.

Priming the Ecotourism Experience

Proyecto Ecológico Quetzal invites you to a natural and cultural immersion with the Q'eqchi' people in the land of the Quetzal.

What is PEQ?

PEQ is a non-profit organization dedicated to protecting the cloud forest in the mountains of Caquipec, Guaxac, and Yalijux. We work with indigenous residents to promote sustainable use of the area's resources and to identify other sources of income. The alternative income sources that we have identified are alternative agricultural products, art work, and ecotourism. The ecotourism program that we have developed has reduced pressure on the cloud forest because farmers realize that it can be more profitable to show the intact forests to tourists instead of cutting the forest to plant more corn."

What are the tour and the accommodations like?

In the ecotourism program you will travel to see and experience the cloud forest and learn about the life and culture of the Q'eqchi' people living near the forest. Your accommodations in a typical Q'eqchi' home are rustic. Their homes are constructed with wood walls and a dirt floor, and there is an open fire inside the home over which your food will be cooked. The typical food includes beans, corn tortillas and eggs. With the corn and the beans the women also make other typical foods including tayuyos, tamales and atol. We have taught the women how to make several types of food for tourists such as rice and pasta with tomato sauce. If you would like drinking water, ask your family for "agua hervida" (boiled water). The adult men in the family speak basic Spanish though their first language is Q'eqchi', but the women in the family may be able to figure out your hand gestures. Your sleeping arrangement includes a bed of a foam mattress located in an area of the house slightly separated from the family. The number of tourists per family is limited to two because you will be staying in the family's home and because this limit ensures an equal opportunity for income to all the host families. You will need to bring a sleeping bag or a blanket because it gets cold at an altitude of 2400 meters in the cloud forest. If you don't have a sleeping bag we have blankets which can be rented.

How do we get there?

Your guide will meet you at 12:00 in the Proyecto Eco-Quetzal office on the day of your trip. With your guide you will first take a bus from Cobán to Carchá. These buses leave approximately every 15 minutes from near the stadium. This trip takes about 30 minutes and costs Q1. Upon arriving in Carchá you will have a chance to find some lunch before getting on the bus to Caquipek. This bus leaves at 2:00 p.m., but you need to get to this bus between 1:00 and 1:30 because this bus often fills up. This ride takes 1½ hours, costs Q4 and will take you through a scenic mountain range covered with pine trees and farm land. On this trip you will need to bring Q10 with you to cover your round trip transportation (your guide's transportation costs are covered), some money for lunch on the first day of your trip, and you may want to bring extra money (in small bills), because some of the families have handcrafts that you may want to purchase. Your guide will then walk with you up to his home in San Lucas or Chicacnab. [The following sentence was added in later.] The last 30 minutes of your hike could be at dusk, so please be sure to have a flashlight with you.

What activities are there?

Upon arriving in the family's house you will be able to rest and have a typical Q'eqchi' dinner. The following day your guide will take you on a hike through the cloud forest. In the evening, be sure to decide with your guide what time you will leave to hike through the cloud forest. If you stay for more than one night you will have more time to see the forest, visit the biological station, and may even have a chance to visit a ceremonial cave in the forest (ask your family about the biological station and cave if you are interested in seeing them). If you wake up early you may even be able to see the quetzal during your forest hike. On your hike remember that we are working to preserve the cloud forest; therefore, please do not take anything from the forest, such as plants, animals, or geological pieces. Through your visit you will be able to enjoy experiencing and participating in everyday life with your Q'eqchi' family. (If you are interested in participating in household activities such as cooking, carrying water, gathering firewood, etc., just offer your assistance.)

Costs: 210 quetzals (about US$25 dollars) for a guide for two days, lodging for one night, and three meals. For each additional night, the cost is increased by 110 quetzals (covering the extra food, lodging, and guiding). Optionally, one may rent boots (Q10), blankets (Q15), and a guide to carry your backpack (Q20).

The majority of your costs go directly to the families and the community of Chicacnab and San Lucas. The fund that goes to the office is the registration fee to cover our administration of the ecotourism program. If you wish to make an additional contribution to the project or to the community please do so in the PEQ office.

What to bring?

Sleeping bag or blanket; warm clothing; boots; rain jacket or buy a "nylon"; toilet paper; flashlight; hat (recommended); sunscreen (recommended).

Evaluation Form

Our families and guides have received training to host and guide tourists. The program can benefit from your constructive comments on how your experience could be improved. Please give us your comments by filling out the evaluation form which will be given to you by your host family. These evaluation forms are also used by us to monitor and pay the radio operators for their work in coordinating your visit so please be sure to return your evaluation form to your host family.

Questions and Answers

1. What is the weather like in the mountain? The climate in the mountain is generally much cooler than in Cobán especially at night and it typically rains at some point during the day.
2. Are there mosquitoes? No there are few to no mosquitoes because of the cold climate.
3. How do I take a bath? If you wish to bathe yourself, ask your family for a bucket of water and ask them where to go to bathe yourself. With this water you can discretely wash yourself.
4. Can I take photos? Yes, please ask for permission to take a photo of the family and then send a copy of your photo back to the PEQ office. The families really enjoy receiving copies of your photos.
5. What things should I avoid doing to respect the Q'eqchi' culture? The Q'eqchi' families are shy about nudity; therefore, please do not show yourself naked in front of the family. The families are quite protective of their daughters; therefore, male tourists should not be alone with the female daughters. The families eat nutritional herbs from the forest and occasionally use medicinal herbs from the forest. On your tour please do not use drugs. During celebration the Q'eqchi' people will drink a special alcohol drink made from sugar cane. Please do not use alcohol on your tour.
6. What if I have any problems? Get in touch with Doña Manuela who lives in San Lucas, who has agreed to help tourists in case of emergencies.

In short, this visual and verbal projection of an ecotour attempted to prime the reader for what he or she was about to experience—what kinds of individual actions and coordinated interactions they should and should not undertake. It treated the ethos of the project, restating their common—and by now familiar—strategies. It explained how to get to the village, and what to expect in the way of travel times, distances, and conditions. It detailed what one would do and experience in the village: eating, accommodations, encounters, and options. It related these activities and experiences to price. It answered potential questions, offered suggestions, and gave negative injunctions. Last, it explained how a tourist could evaluate his or her experience, such that future host and guide training could benefit. Each tourist's visit also provided an evaluation of the NGO's success. And each tourist would engage in an intimate form of surveillance each time his or her activity was coordinated with a villager's by means of so-called immaterial labor such as hosting and guiding. In short, just as the NGO's intervention undergirded the standardization of an ecotourist's potential experience, an ecotourist's actual experience provided an evaluation of the success of the NGO's interventions. Immaterial labor simultaneously acted as its own mode of surveillance. In the next section, I will provide an extended ethnographic example of an ecotour, foregrounding actual value-directed interactions between villagers and ecotourists, to show the types of discrepancies that exist between the NGO's impulse (qua projected standards) and achievement (qua tourist experience).

Being an Ecotourist

It is Thursday morning and three sets of tourists have come into the office, wishing to go up to Chicacnab. There are three Austrian women. Two are sisters; one (age twenty-five) teaches piano to children, and the other (age twenty-eight) works for a software company. The third woman is their close friend, a police officer and a black belt, who threw out her back in the line of duty and now helps train dogs to search for drugs. While the sisters are out of shape and quite lethargic, frequently slipping out of the office to smoke cigarettes, the police officer is husky and energetic, very friendly and instantly likable. There is an Israeli woman and a German woman, who met on a bus and decided to travel with each other for safety. The Israeli woman is studying population biology, and we quickly get to chatting, discussing the relevance of the project's interventions to either science or conservation. And the German woman wants to be an anthropologist and so spends much of the trip quizzing me about the pros and cons of my profession. Trailing after them, but familiar with them for having spent the night in the same hostel, is a couple from Denmark. They are in their early thirties, and newly married. He is a talk-show host for a small Danish TV program, and she is studying to get her masters in psychology. He is just recovering from a bad case of diarrhea, and she does most of the talking, introducing themselves and generally getting the different groups of tourists to chat with each other, the conversation in multiply accented but fluent English. It soon emerges that none of these tourists had known about Proyecto Eco-Quetzal before they came to Guatemala, and they would have avoided Cobán altogether had they not heard other tourists rave about their visits to Chicacnab.

After long waits and a brief orientation, the tourists unload excess weight from their luggage, including travel guides, warm-weather clothing, and souvenirs (mainly textiles they bought before they came to Cobán). At 1:15, they are finally ready to go, but it is now too late to catch a connecting bus to Carchá (where they would then pick up the bus to Caquipek), so Diego offers to drive them to Carchá in the NGO's pickup truck. We pile in the back, sit on our backpacks, and hang tightly to the bed of the truck. Above the sound of the unmuffled engine, the German and Danish women shout about how expensive the tour is, suggesting that this is why no tourists want to spend more than one night. Soon everyone is quiet, staring dully out at the changing scenery, and shifting their weight in preparation for bumps and brakes. The ride is lurching and dusty, but mercifully short.

We arrive in Carchá fifteen minutes later. The big yellow American school bus that will take us to Caquipek is already filled up. There are three people to each two-person seat. Women, couples, and children sit in the front of the bus, and men sit in the back. The rest of us stand in sardine-like conditions. Above us, on metal racks, are market purchases like chickens, tomatoes, batteries, and beans. And above the bus, tied beneath a canvas tarp in case it rains, are our backpacks along with bags of fertilizer, bundles of tin roofing, and other large and unwieldy objects. Children run outside the window selling ice-cream cones and soda. Everyone but the tourists are native speakers of Q'eqchi'.

Ten minutes ahead of schedule, the bus is off. Though ostensibly overflowing already, it nonetheless pulls over wherever there is someone standing on the side of the road, making over three dozen stops in its two-hour trip. Most of the trip is along a one-lane dirt road; the bus swerves, lurches, and jerks; and with every passing vehicle one driver has to back up while the other passes through. We pass village after village. There are corn fields, government signs promising progress, cemeteries with broken crypts, stacked firewood for sale, and little stores painted in the colors and style of Coca Cola and Orange Crush soda. The dust and diesel fumes settle on us through the open windows, making our lips gritty and sour. When we arrive in the small and seemingly empty town of Caquipek—of which we see only the main street, lined by ramshackle *tiendas* populated by chickens and dogs—we are met by two guides.

Disembarking, we exchange names with them. One has a radio around his neck, now playing marimba music interspersed with Q'eqchi'. And the other has been shopping in preparation for the tourists' visit to his house. He shows me his backpack filled with onions, tomatoes, sugar, coffee, and candles. They wear baseball caps and black rubber boots. I know them both from my stay in the village, but they are suddenly shy. Surely the tall gringo women don't help, but the real issue inducing shyness is likely the simple fact that neither has actually been capacitated as a guide; they are adolescent boys standing in for their absent fathers. (Such frowned-on forms of labor substitution, or replacement, will be treated at length in chapter 3.) Does anyone want to buy water or a plastic sheet (in case it rains), the one with the best Spanish asks. Nobody understands his reference to a *nilo*, and so I explain it to them. Most have Gortex jackets, and the thought of wearing a trash bag doesn't appeal to them. Several tourists buy water. The Danish man buys a bunch of bananas that he splits up among the tourists and guides in a gesture of goodwill. It is now almost 4:00 in the afternoon, and the clouds are threatening rain. Wasting no time, we set off for the village itself.

The first half of our hike follows a narrow, four-wheel-drive-accessible road, through several villages. Chickens and turkeys fan out before us. Dogs and small children watch warily from yards. Some women watch us from their doorways, but the only people to address us are a bunch of older kids playing soccer who stop to yell, "Gringo." Other than throwing rocks at their dogs, our only interaction with villagers on this hike is when two small girls ask the Austrian women for their water bottle containers, holding out their hands and saying, "Tumba, tumba." The Austrians are confused, thinking this is a local word for money, until one of the guides explains, "Quieren sus botellas," or "They want your bottles." Good sports, they gulp their water down and give the bottles to the girls.

After about an hour, we veer off onto a steep and muddy single-track trail. Villages recede into the background, and the landscape becomes milpa and scrub, until it gives way to cloud forest. It is much colder now, and the air has become misty, though the clouds no longer threaten rain. The hike has become strenuous. The Austrian women heave as they walk; the German woman jokes that she would have paid the guide to carry her backpack if she had understood how treacherous the trail would be, pointing out how cheap twenty-five quetzals is when framed in terms of Deutschmarks.

By the time we reach the thick of the cloud forest, we have been walking for two hours. Our boots are sopping wet and black with mud. Here, for the first time, our guides stop. This, they tell us, is the cloud forest (*bosque nuboso*). The density of the trees—their trunks, vines, and leaves—shortens visibility to about twenty feet. We hear hummingbirds flit through the woods, and see little red spiders running over moist green leaves. The air is now so wet it might be raining. When we start hiking again, we are so exhausted that we focus only on finding secure footing, not the trees, birds, bugs, and canopy.

Twenty minutes later, we pass two villagers coming down the trail from Chicacnab and get a chance to see local modes of anger in action. When we hear the men talking loudly to each over the sound of marimba music on their radio, we stop hiking and step to the edge of the trail, expecting some kind of brief hello. But when the men see us, they quickly stop talking, shut off the radio, and speed up their pace, passing us quickly without out a word, their eyes glued to the trail. Once ought of sight, the radio is switched back on, and their loud and boisterous conversation resumes. One of these men, I knew, had once taken in tourists at the very beginning of the NGO's work in Chicacnab. However, after allegedly keeping for himself money that David had given to him in trust for the entire community, he was dropped from the ecotourism program. Since then, he has become antagonistic toward tourists, speaking out against them at village meetings and, as some villagers put it, "looking on them with treacherousness" (*xiik' naril*) when they pass. Or, as the Danish man described it, savoring the idiomatic nature of the English phrase though shaken up by the encounter, the men had "given us the cold shoulder."

The guides say nothing about the incident and do not stop again. They talk between themselves in Q'eqchi' and walk quickly. The tourists give themselves over to what is essentially a march. Their experience of the cloud forest at this point, if anything like my own, is reduced to heavy breathing, sweat-stung eyes, and the plopping and sucking sound of boots being planted in and pulled from mud. Finally the cloud forest breaks, and we are at the edge of Chicacnab. Though it is now dusk, visibility is somewhat restored. We walk along the edge of a milpa and can see distant pairs of houses with hearth fires lit. Here we break up into three groups. One guide will take the Danish couple and the Austrian cop to his home (where his mother will host the couple and his sister-in-law will host the cop). The other guide will take the Israeli and German women to his mother's house. I, taking up the slack of the third guide who never showed up, will take the Austrian women to the house where I usually stay. We say our goodbyes and agree to meet up the next morning for a hike through the cloud forest.

It is already dark when we get to our house. Angelina, our host, has cooked dinner. Like the Austrian sisters, she speaks no Spanish. She tells me to tell the sisters that her husband, who should have been their guide, had to travel into town to help a sick villager. She also tells me to tell them that they will have to share a bed, and that I will take the one across (where my sleeping bag and books are already kept). When I explain this to them, they say no problem, and one optimistically points out that it will be warmer anyway. Angelina guides us from the thatch-roofed house where she is cooking, and where she and her family sleep, to the adjacent, tin-roofed house, where a section is partitioned off for tourists' beds. She gestures with a smile to amenities she and her husband arranged for tourists: her two weavings up on the wall; a cord strung across the room where they can hang up wet clothing; two candles with matches; and a thick spongy mattress, with a Disneyland bedsheet on it, where they will sleep. The sisters say, "Gracias, muy amable," and one reaches for her cigarettes.

Smoking in the tourist room, they unload their backpacks and take off their boots. Angelina's six-year-old son comes in to tell us to come to dinner, saying, "Lavar, comer," or "Wash, eat." We wash our hands in a bucket of spring water and go in and sit on little stools around the fire, our hands still smarting from the shock of cold water. A basket with hot tortillas sits on a tall stool. Next to the basket are three bowls of soup, made of water, chili, MSG, noodles, and *ichaj*, a nutritious and bitter plant that grows around housing sites. The two sisters eat in silence, hunched over their bowls, visibly exhausted. Angelina cooks quietly. She puts more tortillas in the basket, offers them coffee with a few murmured words in Spanish, and adjusts the blankets on her youngest son, who is sleeping on a bed by the hearth fire: *hijo, tortilla, caldo, cansado.*

Angelina's husband cannot guide them into the forest the next day, she tells me, because he will still be away. The man hosting their police officer friend will be their guide instead. I translate, and they nod indifferently. When they finish eating, they interact briefly with Angelina's older son, saying in broken Spanish their names, and asking the boy his. This done, they say, "Gracias," to Angelina and go back to our room.

When I arrive, the sisters sit drinking beers they brought with them, zipped into their sleeping bags because of the cold. They talk about the hike and the village, drinking and smoking, a single candle burning on the stool beside them. I ask them what they think about the trip so far; we didn't expect the villagers would be so poor, they say. One had noticed Angelina's son using a discarded corncob as a toy vehicle; the children must be very imaginative, the other notes. An hour later (about 8:00), they have finished their beer and try to arrange themselves comfortably on the small bed. I turn on my Walkman, zip my sleeping bag over my head, and listen to music until I fall asleep.

The next morning, Angelina begins grinding corn for tortillas by five o'clock. I eat breakfast with her at six. The sisters try unsuccessfully to sleep in until 8:30. They get out of bed in a foul mood. I surmise that they are angry about the roosters, angry about the grinding of corn, and angry about the children playing near their beds. They are angry about the wind that comes through the cracks, angry about the tilt of their bed, angry about the quality of the food, angry about the distance to the latrine with their beer-filled bladders, and angry about their wet boots and filthy, chafing socks. They are angry, it seems to me, about all the things I myself have been angry about in the past, and feel irritated about today.

They come to breakfast with sleep scum on their lips, their breath sour from last night's cigarettes and beer. They refuse Angelina's beans and tortillas and content themselves with a cigarette—which they are now bold enough to smoke by her hearth—and some coffee, to which they add their own Nescafé, giving kick to what is otherwise hot sugar water. Revived, they begin to chat a bit. They are here on their annual three-week vacation. So far, they have done the gringo trail, visiting the colonial city of Antigua, the lake of Atitlán, and the temple at Tikal, and diving in Honduras. They resoundingly agree that there is nothing to do in Cobán, emphasizing its lack of bars.

Angelina asks me to tell them that the other tourists have arrived, and that they should leave soon if they want to see the cloud forest, because in two hours they will have to begin their trip back down the mountain. We go outside, where several other neighbors have congregated around the tourists and their guides, each of them with stuff to sell. One man has brought a "dios de maize," or corn god, that he has carved from a local tree. It weighs about twenty pounds and is poorly executed. He learned how to carve such things several years before in Tikal, where he was taught by another NGO. One tourist wants to know how long it took him to make it. When I translate her question, he says, "Tres días," or "Three days." The tourists look askance when he tells them it costs Q75. Another woman tries to sell them some weavings she has made; she points out that she has embroidered a tourist, a quetzal, and a tree in the weaving itself. (And if you look carefully at what is obviously an amateur job, you can indeed see what looks like three distinct spots.) The tourists seem unhappy with both the poor quality, and the fact that it is so baldly "nonauthentic"—representing them and their interests, rather than the "customs and cosmovision" of the Q'eqchi'. Another villager is more successful. He sells a hammock to the cop for fifty quetzals. (A month before he tried to sell it to me for thirty quetzals.) This turns out to be the only successful sale; most of the tourists look uncomfortable at just being offered the stuff. And this discomfort makes sense; most of their actual monetary interactions will have taken place in the project's offices; once in the village, all of one's necessities have already been paid for. Nonetheless, their polite refusals to buy things constitute their most extensive interactions with locals. Villagers' attempts to sell objects constitute their most extensive encounter with the tourists. Hosting and guiding has given way to convincing and selling, haggling and higgling.

The cop has clearly passed a better night. Her Spanish is passable, and she found out that her guide had been in the Guatemalan army, so they could share stories about military life. Both had been shot at and wounded: she, on her arm, where she says a bullet grazed her during a training exercise; and he, in his foot, when he was ambushed. Unlike the other tourists, she is not exhausted by the previous day's hike. She has slept well, eaten heartily, and is on more intimate terms with her guide. She says she took pictures of him and his wife, who posed in front of the house with their children, with whom she spent the morning playing soccer. The Danish couple report being served very good food but complain of the small bed. And the husband says he would be interested in doing an episode of his TV program about village life. The German and Israeli women say they feel cheated that only two guides brought them up, whereas they had paid for four guides. And the Danish woman, quite astutely, as we'll see in chapter 2, jokingly complains that there are more chickens and children than cloud forest and quetzals. The cop, disgusted with this conversation and her companions' petty concerns, leaves to do hacky-sack moves with a beer can left out by the Austrian sisters, and the children are delighted.

By now it is almost ten o'clock—much too late to visit the cloud forest, eat lunch, and hike down the mountain in time to catch the bus. When I tell this to the tourists, they decide to gather their backpacks and hike out before lunch. They will experience the cloud forest on their journey down, they figure. They can buy chocolate and water in Caquipek in lieu of lunch. Any strength they have left, the sisters say, should be saved for the hike. The villages are not happy with this decision. Angelina worries they will tell David that they did not get to go into the cloud forest. The guides are worried that David will find out that they, and not their fathers, had done the guiding. And the cop somewhat resolves the situation by explaining, in efficient Spanish, that her tired friends will see the cloud forest on the way down. Thus, only sixteen hours after having arrived—their interactions with villagers reduced to following guides, accepting food, and declining souvenirs; their experience of the cloud forest reduced to discomfort, exhaustion, and speed; and most of their time in the village spent unsuccessfully trying to sleep—the tourists prepare to leave.

Standards and Singularities

Many tensions underlie the ecotourism experience, as the above story illustrates. In many ways, the NGO's intervention failed *in terms of its own ontology* (qua categories, commitments, and conduct). With routinization, villagers found ecotourists less engaging. For example, in the village of San Lucas, where the project had just begun an ecotourism program, the quality of interaction with tourists, and the range of village life shown to them, was usually much richer than in Chicacnab, where the program had been going on for several years. Concomitantly, as ecotourists became less of a novelty, and care was routinized, standards often slipped.

Tourists' visits, moreover, were highly unpredictable, in terms of when they would occur, how often they would occur, how many and what kinds of tourists would arrive, and so forth. Villagers found other economic opportunities more pressing. Families could not count on ecotourism for a fixed income, so they placed a higher value on everyday economic practices, be they maize agriculture or plantation labor, and made decisions about labor allocation accordingly. The NGO's inability to standardize the supply for ecotourists made villagers unwilling to standardize their delivery of ecotourism.

The capacitation of villagers to standards erroneously presumed that there existed a standard villager to be capacitated. For example, the NGO provided language training sufficient only to articulate pleasantries; the Spanish needed for an actual conversation was best learned on fincas, at school, in the army, or on the street. Villagers' variable ability to communicate with ecotourists was far more a function of their previous experience than their attendance at language-training meetings organized by the NGO.

Crucially, only hosts were capacitated, not guests. Standards applied to tourists with varying success. For example, while the Austrian police officer enjoyed her stay in the village, her two friends found the hike difficult, the food gross, the lifestyle boring, and the locals alternately impenetrable and pushy. In other words, the NGO needed tourists of particular stamina and sociability; and so personality was often the deciding factor as to whether guests enjoyed their stay or not.

With the increasing emphasis on standards, as will be the focus in chapter 4, discrepancies between standards and experience constantly arose. And with relatively coupled and asymmetric roles linking tourists and villagers, every intersubjective interaction became a chance to evaluate whether or not the standards were being upheld. For example, just as tourists grieved that they were not getting their due, villagers felt as if they were always under view (as seen, for example, in the frequent references to David's potential displeasure if word got back to him of villagers not conforming to standards).

While the project fostered instrumental rationality, like cash incentives, as a means to lure the villagers into its ecotourism program, ecotourists were most appalled when they were treated as instruments by villagers—being seen by them as customers, competitors, or commodities.

And last, as seen by the early departure of the tourists, tourists did not want to spend enough time to see village life, because there did not seem to be enough village life for them to see; a plethora of chickens could not capture the heart of a tourist like the promise of a single quetzal.

In short, as radically enclosing as the project's ecotourism program was, it was not nearly enclosing enough. And this was probably to be expected; it is no easy task to create a generalized other (Mead), disciplinary regime (Foucault), or total institution (Goffman), in the middle of the cloud forest. Notwithstanding all the NGO's efforts, the tourists felt cheated, the villagers felt surveilled, the cloud forest receded, and the number of quetzals dwindled. Only the anthropologist walked off with a surplus (of materials).

Or at least this is one kind of story, or interpretation, we could offer. And it would certainly fit in with the NGO's ontology, as well as that of much critical theory. But it is far too easy. Indeed, the most radical forms of enclosure often allow for the simplest forms of escape (say, into one's head); and the most seemingly open of institutions (say, the market) have often turned out to be the most totalizing.

For these reasons, the following chapters will offer decidedly less direct ways of disclosing the effects of the NGO on village life, as well as the effects of village life on the NGO. They will explicate the ramifications of the project's radical and repeated attempts to "incite a coexistence" between different kinds of evaluating agents and different kinds of valued things, through the quasi-intersubjective and seemingly immaterial entangling of their interactions, in local ontological terms, themselves often as fluid and frame-dependent as they were fractious and formidable. Before continuing, and as a means to tie together both of these perspectives in a provisional manner, it is worth theorizing some key relations between labor, value, interaction, and incommensurability as they were at play in the NGO's interventions, and as they have been articulated in several analytic traditions.

Immaterial Labor, Incommensurate Values, and Intersubjective Intentions

To understand so-called immaterial labor, it is best to contrast it with classic understandings of material labor.[7] From one influential perspective, material labor produces a product that "lasts" beyond the production process itself (Marx 2000: 155–74; Smith [1776] 1976: 351–52). This capacity to "last" is not particularly helpful in itself and so should really be resolved into a number of more basic dimensions, which, while in the spirit of Marx and Smith, are not to the letter. Following our discussion of the various senses of portability and enclosure in the introduction, and relatively speaking, the product of material labor is continuously present to the senses (or more or less "objective" in a stereotypic sense). It exists in a permanent form (having more or less the same structure or shape in time, across space, and between persons). It is detachable from the context (understood temporally, spatially, and personally) in which it is produced. It is transportable across such contexts (say, from factory to market, from producer to consumer, and so forth). And it is "handy" relative to the size, strength, skill, and senses of the human agents in question. Materiality (and immateriality as its marked converse) should therefore be understood as a multidimensional, graded, and ontology-specific phenomenon. It is readily assimilated to Cartesian objects (that which has extension in space) and Kantian things (that which serves as a means to an end). In some sense, then, not withstanding its seemingly august origins, it is the most provincial of notions. Indeed, for anthropologists, it is still closely tied to archeology as traditionally understood, that is, whatever can be dug up and/or put on display without suffering undue deterioration. Immateriality, like materiality, is really a pseudocategory—and so not worth theorizing except perhaps insofar as scholars are constantly trying to theorize it (Kockelman 2012a, 2015).

While it might seem like materiality is really just a gauge of the object-like qualities of products (given the particular subject-like qualities of their producers), what really makes it important to critical theory is the way such object-like qualities play into the dynamics of political economy (as classically understood). For example, the materiality of a product is caught up in the productivity of labor; to realize the value created in production usually requires that the product be transportable from the factory to the market. It is caught up in alienation, that is, the ease with which a product may be removed from its producer and appropriated by someone else. It is caught up in displacement, that is, the degree to which the process of consumption may be displaced (in time, space, and person) from the process of production—and hence "circulate" (or rather be widely distributed). It is caught up in the accumulation of capital, that is, the degree to which the finished product of one production process may become the raw material of another. And it is caught up in ownership; that is, the more material a product is, the easier it often is to assign and enforce property rights. In all these ways, then, immateriality is an early way of understanding the relative nonportability of certain products. Somewhat ironically, then, the concepts of materiality and immateriality, as traditionally understood, really sit at the intersection of idealist German metaphysics and classic British political economy and so are themselves difficult to port far afield.

With this intellectual genealogy in mind, itself understood as a critique of the instinct to generate such conceptual distinctions in the first place, I want to offer a more narrow definition of immaterial labor, one of particular relevance to my field site: any activity oriented toward creating and maintaining certain forms of coordinated social interaction, in all their meaningfulness (e.g., signification and interpretation, sensation and instigation) and modality (e.g., commitments and entitlements, permission and obligation), which itself *seems* to produce no lasting product other than the mode of coordination itself (Kockelman 2002, 2006). It is thus a relatively reflexive mode of production, which is orientated toward producing a relatively immaterial commodity—and thus an entity (quality, process, event) that has both use value and exchange value, and so serves a function and may fetch a price, and yet is neither an "object" nor a "thing" (in their stereotypic senses). In the activities at issue in this chapter, the hosting and guiding of ecotourists, such an immaterial commodity turns on inhabiting reciprocal social statuses, expressing and interpreting signs, and thereby being a self in relation to an other. At a higher level of abstraction, it turns on *being an interactant in an intersubjectively shared interaction.*[8]

For present purposes, interaction may be understood to involve the actions (affordances, instruments, roles, and identities) of two or more coupled actors, whose interaction is ongoing, such that the interpretant of one actor is simultaneously a sign that another actor will subsequently interpret (and so on, indefinitely and reciprocally). Such interaction stereotypically occurs in real time (it is immediate, synchronized, ongoing, emergent, and unpredictable), though it need not be. Such interaction is reciprocal (each participant is constantly and simultaneously expressing signs for the others to interpret, however consciously or unconsciously, and interpreting signs that the others have expressed). And such inter- action is multimodal (not only are linguistic signs being expressed and in- terpreted, but also being expressed are bodily gestures, facial expressions, co-occurring material signs in context, and so forth).[9] In these ways, then, interaction is perhaps the exemplar of immaterial labor, that is, the real- time, reciprocal, multimodal coordination of two or more signifying and interpreting actors that often seems to have no product other than the mode of coordination itself. In some sense, by capacitating villagers (in all the ways that will be described in chapter 4) and by priming ecotour- ists (in all the ways described in this chapter), the NGO was attempting to enclose (standardize, utilize, price, etc.) one of the kinds of processes least easy to enclose—interaction understood as a fundamental site of inter- subjectively shared disclosure, and thus a site where individual and col- lective values could be displayed as much as discussed, reflected as much as regimented, produced as much as presumed.

In the tradition of Anscombe ([1957] 1976), as perhaps most usefully articulated by Hacking (1995), philosophers often characterize an inten- tion as an action under a description. What we might say, rather, is that an intention is a relatively controlled behavior within an interpretation. For example, when I raise my hand (controlled behavior, initial phase of action, or sign), your calling on me is an interpretant that projects an ob- ject (in this case a subsequent phase of action, qua function, purpose, end, or intention) onto my behavior. In certain cases, such as the kind focused on by Anscombe and Hacking, these interpretants are articu- lated descriptions, for instance, "Paul raised his hand." But that is only the tip of the iceberg; purpose-projecting interpretants may be affective (blushing) and energetic (ducking) as much as representational (describ- ing or believing), inter alia. In this reading, Hacking's (1995) claim that new descriptions (of actions) may bring about new intentions (for acting) is really a minor point underlying a much larger claim (and indeed a much less surprising claim, given the way semiosis will be characterized in later chapters). With new interpretants of sign-object relations (not to mention new signs, qua behaviors, per se) comes the possibility of new objects (qua purposes or intentions). And with the possibility of new actions and/or intentions comes the possibility of new modes of personhood (Kockelman 2010c, 2013a), understood as the prototypic instigator of actions, and thus a key unit of accountability.

But this criticism and generalization aside, what is so important about descriptions per se is that they are caught up in the conceptual structure of language, and reason giving more generally. This means not only that the intentions (in this case, the states of affairs being described) can be richly articulated, but also that the descriptions themselves can be easily called into question, and the intentions themselves can be subject to justification. Intentions—qua actions under descriptions—do not have just causal-indexical fruits (in the sense that they bring about the states of affairs so described); they have also rational-inferential roots (in the sense that they are subject to reasoning). And the reasons actors give for their actions turn on values in the most stereotypic sense, be they mundane or otherworldy, personal, or categorical. *Why did you open your umbrella? Because I wanted to stay dry, check its springs, protect my clothes, hide my face, disguise my origins, signal my accomplice, protect a tourist from the rain, do unto others as I would have them do unto me, act such that my action could become a universal maxim,* and so on, and so forth.

(Needless to say, while many anthropologists are wary of ascribing allegedly Western [European, modern, etc.] forms of intentionality onto others [as seemingly private, psychological states], human interaction would be impossible if we did not project [affectively, energetically, discursively] purposes [qua possible and probable outcomes] onto the behavior of others, any more than if we did not project objects onto each other's signs through our interpretants. In other work [Kockelman 2010b, 2013a] I have treated at length the relation between "intentions" [in a so-called Western-European folk-psychological sense], intentions as just characterized here [from a semiotic stance, following a tradition in analytic philosophy], the purposeful behaviors of animals, and the ways speakers of Q'eqchi' Maya ontologize related processes. For present purposes, it cannot be stressed enough that intentions, for Anscombe and Hacking, are not "mental states" in such a stereotypic sense; they are simply actions under descriptions. And so simply to describe another's behavior [the tourists went to the cloud forest, Angelina is making dinner, he tried to sell us a hammock] is to project an intention onto it.)

What Anscombe did not consider, what has been left out of the secondary literature on her ideas in critical theory (such as in Hacking's important and widely cited work), and what is particularly germane to my current interests, is the fact that many actions—indeed, many of the most interesting and consequential actions—are really *interactions* undertaken by two or more interactants. In particular, while interactants may each have their own small-scale purpose or intention (you are holding the nail in position while I am hammering it in), the large-scale intention may be more or less identical, and more or less self-consciously so; that is, we are making a desk, fixing a chair, preserving an heirloom, producing a commodity, covering our asses, overthrowing a dictator, and even increasing the wealth of the nation (as will be discussed below).

And, in the case of immaterial labor, which is very often a mode of "semiotic labor" (Kockelman 2006), when the intention is not to produce a relatively lasting object, the joint intention may be simply to share an experience, shoot the shit, establish a price, formulate a plan, undertake a transaction, maintain a convention, stay in touch, and so forth. Thus, while it may not be material in the stereotypic sense, it may be incredibly consequential in every other sense; the state of affairs brought about may have deep and lasting repercussions; and the values justifying such an action may intimately touch every aspect of social life. Such joint intentions are often the condition for, and consequence of, joint attention; that is, we act together such that we may perceive together (and vice versa); and what we perceive together is often our own and others' actions. And they are a crucial site for the emergence of distributed agents, or dispersed modes of personhood (Kockelman 2005, 2011; Enfield 2013); we act (in part) as one, and so we may each (in part) be held accountable for the result of our action. Moreover, not only can we each—individually or collectively—be held accountable for the causal fruits of our actions (what comes about because of them); we can also be held accountable for their logico-rational roots, that is, the reasons we may give (or have) for undertaking them, and the kinds of values these are grounded in. That is, accountability for interactions is usually radically distributed (even if there is a fall-guy, qua fetishized villain, or designated hero, as there so often is). And, of course, both kinds of processes can go awry—indeed, as we saw in this chapter, and as we will return to in the conclusion, this *capacity to fail may be the very essence of action*, either in bringing about various causal fruits, or in being grounded in various rational roots. That is, just as our actions may prove ineffective, our reasons for them may be judged inadequate.

Values may be understood in many ways, but a classic move from scholars ranging from Max Weber (1968) to Charles Taylor (1989), and certainly in line with the NGO's interventions, frames value in terms of second-order desire. As the story goes, there are too many desirable objects and outcomes, and not enough resources to secure all of them, so choices must be made. And to make such choices requires a standard of value—some way of assessing the relative desirability of different desires, such that an actor (or interactor) can determine which one to act (or interact) for. In this tradition (Kockelman 2010c, 2013a), there are relatively instrumental values (Weber) or modes of weak evaluation (Taylor) that are grounded in notions like cost, efficiency, or utility. And, conversely, there are relatively existential values or modes of strong evaluation, which are grounded in notions of the "good," the "just," or the "true."

Moreover, as a function of such evaluative standards, not only may different desires be more or less commensurate (insofar as they may or may not be graded as to their relative desirability via such an evaluative standard), but so too there may be different kinds of evaluative standards, qua second-order desires or "values" (insofar as they may or may not be used to evaluate the same kinds of actions, lead to the same decisions when used, or be translated into one another's terms).[10]

As shown in this chapter, many of the (putative) second-order, or existential values of tourists and funding agencies are easily listed. There are quasi-theological values; for example, the quetzal is understood as being integrally related to either the Mayan soul or Guatemalan national identity. There are quasi-aesthetic values; for example, the project's interventions are designed to be beautiful and/or simple by being minimally intervening, self-reinforcing, and maximally transparent. There are quasi-modern values; for example, Q'eqchi' culture is characterized as authentic, and the environs of the Q'eqchi' are characterized as pristine. There are quasi-moral values, for example, women's participation and economic justice. And there are ecological and/or political values, for example, sustainable development and biodiversity. In other words, these are all reasons that the NGO (and many ecotourists) gave for their actions—why they undertook the interventions they did, and what kinds of effects they hoped their interactions with villagers would have.

As seen in the introduction, at the heart of the NGO's intervention was a radical assumption about what motivates different kinds of people; they foregrounded the instrumental nature of villagers (by using cash as an incentive) to tap into the existential values of tourists and granting agencies (such as authenticity and biodiversity). Indeed, the strategy was perhaps more interesting and insidious than this; by using existential incentives with tourists, the NGO accommodated such incentives to their own economic values; and by using instrumental incentives with Q'eqchi', the NGO assimilated such incentives to their own existential values. Insofar, then, as seemingly instrumentally rational villagers were engaged in co-ordinated interactions with existentially motivated tourists, or vice versa, each of their actions could often be interpreted in two or more idioms at once—not just in regards to what kind of action, or interaction, was being undertaken, with what causal effect, but also in regards to why it was being undertaken, with what value-based reason.

Of interest in this chapter, then, is the relation between the articulated (and ascribed) intentions and values of particular interactants (such as Q'eqchi'-speaking villagers and ecotourists), and the degree to which these intentions and values were actor specific or mutually shared. In some sense, we might think of this chapter—and, indeed, one important thread of this book—as an examination of what happens when actors who are accustomed to acting under radically different descriptions, and for radically different reasons, are capacitated (in the case of villagers) or primed (in the case of ecotourists) to *interact under the same description—or, at the very least, to smoothly interact under ontologically different local interpretations in ways that can causally, performatively, and perhaps unconsciously bring about the possibility for interacting under similar global descriptions.* This is arguably the most insidious—and hitherto uncommented on—kind of commensuration, a mode of governance that channels first-order difference into second-order equivalence. As will be shown, this making and breaking of various scales of commensurability often turned on the most visible of hands—themselves hard at work, so to speak, producing the conditions of possibilities for modes of immaterial labor to function, such that the value of social relations and semiotic practices could be captured.

CHAPTER 2

A Mayan Ontology of Poultry

SELFHOOD, AFFECT, AND ANIMALS

Birds as Emblems of Eras and Identities

Let us now move from analyzing the categories and values underlying an NGO's protection of endangered avifauna to the modes of significance that organize how and why the Q'eqchi' care for chickens.

The chicken was brought to the New World by the Spanish colonizers five hundred years ago, displacing the turkey as the preferred domestic bird in many parts of Mesoamerica. *Gallo*, the Spanish word for rooster, is also the name of the national beer of Guatemala. European immigrants, lured by the coffee-growing potential of the chilly, mountainous homeland of the Q'eqchi' Maya (itself located in the department of Alta Verapaz, Guatemala) began to arrive in the late 1800s and soon displaced many of the Q'eqchi' from their land and were using many of the Q'eqchi' for labor. *El Gallo* is also the name of the formerly German-owned department store (circa 1872) in Alta Verapaz's capital city Cobán—the first place in Alta Verapaz where one could buy a wide array of constantly stocked European-made commodities. (Also, *el gallo* functions as a superlative in Guatemalan Spanish; for example, one can say "the cock of soaps," or "the best soap"—making all other brands of soap, as it were, mere hens.) Atop this department store, and higher than everything else but the cross of the local church, still stands a metallic rooster astride a weather vane and compass, being not only an index of weather, but an emblem of dawn, a geocentric origo for national territory, a symbol of ladino masculinity, in contiguity with a plethora of consumer commodities, and a trace of history. Signs of time, space, history, identity, economy, gender, nationality—and even beer—all find their expression here.

As introduced in chapter 1, the village of Chicacnab is located within half a day's journey from Cobán. To get there, one must ride in a bus for two hours; and then, one must hike up a trail for three hours. Because of its distance from roads and altitude (more than two thousand meters), Chicacnab is surrounded by one of the largest cloud forests in Guatemala (with an average rainfall between two and three meters per year), and has one of the highest densities of the resplendent quetzal, a rare and beautiful bird. The tail feathers of the male quetzal are an iridescent green, and can be more than three times the length of its body. Such is their beauty that they have been a sumptuary item, and at times currency, in Mesoamerica for thousands of years. Indeed, Guatemalan national currency is called the "quetzal," and elders in the village, when tipsy, sometimes trace the dwindling of quetzals in the cloud forest that surrounds their homes to the devaluation of national currency. The chicken might be figured as a foreign imposition, but it is the quetzal that functions as a universal equivalent; that is, the one commodity that can be used to measure the value of all other commodities—and hence one of the most portable of commodities.

Quetzal (from Nahuatl *quetzalli*) is a nominalization of the Nahuatl verb *quetza*, which means "to erect." And, indeed, the male quetzal tail feathers are long and stiff backed. If one remembers that *quetzalcoatl*, the famous "plumed serpent" of Aztec mythology, is composed of this same root, one is tempted to retranslate the entire construction as "erect serpent," or simply *tumescent penis*—a point to which I will return.

So if the quetzal is a sign of national currency, and the rooster is a sign of national masculinity, the two come together in the money that Q'eqchi' men spend on beer. Indeed, there were two vices in the village that various organizations explicitly thematized: drunkenness (*kalaak*) and excessive childbearing (*kok'alib'k*). In particular, when speaking about dissolute Q'eqchi' men, those with "bad habits," one made reference to alcohol—specifically *tzo' kaxlan*, the Q'eqchi' word for rooster, and the local code word for beer (borrowing from the trademark *Gallo*). Indeed, a favorite way to trip up the anthropologist was to ask him, "Ma nakaaket li tzo' kax-lan?," which means both "Do you eat cocks?" and "Do you drink beer?" (It might also mean "Do you give head?," but I was too shy to pursue this.) In this way, the relationship between chickens and Guatemalan national culture permeated the village (and sometimes inebriated the villagers).

Furthermore, as also seen in chapter 1, the NGO was sending ecotourists into this village, using the existence of cloud forests and quetzal birds as a lure. However, one of the ironies of village life was that while ecotourists would backpack in to see the quetzal, not only was the journey boring, but the quetzal was rarely seen. In its stead, the average ecotourist saw hundreds of chickens, all of whom bore a particularly textured relation to the Q'eqchi' and, indeed, a particularly textured historical relationship to the ecotourists themselves. In other words, the villagers would receive quetzals, qua scarce currency, for showing tourists their quetzals, qua rare birds; the trouble was that the Q'eqchi' had very few quetzals (in either sense), and so tourists only ever saw their chickens, which were in abundance. To quote Wallace Stevens, "O thin men of Haddam, why do you imagine golden birds? Do you not see how the blackbird walks around the feet of the women about you?" (from "Thirteen Ways of Looking at a Blackbird").

In short, when the chicken (as the female member of the species *Gallus gallus*) is contrasted with other birds—such as roosters, quetzals, and chicken hawks—it gets figured as not just female and foreign, but also worthless and weak, prosaic and prey. Or, inverting the frame, as the cock is a sign of one hundred years of world-market domination (and God only knows how many years of world-male domination), as the chicken is a sign of five hundred years of colonialism, and as the quetzal is a sign of two thousand years of Mesoamerican elite life (not to mention twenty years of ecotourism), so the chicken hawk is a sign of timeless nature: a bird of prey or raptor, symbolic not only of predatory precapitalism, but also of instinct laid bare.

Frames of Value

As a means to complement our analysis of ecotourists in search of quetzals, and NGOs aiming for conservation, this chapter focuses on women's care for chickens among speakers of Q'eqchi' Maya living in the village of Chicacnab. It is ethnographically organized around local ways of framing the relation between women and chickens, the relation between chickens and other species, and the relation between women and other identities. I analyze these frames in terms of three key themes: *ontology* (what kinds of entities there are in the world), *affect* (cognitive and corporeal attunements to such entities), and *selfhood* (relatively reflexive centers of attunement).

The first part of this chapter is the most stereotypically linguistic and symbolic. In it, I detail five broad frames: the complementary relation among four kinds of birds (hens, roosters, quetzals, and chicken hawks), each of which is emblematic of a particular era or identity; the etymology of the word *kaxlan*, which denotes chickens and connotes alterity; lexical taxonomies surrounding domestic animals, with a particular emphasis on birds, and the relatively tacit semantic associations that these index; animal calls, naming practices, and kinship designations, which in turn interpellate chickens as quasi-subjects. Finally, I analyze ontological qualities related to *not* being a mammal and *not* having a self that are revealed in the context of discursive disruptions. The second part of the chapter is the most stereotypically economic and material. In it, I detail the wide range of social relations mediated by the circulation of chickens. The third part is the most stereotypically psychological and person centered. In it, I detail five broad frames: illness and the relation between pregnant women and brooding hens; attributions of desire and reason to animals; the relation between children and chickens; signs of fear, cowardice, and anxiety; and the attack of a chicken hawk in relation to the collapse of selfhood. I argue that the chicken is a particularly rich site for research because it is simultaneously self, alter, and object for its owners. Chicken ontologies reveal not only the inadequacies of person/thing and subject/object ontologies, but also the inadequacies of the critics of such ontologies.

I chose these frames because they constitute empirically rich and analytically replete semiological structures and semiotic processes, which in turn mediate a range of social relations. As will be seen, the nature and culture of my object (the chicken) requires me to take into account (and often leap across) various temporal and spatial scales—from the Maya to Mesoamerica, from narratives of conquest to modern ethnographies, and from grammatical categories to breeding strategies. It also thereby shows some of the long history of ontological entanglement between birds and humans, and Mesoamerica and Europe, that were prior to the NGOs' interventions.

A Brief History of Loan Words and Loan Birds

In Q'eqchi', the word *kaxlan*, as a noun, refers to "chickens." In compound constructions (in which it functions like an adjective), *kaxlan* is used to refer to the newly introduced, nonindigenous analog of the object usually referred to by the noun. Thus, if *winq* refers to "men," *kaxlan winq* refers to "Ladino men" (i.e., nonindigenous, or nonindigenous-identifying, Guatemalan men). If *aatin* refers to "language," *kaxlan aatin* refers to the "Spanish language." If *motzo'* refers to "worms," *kaxlan motzo'* refers to "noodles." The objects denoted are typically nonmetallic objects, for example, artifacts, species, professions, food, or ideas. Loosely speaking, the word *kaxlan* denotes poultry and connotes alterity.

The word *ch'iich'*, as a count noun, refers to "machetes" and, as a mass noun, refers to "metal." In compound constructions with another noun, it refers to the newly introduced, nonindigenous analog of the object referred to by the other noun. Thus, if *so'sol* refers to "vultures," *so'sol ch'iich'* refers to "airplanes." If *ulul* refers to "brains," *ulul ch'iich'* refers to "computers." The objects typically referred to by such constructions are made of metal, or perceived as such.

Note then that *ch'iich'*, "machete," and *kaxlan*, "chicken," are in complementary distribution with respect to the newly introduced and nonindigenous objects denoted in such constructions. In this way, a threefold ontology comes into view, namely, Q'eqchi' things, and Spanish-introduced metallic and nonmetallic things. Note as well that, among the Q'eqchi', machetes are quintessentially male possessions, whereas chickens are quintessentially female possessions. And finally, note that while machetes are used to kill chickens, chickens are not used to kill machetes. In this way, gender and hierarchy are metonymically built into the ontology.

Evidence suggests that the Nahuatl-speaking Aztecs, upon hearing that the Spaniard conquistadors were from Castilla, assimilated the word to their language and heard "Castillan" (Lockhart 1992: 276–78). Given that the Nahuatl locative suffix is *-(t)lan*, this would have made *Castil(li)* a noun referring to some notable feature about the place of origin of the Spaniards. As the Spaniards brought with them, and were in constant contiguity with, chickens, it is not surprising that early Nahuatl dictionaries have an entry *Caxtil*, which is said to denote "chickens." *Castilla(n)* seems to have meant for the ancient Nahuas, then, "land of the chickens" (Lockhart 1992: 276–78). To speculate on historical process, when the Spaniards subsequently invaded what is now Guatemala, their Nahuatl-speaking assistants may have brought this word with them, and, with some phonological shifts, it became the Q'eqchi' word for "chicken" and, as seen above, "foreign." Nonetheless, it should be emphasized that, during my fieldwork, most villagers did not consider *kaxlan* a loan word. In this way, otherness came cloaked in darkness.

That said, this grammatical construction could still be used to ridicule those foreign others. In particular, there was a nice slippage between *kaxlan aatin*, "the Spanish language," and *r-aatin kaxlan*, "the language of chickens" (lit. "its-word chicken"). For example, several times during the course of my fieldwork, a young man, watching me watch his wife's chickens—and both of us in the midst of a cacophony of clucks—would say, "ab'i', li kaxlan aatin," or "Listen, [they're speaking] Spanish."

Taxonomies as Denotational and Connotational Domains

Kaxlan, functioning as the Q'eqchi' word for chicken, is unmarked with respect to gender. Nonetheless, it primarily refers to female members of the species *Gallus gallus domesticus*. *Tzo' kaxlan* is used exclusively to refer to (adult) male members of this species. Chickens share such a gendered feature (unmarked female) and such a linguistic form (*tzo'*) with turkeys (*ak'ach*) and ducks (*patux*). For example, if *ak'ach* refers to "turkeys," *tzo' ak'ach* refers to "tom turkeys." In other words, domestic fowl have the semantic status of unmarked female; marking the male animal requires the form *tzo'*. This inverts the typical gender hierarchy of unmarked male and marked female. Such inversion is frequently found in particular nominal kinds, such as *widow* and *widower*, and in the restricted domain of domestic animals.

Domestic fowl share this gendered feature with pigs (*aaq*), cows (*wakax*), and dogs (*tz'i'*). The linguistic form used to mark male members of these latter species is not *tzo'*, but rather *k'ol*. For example, *k'ol wakax* refers to "bulls," *k'ol aaq* refers to "boars," and so on. All these species (fowl and nonfowl) belong to the superordinate category of domestic animals, lexicalized in the folk taxon *ketomj*, which is a marginal member of the class of inalienable possessions (Kockelman 2007b, 2010b), and which itself is probably related to the verb *ketok*, which means "to eat (or drink)."

Xul, as a noun, refers to all animals but can be glossed as "nondomestic animal." Domestic animals (*ketomj*) are the most marked members of this category. When *xul* ("animal") is contrasted with *kristyan* ("human"), *ketomj* ("domestic animals") are included within *xul*. However, when *xul* is contrasted with *ketomj*, domestic animals are kept distinct from animals. In formal genres, animals (*xul*) are linked—through parallelism— to forest and field, while domestic animals (*ketomj*) are linked to the homestead and hearth. Similarly, forest and field are typically associated with men (insofar as they are the locales of daily male work), whereas the homestead and hearth are associated with women. In this way, domestic animals such as chickens were associated with women and home, whereas nondomestic animals were associated with men and fields (or forest).

Xul, as an adjective, can mean "unbaptized," when occurring with the noun *winq*, "man" (unmarked human male), and contrasting with the word for *kristyan*, meaning "person" and, here, "Christian." *Xul* can also mean "wild," when contrasting with the adjective *tuulan* "tame" (which can also refer to nondangerous but otherwise wild animals, such as deer). And it may mean "mischievous" or "unruly" when occurring with the noun *al*, "child." Insofar as *xul* contrasts with *ketomj* (as nouns), the members of the category denoted by *ketomj* were associated with the antonyms of the adjectives for which *xul* is used. In other words, in contrast to nondomestic animals, domestic animals such as chickens could be associated with the ideas of baptism, tameness, and obedience.

Besides *xul* there is another construction used to refer to "wildmen" or the "unbaptized," namely, *choolwinq*. This construction seems to refer to speakers of the Mayan language Chool, who had some geographic overlap with the Q'eqchi'. When the Dominican friars, headed by Las Casas, first tried to conquer the area, the Chool reportedly could not be contained in the "reductions" (a kind of spatial, religious, and linguistic concentration of previously dispersed peoples). And so this linkage of animality, heathenness, and disobedience probably has a long, tragic, and bloody history. In some sense, then, to be wild is to resist enclosure. And chickens with their coops, just like cows with their corrals, are as unwild as can be. From this vantage, chickens, in contrast to chicken hawks, and the Q'eqchi', in contrast to the Chool, are "reductions" of their former selves.

As mentioned, *xul*, as a noun, refers to all animals, including birds. To speak about birds directly, there was no simple word, but rather an adjectival modification of *xul*, constructed with the diminutive-plural marker *kok'*. Thus, *kok' xul*, which literally means "small, numerous animals," referred to birds (and also to prototypically flying insects). There was a superordinate category of bird, marked by the word *tz'ik*, but it was almost exclusively used to refer to the penis. It could no longer be said without making children giggle and adults look uncomfortable. Indeed, the derived verb *tz'ikib'k*, "to be birding," referred to the activity of having sex. (The other key euphemism for having sex was *aatinak*, "to speak to" or "to have a conversation with.") The nonmetaphorical (and nonvulgar) word for penis, *kun*, was exclusively used to refer to the penis. Birds, then (but probably not chickens, as we will see below), were associated with the penis, and sex more generally.

Indeed, while this section has treated the set of taxa surrounding chickens, I will show in later sections that chickens were more like artifacts than living kinds. That is, the chicken's inherent relation to other animals was determined more by the instrumental functions it served, the associative semantic chains it was entangled with, and the ritual meanings it expressed, than by any inherent biological qualities it might possess. Insofar as the chicken had such a relation to other animals, if one knew some fact about a chicken (for example, that it succumbed to a particular kind of illness, or that it had a certain type of defense strategy), one could generalize this propensity more easily to other domestic animals, or even to children and women, than one could to other birds. Thus, the types of inductions chickens allowed for were conditioned by their pragmatic function and ritual meaning as much as their taxonomic placement. In some strange way, then, the chicken was removed from its life-form (qua biological class, that is, *aves*) by its positioning in a particular form of life.

Chickens as Addressees and Affines

Of all animals, only dogs and cats were typically named and given status designators. Dogs, for example, were given the nonelder status designator *aj* or *ix* (regardless of their age), depending on whether they were male or female, respectively. For a name, nonproper nouns from Spanish were typically chosen, for example, *Conejo*, "rabbit," *Chapín*, "Guatemalan," *Camarún*, "Camaroon," and so on. Cats were often given proper nouns from Spanish and, if they were old enough (and surly or aloof enough), an elder status designator *qawa'*, "don," or *qana'*, "doña," *Carlota, José,* and the like. In contrast, chickens were usually identified using the definite article *li* and a size-color-pattern predication. (Since there was typically only one rooster per flock, specifying sex was not helpful.) For example, *li ch'ina-q'eq* referred to "the little black one." It should be said that such a definite descriptor did not hold in "any world" (as a proper rigid designator should) but only until growth, death, or sale of a chicken occurred. Thus, unlike proper names, such descriptions uniquely identified their referent for at most a few months. Indeed, small chickens were not often differentiated. Rather, they were referred to using deictics when the speaker and addressee shared a common phenomenal field, for example, *li ch'ina kaxlan a'an*, "that little chicken." (Nonetheless, women were quick to point out that they were "familiar with"—*na'ok u*, qua German *kennen*, or Spanish *conocer*—or could uniquely identify, each of their chickens.) Wild animals were never named. They were referred to by their folk taxon and the definite article *li*. Of all animals, only dogs were usually addressed. When asked why chickens are not named, women usually answered that it was because "they wouldn't understand them" (*li kaxlan moko te'xtaw ta li ru*). In this way, understanding—the recognition of oneself as the referent of a word—was a prerequisite for interpellation. Chickens, then, unlike dogs, would not answer if called.

The fact that chickens were not named did not mean that they could not be hailed by other means. In particular, to call chickens to come and eat, one said, "achik chik chik chiiik." For example, a woman might grind corn for the chickens up to three times a day (in the midst of grinding corn for her family). She could take out a small basket of corn (for the mature chickens) or a handful of ground corn (*b'uch*) for the chicks, walk around the house, peer into the underbrush and behind stumps, and use this call half a dozen times. After the chickens had gathered in front of her house, she could then scatter the feed. To call chickens back to the house for safety and counting after a predatory engagement, or into the chicken coop at dusk, one could say, "awú chu chu chu chuuu." To get chickens out of the house, one could give the command "ayu," or "go," in the same syllabic-stress-length pattern as other chicken calls, for instance, "ayú yu yu yu yuuu." Alternatively, one could use the noun for "fear" (*xiw*) as a command to flee, for instance, "axíw xiw xiw xiw xiiiw." In short, there was a form class (determined by a syllabic structure and prosodic envelope, as much as deictic centering and directionality) that had four members:

come and get it, come home to roost, go away, and get out (or "shoo"). Such animal calls are a subset of interjections (Kockelman 2003, 2010b), themselves a sign that is often erroneously understood by linguists and lay folk alike to be at the margins of language, a kind of locale where human voice is still mythologically entangled with animal sounds because of its alleged iconic transparency and indexical immediacy.

For example, if the chickens had not yet been fed, then, while a woman cooked, they could slowly encroach on the hearth. An immature one might even singe its feathers on the fire, or burn its feet on the frying pan. A woman could shoo them out herself, or enlist her children to clap their hands, shoo, and chase. Thus, although semiotic beasts, actual fright (the waving of hands and the chasing by children) was often required to induce them to leave the house; and, similarly, food, predators, or rain were required to make them return. Deception also worked. For example, I saw women stop their *xiw*ing and hand waving (from behind the chickens), and instead move in front of the chickens giving the command "to come to eat," "a chík chik chik chik chiiik," even though they had nothing edible to offer. In this way, women could lie to their chickens—at least via gestural feigning, if not symbolic deceit.

Although all domestic animals could have their offspring referred to using the kinship term *r-al*, "son-of-mother," only chickens could be referred to using other kinship terms (themselves also members of the class of inalienable possessions). In particular, a rooster-owning woman could speak of a "daughter-in-law chicken" (*alib' kaxlan*), in cases where a roosterless neighbor lent the "mother-in-law" in question a chicken to breed with her "son" (the studded rooster). In cases where a woman's rooster was being used to service a roosterless woman's hens, the latter could refer to the to-be-serviced hens she was lent as "daughters-in-law." Although breeding took place in the home of the rooster's owner, brooding was done in the home of the owner of the hen. And the offspring of such a match could be divided evenly between the women. It should be emphasized that only the term for "daughter-in-law" was used. I never heard the woman with the rooster refer to it as her "son," and the offspring of the mating were never referred to as their "grandchildren." Also note that, in contrast to the use of *r-al* to mark kinship relations between animals, *alib' kaxlan* was used to mark kinship relations—although affinal, to be sure—between humans and chickens. In this way, such chickens were explicitly treated as first-order-descending female affines; and, implicitly, cocks were treated as first-order-descending male consanguines.

Ontologies Disclosed in the Midst of Discursive Disruptions

A young boy once threw a fit. His mother, unexpectedly called to help a friend cook, had just pulled her nipple from his mouth, placed him on the ground, and dashed off. Chagrined, he jumped up and down screaming. All the older children sitting around the hearth imitated him, raising their arms over their heads and pretending to yell. The boy's elder brother, seven years old, said, "ma a'an xtu' tz'i' la?," or "Is that a dog's tit, you?" The other family members laughed. This boy's cousin, who just turned five himself, then said, "ma a'an xtu' mis la?," or "Is that a cat's tit, you?" The family members laughed again. Finally, the younger brother of this last boy, himself the most recently weaned, mimicked the words while jumbling the sense, saying, "ma a'an xtu' kaxlan la?," or "Is that a chicken's tit, you?" He himself then laughed, thereby conflating both the joke and the audience's response, or his own participant role and theirs. And then the real fun began; this last child's own mother repeated not only what her son said but also his misplaced laughter, while the rest of us continued laughing—both for a child having mistaken a chicken for a mammal, and a speaker for an addressee.

Note, then, that the real laughter of the older participants didn't begin until after the boy attempted to laugh for them. And then their laughter was much more vigorous, for it was not just another animal's tit, and it was not just an animal that didn't have a tit (though clearly this was funny in itself), but it was the confusion about how to be funny that was so funny. Here, then, was a beautiful instance of the implicit disclosure of a local ontology (what kinds of things there are in the world) and ontogeny (what kinds of developmental processes do such things go through). Whereas nobody would explicitly thematize this quality of a chicken (nonmammal or "breastless"), or this quality of a child (nonself or "reflectivity-less"), both were therein revealed.

Ontology

We have just seen the ontological placement of chickens, as figured through five frames: the etymology of the word *kaxlan*; the complementary relation between four kinds of birds; lexical taxonomies surrounding domestic animals; semiotic practices that interpellate chickens as quasi-subjects; and finally, covert ontological qualities evinced in the context of discursive disruptions.

While there was a striking resonance across such diagrammatic relations, as well as a relative coherence within them, there was also a great degree of ambiguity—chickens having properties that figure them as self, alter, and object for their owners. As we will see in later sections, this ontological ambiguity has important ramifications for local modes of affect and selfhood. For the moment, note that while the methodological focus so far might be considered relatively linguistic and symbolic, the key relations were relatively iconic and indexical. More generally, the ontologies disclosed were relatively tacit (versus explicit) and associative (versus referential). While we are not yet done with ontology (as later sections will offer relatively economic and psychological framings of such relations), it is worthwhile offering a more extended discussion of the way this term is being used in this chapter.

Each of the frames of this chapter was used to disclose and enclose a range of semiotic processes and semiological structures, which themselves figured the social relations between women and chickens, the social relation between chickens and other animals, and the social relation between Q'eqchi' women and other identities. As used in this chapter, then, ontologies turn on the objects (signs and interpretants) projected from, and generating of, such processes and structures. In particular, such objects (signs and interpretants) stand at the intersection of two kinds of relations between relations. First, we have Saussurian semiological structures: sign-object (or signifier-signified) relations analyzed by their relation to virtual assemblages of other sign-object relations. For example, the way a word gets its "conceptual value" (or meaning) in relation to other words that combine with it (in a sentence), or could substitute for it (in a slot). And second, we have Peircean semiotic processes: sign-object relations analyzed by their relation to sequential unfoldings of interpretant-object relations (where an interpretant is whatever effect a sign has insofar as it stands for an object). For example, just as an answer is an interpretant of a question, my change in attention (say, turning to look) is an interpretant of your gesture that directs my attention (Kockelman 2005).

From such a semiotic stance, taxonomies and partonomies project out ontologies, as do lexical fields and grammatical categories, as do pecking orders and seating arrangements, as do interactional sequences and affective processes, as do value regimes and commodity circuits, as do predation relations and mating practices. Such objects range from the concepts and referents of words to the purchases of affordances, from the statuses of roles to the functions of instruments, from the purposes of actions to the values of commodities, and from modalities of intentionality (e.g., beliefs and desires) to techniques of the body. Anything that signifies and interprets has an ontology in this sense, whatever its degree of semiotic agency. And anything that is signified or interpreted is ontologized in this sense, whatever its degree of complicity. Finally, ontologies are concomitant with ontogenies; that is, the latter describe how the former develop—either in history (as the conditions and consequences of their coming-to-be), or in practice (as the processes, practices, and relations through which their being is constituted). Ontologies, then, mediate assemblages, processes, and scales far beyond the human-specific, linguistic, or ideological (Kockelman 2011, 2012b, 2013b, 2015).

Such an approach allows us to both incorporate and critique other approaches to ontology. For example, perhaps the most widespread approach to ontology, qua "cultural logics," is through the lexicon. Given that we are focused on chickens, perhaps the most important scholarship in this regard turns on taxonomic approaches to natural kinds—as undertaken by anthropologists like Conklin (1954) and Berlin (1992), psychologists like Keil (1989) and Medin and Atran (1999), and philosophers like Quine (1969a, 1969b) and Griffiths (1997). Such a lexical-conceptual approach to ontology is very useful, so long as it isn't privileged; it is one important frame among many possible frames. And, indeed, the section on taxonomies presented the most relevant piece of the local taxonomy. Nonetheless, chickens partially fall out of such taxonomies because they often seem more akin to artifacts than living kinds (in the stereotypic sense of these words). Moreover, the form classes and associative chains (or indexical "connotations") that words enter into, via grammatical and lexical constructions, are often far more interesting than their sense and reference per se. In the terms of George Herbert Mead (1934), the ontologies developed here are gestural as much as symbolic, embedded and embodied as much as enminded and encoded.

Complementing such lexical approaches to ontology is another great tradition—the Boasian emphasis on grammatical categories, and the kinds of conceptual structures and cultural commitments these reveal (Boas [1910] 1989; Sapir [1927] 1985; Whorf 1956; Silverstein 1976, 2006; Hill and Mannheim 1992; Lucy 1992a, 1992b; among others). Depending on where one draws the divide between grammar and lexicon, much of what is discussed in this chapter, and in allied works such as Kockelman (2010b), undertakes such a Q'eqchi'-specific grammatical ontology. However, while the grammatical categories that interested Boas (evidentials, status, tense, number, etc.) were relatively tacit, habitual, and obligatory, many of the categories discussed here, while tacit and obligatory, are relatively infrequent—evinced in grammatical and lexical constructions that are not present in every utterance, but only in particular moments of particular registers by particular kinds of speakers. Finally, in contrast to both lexical and grammatical approaches to ontology, many of the frames in this chapter turn on nonlinguistic semiotic practices and semiological structures, and the objects (signs and interpretants) therein revealed.

A closely related approach to this chapter may be found in Kockelman (2006), which provides a semiotic ontology of the commodity, and the categories of political economy more generally. While that approach attempted to critique, incorporate, and extend the usual Marxist ontology (Postone 1993, among others), its categories were grounded in a general theory of semiosis rather than community-specific categories. In this chapter I have moved the semiotic machinery to the background, serving mainly as a methodology for analyzing Q'eqchi' categories. Moreover, while Marx focused on the commodity because it was, in some sense, the master object (or, rather, relational nexus) of capitalist societies, the chicken is a relatively marginal object—locally figured as female, nonindigenous, nonexotic, and so forth. Indeed, this marginality (as well as liminality and interstitiality) is part of what makes it so interesting (and challenging) to analyze. In this last regard, classic work on domestic animals by Leach (1964), Bulmer (1967), and Tambiah (1969) is relevant; and, in particular, Evans-Pritchard's (1940) notions of value, structural distance, intimacy, and relations between relations undergird this entire chapter.

I now turn to the paths through which chickens, and their parts, circulated as items with use value and exchange value, showing the wide range of social relations mediated by such travels. Along these paths, I will highlight local modes of intimacy that related women and chickens, in relation to men and predators. And I will highlight some of the tensions that existed in this field—from double-edged deontic modality and wrinkled time, to tender care and constant death. This will prepare the way for my analysis of selfhood below.

Social Relations Mediated by Chickens

Chickens were one of the few objects in the world a Q'eqchi' women could be said to personally own. Woman possessed chickens independent of their husbands (unlike other gifts they received). This possession entailed more responsibilities than rights. As wedding presents, mothers gave their daughters several egg-bearing chickens and a few chicks from their own flock. These were cared for exclusively by women but fed a small portion of corn (sometimes rotten) from the household store. In turn, chickens could be sold for cash, controlled by women, for the purchase of household supplies: sugar, oil, coffee, gas, and so on. Mature, meat-bearing chickens could be slaughtered to feed familiars in festivals, or sacrificed to feed deities in rituals. Originating in the domain of status (inherited through relatively immediate familiars), chickens often terminated in the domain of contract (as something transacted to strangers), commensality (as something eaten with relatively distal familiars), and sacrifice (as something given to the gods). In the rest of this section, I will analyze the various regimes of value through which chickens circulated.

Chickens were inherited through complicated patterns following their owner's death. When a woman died, her chickens would usually go to her daughters (evenly divided, if all lived within similar proximity). If a woman had no daughters, her chickens would go to her stepdaughters, and then to her sisters. Such norms were complicated by the fact that the surviving husband was often dependent on these daughters or sisters. Chickens would likely go to the woman most instrumental in caring for the dead woman's husband—and this was a virilocal community. Thus, while chickens were the possessions of women, their circulation was directly tied to men. For this reason, it is more accurate to say that chickens were the possessions of a single social person (the household) in regards to use rights and exchange rights, and the key possession of the wife in regards to care responsibilities. Women's anxiety regarding chickens is clarified in the light of this double-edged deontic modality. In particular, women were solely responsible for the effort of caring for chickens, whereas their immediate family had collective rights to their achievement.

Women in the village had anywhere from two to one hundred chickens—as a function of a woman's age, social standing, the time of year, or the number of her coresiding daughters-in-law. A typical household (say, married between five and fifteen years, having between two and six children, living near the husband's father's house, and probably sharing a pasture) could have twelve chicks, five full-grown chickens (not all of which were regular egg layers), two immature chickens, and one cock. If well fed, a chicken could lay eggs after six months. A brood was on average about five to fifteen chicks and took about three weeks to hatch. Typically one-third of the chicks would survive into adulthood—the others could die from sickness, cold nights, rain, careless children, and predators. Indeed, on average, 20 percent of fertilized eggs didn't even hatch in the first place. Thus, although a chicken's "natural" life span is about six years, I never met one that made it past middle age.

Chickens were said to be able to lay eggs in any possible month. A good brooding hen could lay four to six clutches a year. Nonetheless, because of the cold and rain, it was agreed that chicks had the least chance of survival if hatched in October, November, or December. Indeed, many women reported losses of around fifty chicks per year because of weather, and thirty chicks per year because of chicken hawks. (Missing chicks were always blamed on the chicken hawk.) If a woman had two to four egg-laying hens, each of which could lay four to six inseminated clutches a year, of four to twelve eggs apiece, she might oversee the birth of between thirty and three hundred chicks per year. The range is of course enormous. Chickens died at all stages of life. Chicken owners watched many of the chickens born under their care (and for whose lives they were accountable) die as a result of agencies other than their own. (Indeed, it's hard to imagine a more difficult place to raise chickens.) A central preoccupation of women, then, was indeed care. But care meant the staving off of death more than the fostering of life. (Indeed, there was a whole genre of narrating the various misfortunes and untimely deaths that befell chickens, and who was at fault.)

A woman could give her chickens' eggs to other family members for eating. If there weren't enough to go around, the order was usually children, husband, owner. If the number was in excess of a family's needs, or if cash was scarce, eggs could be sold to neighbors, or exchanged with them for various garden plants (for example, chili, cilantro, and tomatoes). If a woman had many egg-laying chickens, their eggs could also be brought to the market for sale (and most people had cardboard egg crates for transporting delicate eggs along the steep, slippery, and often muddy paths). If eggs were sold to neighbors, they could cost between twenty-five centavos and one quetzal (US$1 equaled approximately Q7.75); if sold in the market, their cost could double. That said, eggs were also gifted back and forth between women living nearby, often in-laws and siblings, on timescales that rarely exceeded two weeks.

Eggs were praised by Peace Corps volunteers, and other foreigners, for their nutritional value and lack of chemicals (in comparison to store-bought eggs or non-Q'eqchi' foodstuffs). Many women had internalized these narratives and would repeat such praise to me. There was talk of creating a women's cooperative to market eggs. Women, as such, had a sense of the village-external recognition of their eggs' value in nutritional terms.

Chicks could be sold for five to ten quetzals to Q'eqchi' speakers from other nearby villages in the biweekly market in the nearby town (which itself was connected by an all-weather road to the department capital, Cobán). Some chicks traveled quite far, making it all the way to Guatemala City. At that altitude, and under such relatively harsh conditions, chicks took about eleven months to fully mature into chickens. Once mature, they could be (re)sold in the market for forty to sixty quetzals. They were not usually sold among villagers, although excess meat from one's own slaughter could be sold in the village. Some women explicitly purchased chicks, or raised them on their own, to sell as chickens, thereby converting many pounds of their family's corn and many months of their own care into cash. For example, one woman who had about ten mature chickens sold between five to ten per year, thereby making between two hundred and four hundred quetzals. This provided one key means for women to turn their labor into cash, or their chickens into quetzals, which could then move on far wider circuits.

As has often been argued, however, this seems to be an economically losing conversion (see Carter 1969; Wilk 1991; Wilson 1972). Note, for example, the following: a mature chicken could eat between four to six ounces of corn a day, or between seven and eleven pounds per month. In

2001, corn cost about sixty centavos a pound. In this way, a six-month-old chicken "cost" between twenty-five and sixty quetzals. Yet at this age, a chicken at the market was worth only about twenty-five quetzals. And by the time most women usually sold a chicken (after about eleven months), the chicken "cost" between seventy-seven and 121 quetzals, yet only sold for between forty and fifty-five quetzals. Indeed, as mentioned above, women usually waited as long as possible before selling a chicken—and so the seeming irrationality of the conversion was only heightened.

Such an economically losing strategy is usually justified by noting that domestic animals, in this case chickens, act as storage banks; they can be fed corn unfit for human consumption, surplus corn that would otherwise rot, or entropic corn (that has fallen out of baskets, and is otherwise too sparsely scattered to be easily picked up). Moreover, chickens convert carbohydrates into much needed protein. In this way, chickens may be thought of as wrinkles in time and value, allowing a woman to turn the family's corn supply into personal cash, carbohydrates into protein, disordered spoilage into ordered vitality, and current resources into future benefits.

Perhaps more important, however, than their use as storage facilities and protein-conversion factories, chickens mediated any number of social relations, thereby constituting a medium of exchange in the social economy. For example, mature chickens (especially roosters) were slaughtered to feed groups and gods at various ceremonies (be they "Catholic" or "autochthonous"). Indeed, the serving and eating of chicken meat was necessary for a ceremony; it was the dietary sine qua non that something special was happening. Chicken-consuming ceremonies took place at all stages of the agricultural cycle (planting, clearing, and harvesting) and religious calendar (weddings, baptisms, funerals, and saints' days).

In such modes of commensality, many kinds of social relations were mediated, for example, kin, ritual kin, close friends, intimate neighbors, and members of the village-based community. Chickens also linked *cofradía* members to the priest who came one Sunday a month to lead mass, so far as the female members were in charge of his main meal. Chickens were sacrificed (rather than served), and their carcasses given to a god, during ceremonies of house building, to cure fear-based illnesses, during festivals for saints' days, and during ceremonies used to propitiate the local earth-god, or *Tzuultaq'a*. Indeed, in this last form of ceremony, a woman would slaughter a chicken while praying for the health of her family, crops, and chickens. That is, chickens simultaneously played the role of ceremonial means and ends. One might sacrifice a chicken while praying for the current health or future accrual of chickens.

At different phases in their development, chickens entered into very distinct regimes and repertoires of value. Only a mature chicken served as the culinary emblem of a ritual meal. To serve this symbolic function, a chicken's owner had to take the life of the "animal" up close and with a machete, blood spilling over and organs jumbling out; and of an animal she had cared for all its life, stopping others from taking its life prematurely. At this highly social and symbolic moment, when a chicken was fully mature, a woman finally stood in relation to the chicken as predator to prey.

Scholars often speak of the metamorphism of value—how commodities and money, or use values and exchange values, can be exchanged with each along endless circuits: C-M-C'-M', or commodity-money-commodity-money (and so on, indefinitely). Regarding chickens, metabolism, a biological process, is a key agent behind the metamorphism of value. Moreover, scholars are often excited by the fungibility of money—its ability to be converted into any other object, and to be divided and multiplied indefinitely. Here, we see the extent to which chickens have such fungibility. For example, they reproduce themselves (with a little help); their offspring could be converted into just about any other good imaginable— from the extension of social relations to the increase of one's income, from securing the recognition of gods to satisfying the hunger of children. (In Q'eqchi', interest was called the "child" [r-al] of money; and capital was called the "mother" [x-na'] of money. That is, money had inalienable possessions in the form of kinship relations; and so the trope of reproduction, of female fecundity and offspring, rather than production, was also the central metaphor of such capitalist endeavors as money lending and merchandise capital.) It is therefore tempting to stand Marx's chain on its head, or rather flip it on its back, giving C-W-C'-W', or Chicken-Woman-Chicken-Woman (and so on, indefinitely). Indeed, just as the essence of capital, as self-expanding value, cannot be understood without looking at the entire circuit that commodities and money go through, so too one needs to examine the entire "circuit" of women and chickens. Unlike the quetzal, moreover, chickens hold their value; and unlike money more generally, chickens can be eaten. All of this is not to say that chickens are the universal equivalent (the one commodity that is used to measure the value of all other commodities), but that (with corn) they are universal mediators (the one good that can be used to evince or extend any social relation). Chickens, then, were highly portable in important ways.

That said, many foods in the village were flavored with an imitation chicken broth, consisting mainly of MSG and salt. It was a pervasive background taste in rice and bean recipes, in ceremonial broths, and in noodle dishes. In this way, one was always eating synthetic chicken. It should also be mentioned that the ecotourists, whom some families hosted, were supposed to be given the choice between coffee with or without sugar, and soup with or without chili. However, much to the chagrin of these tourists, as we saw in chapter 1, coffee without sugar, like soup without chili, was just hot water (that at least had been boiled). Only when such a flavoring packet was added did Q'eqchi' food—for the average ecotourist—come alive. The MSG was like a counterfeit coin in the symbolic economy, passed off to tourists in place of real chicken. To be sure, it is not necessarily the case that fake chicken was given to ecotourists to shunt off a potential social relation; it could be that the Q'eqchi' were just being chintzy.

Selfhood

We just saw how a chicken relates to the possessions of a woman—not just as her property (to buy, sell, raise, slaughter, sacrifice), but also as her properties (a means to behold and measure herself). More generally, and loosely speaking, we have been focused on a wide range of material processes, semiotic practices, and social relations, through which chickens (and their parts) get caught up—however directly or indirectly—in use value (as the means and ends of actions), exchange value (in the give and take of transactions), semantic-value (through the sense and referents of discursive acts), and much else besides.

Crucially, such evaluated entities are bound to evaluating agents. Whoever wields, exchanges, and refers (and often whatever is wielded, exchanged, and referred to) can be framed as an agent (e.g., a manipulator of means, a chooser of ends). They can be framed as a subject (e.g., a bundle of cognitive representations, an ensemble of social relations). They can be framed as a self (e.g., the ends of their own actions, the objects of their own thoughts). And they can be framed as a person (e.g., the bearer of sociopolitical rights and responsibilities). Loosely speaking, they are simultaneously a locus of causation, representation, reflexivity, and accountability. While each of these capacities (or potentia) deserves a chapter in itself, and while all are irreducibly interrelated (and much more complex than this quick sketch allows), in what follows I will limit my attention to a few aspects of selfhood, qua value-directed locus of reflexivity, as they emerge in the ethnographic details of this chapter.

Ontologies disclose agents' commitments regarding what kinds of entities (things, qualia, processes, causes, etc.) are in the world. They also disclose agents' commitments regarding what kinds of agents there are in the world—as well as what constitutes an agent, person, or "self," in the first place. In this regard, four general claims are at stake in this chapter. First, selfhood is constituted by a kind of ontological reflexivity; that is, there exists an ensemble of entities (people, things, events, processes, relations, qualities, etc.) that is ontologically recognized in the semiotic practices, semiological structures, and social relations of some community, however tacitly or elliptically, as reflexively relating to itself. The task, then, is to delimit both the ensemble of entities and the range of reflexive relations. Second, such reflexive relations are distinct from, and yet a condition for, more stereotypic modes of self-reflectivity (turning on mirrors, symbols, techniques of and narratives about the self, and so forth). The rest of this section will develop these points in detail. Third, to return to key notions explicated in the introduction, the very processes that signify, and thereby disclose, such ontologically reflexive ensembles tend to simultaneously enclose them—framing them as relatively bounded and coherent wholes. And finally, as will be seen in the last part of this chapter, just as selfhood cannot be understood without reference to ontology, affect cannot be understood without reference to selfhood.

So what belongs in that ensemble we call the self? For William James (1985: 44), it included one's body and mind, one's clothes and house, one's spouse and children, one's ancestors and friends, one's property and bank account. For Thorstein Veblen ([1898] 1998), it included one's shadow, reflection, name, tattoo, totem, footprint, nail clippings, hair cuttings, exhalations, excretions, clothing, and weapons (or what he called the "quasi-personal fringe"). And for Michel Foucault (1997: 225), it included one's body, soul, thoughts, conduct, and ways of being in the world. Crucially, the interesting question is not so much what belongs in the ensemble per se, but rather what criteria or evidence one uses to determine what constitutes a part of such a whole, or a relatum in such a relation, in the first place. Extending James's ideas, there are three key criteria for delimiting the ensemble he described: (1) one's actions are oriented toward the care of such constituents (one acts both for them and with them, such that one's actions are both autotelic and autotechnic); (2) one's moods are reflective of the status of such constituents (their flourishing or foundering registers on one as positive and negative affective unfoldings); and (3) one's self is accountable for the effects of such constituents (they belong to one in ways that may be both normatively and causally regimented). In short, the key signs of selfhood are relatively reflexive desire, affect, and accountability.

It should be emphasized that this ensemble is thereby defined in terms of three relatively distinct modes of reflexivity, and that, with certain caveats, such reflexive relations probably hold for nonhuman animals as well as for many other forms of life (Kockelman 2011, 2013a). Crucially, the relative coherence, continuity, or boundedness of the self turns simply on the relative coherence, continuity, and boundedness of such an ensemble. While key characters in the history of literature, key identities in the ethnographic record, and key moments in the life course of any individual may diverge from one or more of these dimensions; while the actual contents of the ensemble may be community specific; and while the individual in question may be a corporate (and, indeed, incorporeal) entity, the dimensions per se seem relatively robust.

Such relatively panspecies and prereflective modes of reflexivity should be compared with what are (allegedly) more human-specific modes of self-reflection—such as knowing oneself, representing oneself, performing oneself, and acting on oneself (for the sake of oneself). In particular, each of these has a great tradition behind it in the philosophical, psychological, linguistic, and anthropological literature. Crucially, these more canonical and well-mined modes of self-reflectivity presuppose the first kind; for all the things a knower could know (a signer could signify, a performer could perform, or an actor could affect), only some belong to the ensemble that constitutes the knower (signer, performer, or actor). And, aside from the various modes of reflectivity per se (and their criterial significance for the constitution of human-specific modes of selfhood in certain ontologies), it is really the fact that such things belong to the reflexive ensemble that gives them their importance in the first place (such that reflecting on them, or failing to reflect on them, is so fraught). Nonetheless, most analyses of various forms of reflectivity presume, or elide altogether, modes of reflexivity—and thereby fail to account for the ensemble's local contours, conditions of possibility, or consequences.

To return to speakers of Q'eqchi', the self-qua-ensemble includes at its prototypic core many body parts (including the heart, the center of emotion and motivation), most kinship relations, one's name, home, and field, one's clothing and community, and—more peripherally—one's domestic animals (*ketomj*), and one's shadow and breath (Kockelman 2007b, 2010b). This ensemble is evinced in a range of grammatical categories, discourse patterns, ritual practices, and everyday activities. These categories, patterns, practices, and activities resonate with James's three dimensions of reflexivity (motivation, affect, accountability) and also stand at the center of the four kinds of reflectivity (knowledge, power, performance, and signification). In some sense, the entities that make up such an ensemble may be understood as relatively inalienable parts of relatively personal wholes (and hence radically nonportable entities, in one important sense), such that whenever one relates to such things, one relates to oneself at one degree of remove.

In sum, we can see that this chapter is precisely a detailed look at the relatively reflexive relations between certain kinds of "selves" (Q'eqchi'-speaking women in a particular village) and certain kinds of "things" (chickens, and domestic animals more generally). Chickens do not just constitute part of a women's reflexive and reflective self (even if at the periphery). They are also relatively reflexive selves in their own right (even if only marginally—at least in my own, and the Q'eqchi's, ontology). In the third and final part of this chapter, I will ground affective relations—in particular, fear and desire—in terms of both this reflexive ensemble and this ambivalent ontology.

Brooding Hens, Tabooed Acts, Corporate Units of Accountability

Women's actions affected the health of their chickens. A relationship of contiguity and similarity was understood to exist between a woman's just-hatched chicks and her own actions during the weeks her hens were brooding. For example, after a woman placed a basket over her brooding hen (for peace and quiet as much as protection), if she were to go out on a long walk, the chicks, when born, would tend to wander far distances from the house, thereby making themselves easy prey for predators—in particular, the chicken hawk. If she (or, as was more likely, her children) went out to play soccer, her chicks would suffer a disease known as *mosq'ok*, in which their skin would swell and become bumpy like a soccer ball with its inflation and bumps, causing them to die. If she was out looking for firewood and collected the *q'otq'ob'il che'*, or any other tree branches that were particularly twisted, then the legs of her chicks would twist as well. Because of this infirmity, they would be unable to walk or forage for themselves and would die. If she let her griddle (*k'il*) heat up on the fire without maize dough (*q'em*) on it, her chicks would not even hatch. If she went out to do the wash after she had basketed her brooding chicken, the eggs would have only water, and no little chick (*xul*) would have formed. And if she slept in a fetal position, with her arms curled around her head, the wings of her chicks would be twisted. In this way, her chicks would not be able to get themselves out of their eggs, and they would die. In sum, at certain times a women's personal boundaries, both her actions and experiences, overlapped with those of her brooding chickens—and thereby had consequences for the health of her newly hatched chicks.

These kinds of sympathetic, or "iconic-indexical" relations are the low-hanging fruit of anthropology—insofar as they are quickly elicited, ubiquitous, and too easy to make too much of. That said, no other animal, domestic or wild, had such relations to women. And the only other humans that were involved in similar relations with women were their own children. Moreover, the real importance of these relations lies in the fact that various activities of women could be inferred from the health of their chickens; newborn chicks acted as mirrors, reflecting the actions of their owners while their mothers (i.e., the hens) were brooding. Moreover, such relations lent themselves to a form of self-consciousness, qua reflectivity; in particular, the constant attention to one's own behavior in order to understand its consequences for another's health. And as for reflexivity, when chickens were brooding (just as when women were pregnant), they and their owners (just as children and their mothers) constituted a single unit of accountability, if not a single corporate body. In short, just as chickens could be representative of women (qua living symbols, or lively signs), women could be representatives for their chickens (qua spokespeople).

Reason, Desire, and Domestic Animals

If one examines the types of mental faculties, or semiosocial facilities, attributed to chickens, one finds that they are relatively unique among animals. Let me discuss "reason" (*na'leb'*) and a form of desire known as *ataw*. *Na'leb'* is the instrumental nominalization of the verb *na'ok*, which means "knowing that," "knowing how," and "knowing someone" (depending on the form of its complement). As a noun, *na'leb'* may be given the basic gloss of "instrument for knowing (how)." In such a capacity, it is a count noun and may be pluralized, spoken of in the singular, and possessed. Depending on context, this word may be translated as "habit," "custom," "idea," "example," "advice," "sense," or "reason."

For example, to say that someone has a na'leb' (*wan lix na'leb'*) is to say that that person is "wise" or "experienced." To say that someone does not have a na'leb' (*maak'a' lix na'leb'*) is to say that they are "ignorant," "naïve," or "callow." To describe someone's na'leb' as *tz'i'ej*, "doggish," is to imply that they practice immoral or disgusting acts. At age three, a child can be said to have a na'leb' insofar as it can play imitative games with its parents. For example, while digging post holes for his new house, a man noticed that his three-year-old son was patting dirt around the post holes just as he himself had tamped in dirt with a pole. He said to his assistant, *wan xna'leb'*, "he has sense" or perhaps "he has a trick or habit." The friend grinned, and they continued working. Besides such metaphorical or humorous extensions of children having a na'leb', they are usually said to have only one up until the age of twelve; namely, they can play.

Nonhuman animals could also possess a na'leb', but usually only in the sense of a typical action they engaged in, itself caught up in human concerns. For example, a dog was said to have a na'leb', in that it would greet its owners when they returned home, and barked when an intruder approached the house. Thus, a dog's na'leb' allowed it to distinguish between its owners (and their familiars) and strangers, evincing this distinction by the response it gave. The quetzal was said to have a na'leb', in that it showed itself only when the tourists who came to see it had gone home. And chickens had a na'leb', in that when you scared them, they were frightened and ran away, and in that when they got hungry, or were called, they came to eat. (Turkeys were said to have such an insignificant na'leb' that they didn't even come to the house in the evenings for food or protection—whereas even newborn chicks did that.) Such domestic animals, then, had na'leb's that depended on the actions of their owners—that is, certain types of sign-interpretant relations that owners could expect, and which turned on the timing and location of certain human practices. Note, then, how the authochthonous domestic bird was said to be far more stupid than the nonautochthonous domestic bird. And note how the wild bird had a trick that frustrated, rather than facilitated, human involvement; and that its actions were oriented toward ecotourists, qua outsiders, rather than Q'eqchi' speakers themselves. But, that said, such a na'leb' had repercussions for villagers, in that tourists who didn't see a quetzal could go home unhappy (and the tourism economy might suffer as a result).

Chickens also had such frustrative na'leb's. For example, a woman spent one morning watching her chicken rooting about in the underbrush, thinking that it had left a number of eggs there. She told me that it had a na'leb', in that it didn't want her to find its eggs. Similarly, when a chicken flew through a window into a home, the owner joked that it had a na'leb'. When I asked why, the owner said, "molb'ek traj," or "It wants to lay eggs." In this way, although slightly humorously, chickens had other na'leb's, which turned on the shenanigans they engaged in while trying to lay eggs—for instance, protecting them from humans and finding nests. In this way, chickens had na'leb's that mediated between, if not helped to institute, their own instincts and human institutions.

In this last example, the na'leb' of a chicken was described in terms of a desire (to lay eggs). However, if asked directly what the desires (*ajom*) of chickens were, I usually heard that chickens (and other domestic animals, such as turkeys) did not have desires, although wild animals did. Instead, it was emphasized that owners had desires over their chickens—which I understood to mean that owners were in control of the ends to which their chickens were put, because the chickens were their possessions, and thus could be disposed of how they (that is, the owners) wished. The desire of animals, in this most general way, required a kind of freedom from possession that only wild animals could be said to have. In other words, domestication, as the enclosure of animal instincts in human institutions, had the effect of destroying desire.

However, chickens were said to have one type of desire known as *ataw*, which itself was usually predicated of women. In particular, a person was said to have such a desire if he or she really wanted something (such as a house or clothing) but could not buy it (usually for lack of money). While this is a wide gloss, it conveys the sense of wishfulness—that is, desiring something that cannot be obtained. More frequently, women experienced ataw when they were pregnant, as evinced in their marked hunger for certain kinds of foods (often meats, like chicken, as well as sweetbreads, and so forth). In particular, if one did not offer such foods to them (say, while they were visiting), their children could be born with certain defects— akin to the ones to which chicks were subject. Thus, one was often under a loose compulsion to give a pregnant woman whatever she asked for. In this way, pregnancy (like brooding, in the case of hens) allowed a woman to expand the scope of her desire, and more easily secure the objects to which it was directed. In this way, such taboos could expand a woman's agency as much as limit it.

Various kinds of ataw were also ascribed to domestic animals. For example, older chickens were said to have ataw insofar as they wanted the cooked corn (*b'uch*) that was scattered out to the young chicks. In this way, they had a kind of desire that was thwarted by humans—who had to tie them up or keep shooing them away. Similarly, dogs were said to experience ataw insofar as they wanted to eat the eggs of chickens, but were prevented from doing so by their owners. (Dogs could often be trained to not eat eggs, but most would still do it when not watched, and, for this reason, egg-laying chickens were kept inside the house.) And cows were said to have ataw insofar as they wanted to eat corn in the fields, but were prevented from doing so by being tied up or fenced in. In this way, while the frustrated desires of domestic animals were cross species, that which did the frustrating (money, training, fences, and so forth) was species specific, and yet always human related. In each case, then, the metaphor was one of the corral; that is, a quasi-instinctual desire was thwarted by a human-specific instrument or enclosure—fences, twine, or obedience training. And desire itself was constituted as a back formation, that which was evinced in its frustration or thwarting.

Chickens and Children

The tales of chickens and children are many. For example, a boy, grab-assing with his cousin by the hearth, stepped on a chick. Several hours later, half-dead, it was discovered by the boy's mother when she returned from the market. When asked if they knew what happened to it, the boys said no. Indeed, the one who stepped on it said to her, rhetorically, "k'a tawi' ru ninnaw k'aru xk'ul," or "How would I know what it received!?" His eyes flicked up to mine, knowing I knew. Satisfied with the answer, the woman crushed the remaining life from the chick beneath the naked heel of her foot. I helped her bury it behind the house, in the marshy soil, near an old stump.

On another occasion, a two-year-old boy, Munter, advanced on a chicken, saying, "kaxlan, kaxlan," or "Chicken, chicken," one hand raised above his head in a fist (as when he would threaten his older brother), and the other gripping a stick. He called out to a big chicken, "laa'at," or "You," took an unsteady step toward it, and sent it running away. (Note, then, that children could address chickens—indicating their relative proximity in terms of structural distance.) Munter then scooped up one of its chicks, gripping it tightly. It did not peep; it could not breathe. The big chicken—its mother—returned. Munter set down the chick, which was dazed and unsteady, giving Munter just enough time to whack it on the back with his stick. Ingressively peeping for lack of air, it ran away. The boy's mother, watching me watching him, called his name. Wide-eyed, perhaps ashamed, he looked back to her and said, "xiwak," or "It got scared."

Q'eqchi' children were indeed often equated with, and seemingly jealous of, their mothers' chickens, as readers predisposed to psychological explanations might point out. Indeed, one of the first emotion terms children learned (and perhaps the first emotion they learned to intentionally induce in others [in particular, chickens]), was *xiw*, "fear." This word for fear, the reader might recall, was also the command given to chickens to shoo—and thus a sign that simultaneously denoted and induced an emotion, functionally akin to John Austin's description of primary performative utterances. The beating of chickens by small children can also be seen as their attempt to recoup the prominence won over by chickens—reestablishing, as it were, the village-wide and interspecies pecking order. And all the ways in which a woman's chickens were treated similarly to her children come to mind as well, from the care spent on their upbringing, through the birth-defect pathologies they were caught up in, to the responsibilities they had for them. But let me leave such developmental stories aside and, in their stead, begin our segue to affect.

Signs of Fear, Cowardice, Anxiety, and Gender

As detailed in Kockelman (2010b), *xiwak*, "to become scared," belongs to a form class that includes *titz'k*, "to become exasperated, or fed up," *lub'k/tawaak*, "to tire," *raho'k*, "to get hurt," *yib'o'k*, "to get disgusted," *jiq'e'k*, "to get choked up," *q'ixno'k/tiqwo'k*, "to get angry/hot," *josq'o'k*, "to get angry," and *xutaanak*, "to become ashamed." Such verbs are intransitive state changes (where the subject undergoing the state change is accorded relatively little agency); all have nominal counterparts from which they are derived (e.g., fear, anger, pain, disgust, etc.); and all may take nonfinite complements (which indicate the event or experience causing the change in state). Most of these words can be predicated of animals, as well as people. And in many ethnopsychologies, including my own, most of the predicates within this form class would be understood as referring to "feelings" (or even "emotion").

Xiwak, to become scared, could be further derived into the participle *xiwajenaq*, "scared" or "frightened" (also referred to as *seb'esinb'il*, the participle form of the verb "to scare [someone]"). In this form, it was often used to refer to the local elaboration of *susto* (or "magical fright," as it is often called in the ethnographic literature on Mesoamerica). As detailed in Kockelman (2010b), this illness was usually caused by moral transgressions, and was intimately linked to relatively inalienable possessions (qua reflexive-self) in its origins, symptoms, and cure. Like desire, fear constituted a highly elaborated lexical domain, and was thus what Levy (1973) would call a "hypercognized" emotion. In what follows, we will move from such relatively lexical signs of feeling, and such relatively medicalized and well-studied forms of emotion, to more elliptical, covert, embodied, and quotidian modes of affect as they mediate the relation between women and chickens.

There were two ways to refer to "cowardice" among speakers of Q'eqchi'. *Kapun* was an adjective meaning "cowardly." It may be thought of as a trait—that is, an adjective predicable of a person as part of their underlying personality, in the sense that it is relatively predictable or stable. In this regard, it was in a class of words with "sensitive" (*ch'impo'*), "abu-sive" (*eet*), "stubborn" (*jip*), "angry" (*josq'*), "dumb" (*mem*), "smart" (*seeb', q'es ru*), "humble" (*q'un*), "tame" (*tuulan*), "jealous" (*sowen*), "crazy" (*kaan, look*), "arrogant" (*b'ach'b'ach'*), "rude" (*q'etq'et*), and "nice" (*b'it'b'it'*). It was also one of the great unsung loan words of Q'eqchi', coming from the Spanish word *capón*, meaning either "castrated" (as an adjective), or "cas-trated cock" (as a noun). In English, for example, we have *capon*, a rooster castrated to improve the taste of its flesh. Another way to say coward was the compound form *ixqiwinq*, consisting of three morphemes: *ixq*, the noun for "woman"; *i*, a compounding infix that was attached to some nouns; and *winq*, the word for "man." Thus, a coward is something like a "womanish-man." Note that in the case of *kapun*, the underlying trope was diminished masculinity, whereas in the case of *ixqiwinq*, the under-lying trope was heightened femininity. In this way, to attribute either of these traits to women was relatively nonsensical. In short, cowardice—a type of personality that all too easily gives in to fear—was lexicalized in Q'eqchi' using words originating in the domains of chickens and women and yet could not be easily predicated of chickens or women.

Many families, especially those living on high and exposed hills, set up long poles with brightly colored plastic bags attached to them. These were said to scare off chicken hawks, who nonetheless made enough visits to make the ethnographer wonder if they were at all worthwhile. Indeed, their main purpose seemed to be indexing the owner's fear of chicken hawks. In this way, they were like flags announcing the shared anxieties of an otherwise anonymous community in regard to an event that may best be described as a *replicated singularity*.

Ride of the Chicken Hawks, Effervescence of a Community

Compulsively looking out windows, sending children outside to scan the sky, growing more restless as the afternoon wears on, staking hens to posts near the house to keep their chicks in place . . . Sometimes it seemed not only that women would not count their chickens before they hatched, but also that they would not count them until they had grown too large to be snatched away.

These constant, low-level indices of anxiety aside, no one would see the chicken hawk (*k'uch*) descend when it finally did. A woman might be grinding corn for dinner; her children fussing by the fire; the men still out clearing their milpa for planting. Perhaps only the chickens suspected, for they were silent. The kind of silence that is retroactively inferred after the chicken hawk's dive punctuates it—by the hens cackling, the dogs barking, and the children screaming. In just this order. And then she would drop her work to come running out, door banging, feet thumping, and newly wielded machete whishing.

On the ground, children from each of the houses circling the valley might be at the edges of their housing sites screaming a high-pitched *iiiiiiii*. Punctuating this would be the low voices of women urging their dogs on to keep after the hawk, saying, "hach' hach' hach' hach' hach'," or "Bite it, bite it, bite it, bite it." They would try to make sure the hawk could not land lest they lose sight of it and be attacked again.

A young woman, her mother-in-law, her sisters-in-law, her older sister, and most of their children would follow the dogs hot in pursuit of the chicken hawk. They would race down the individual trails linking their houses, slipping in the mud, or heelless sandals slapping on dirt and stones. Their paths reliquescing in this way, not only was chaos constituted by the chicken hawk, but also community.

At no other times, and certainly not on a weekly basis, would women move that fast. The only other activity that came near such a frenetic pace was soccer played by men on Sundays. This was hot sweat and strewn hair.

One rarely saw a direct hit. It was always too quick. Too quiet. Usually I figured out what had happened only when I saw the slow, heavy flaps of the hawk, postkill, as it moved toward the thermal at the edge of the valley. There, it would slowly circle with its putative load, rising out of the valley in the heated air until it was no longer in sight.

Such an event could happen once a week within the same family compound. After the event, the afternoon would be spent combing the underbrush for remains—or even the chick. Perhaps the hawk had dropped the chick; perhaps it had never gotten it but had only scared it outside the housing site and into the underbrush. Chickens, and especially chicks, were difficult to account for. If anxiety would precede an attack (would it happen?), uncertainty would follow (just what had happened?).

"Mare wan sa' pim xb'aan xiw," or "Perhaps it is off in the bushes because of its fear," said a little girl about the chick her mother couldn't find. And several days after the attack, when I asked her mother whether the chicken hawk had actually got the chick (whose body was never found), she said, "hehe', xchap li ch'inakaxlan, kikam," or "Yes, it grabbed the little chicken; it MUST have died." Just as the girl used the modal adverb *mare*, "perhaps," to say that she wasn't sure where the chick was, her mother used the unexperienced evidential verbal inflection *ki-*, indicating that the event of death was not actually experienced, but only inferred. She never knew for sure whether the chicken hawk killed the little chicken.

Affect

The previous part of this chapter foregrounded two modalities of affect, fear and desire, as they played out in relations between women and chickens. While I began by focusing on the lexical and ethnopsychological elaboration of fear and desire, I ended by ethnographically detailing a chicken hawk attack, itself figured as a kind of replicated singularity. In this section, I offer a more analytic framing of this event, focusing on signs that might be considered relatively less mediated and relatively more deferred.

Scholars trained in a semiotic tradition often speak of the "grounds" of signs, usually understood as the relation between a sign and its object. In particular, relatively iconic signs share qualities with their objects; relatively indexical signs are causally contiguous with their objects; and relatively symbolic signs are related to their objects by convention—itself typically couched in terms of a mediating idea, or concept, that is intersubjectively shared within a community (Kockelman 2005; Parmentier 1994; Peirce 1955b). In this chapter, I have been focused not so much on "signs of the self" (be they icons, indices, or symbols; be they evinced in performance or described by narrative; etc.), but on *selfhood as a ground of semiosis*. In fact, I propose that the reflexive self may be understood as a kind of *metaground* (Kockelman 2012a, 2013a). Crucially, the reflexive self as ground does not just mediate relations between signs and objects, but rather relations between interpretants and such sign-object relations. What is at stake in such interpretants is not "what is the object of this sign," but rather what is an appropriate and effective interpretant of this sign-object relation given the selfhood of the interpreter, with its distinctly reflexive modes of desire, affect, and accountability. To conclude this chapter, we draw out the repercussions of such metagrounds as they play out in the attack of a chicken hawk.

The self is at stake in any semiotic process. But in the context of emotion, and affect more generally, its fundamental relation to interpretation is perhaps most transparent. To make this claim as clear as possible, it is worth discussing such putatively psychological processes at length. Many serious scholars of emotions (Averill 1985; Ekman and Davidson 1994; Frank 1988; Griffiths 1997; Wilce 2009; among others) long ago gave up thinking of them in terms of relatively subjective states, or private feelings. Instead, emotions are usually understood as relatively complicated groupings of one or more of the following kinds of components: an eliciting event or situation (e.g., a loss or the threat of loss), a physiological change (e.g., autonomic nervous system arousal), a relatively reflexive signal (e.g., a gasp, interjection, or facial expression), some stereotypic affective experience (i.e., a "feeling"), a relatively controlled action (e.g., fleeing from a threat or fighting to forestall a loss), and a second-order interpretation of this grouping of components, whether by the experiencer or by an observer, as relatively uncontrollable, subjective, and natural. No single one of these components is an "emotion"; rather, any affective unfolding may involve all of them, with more or less elaboration. Moreover, despite the common assumption that the key component of an emotion is a subjective state or "feeling" (qua putative psychological kind), the ethnographic record shows that local understandings of this grouping are just as often rendered in moral, spiritual, and physical idioms as in psychological ones (see Levy 1973; Rosaldo 1980; Shweder 1994).

Not much has been resolved in this domain. We still find contentious debates about what components are involved, how fixed or fluid are the groupings, what is the order and intercausality among the components, how much control one has over any particular component, and whether and to what degree emotion (as a genus phenomenon), or any particular emotion (anger, surprise, etc.), is a natural kind or social construction in the first place. My goal in what follows is not to enter into these debates per se. Rather, I want to reframe such a grouping of components from a semiotic stance (Kockelman 2005) that is itself grounded in reflexive (and reflective) modes of selfhood. Such an endeavor involves bringing together and retheorizing Peirce's understanding of interpretants and James's understanding of the self. My point then is not to define "what emotions really are," but rather to map out the relevant semiotic and intersubjective dimensions of what is usually understood as a psychological and subjective domain.

We must first remember that to appraise a situation is to interpret it

(Averill 1985). Any situation so interpreted is thus a sign, however immediate or mediate, of an event (qua object) that concerns the self as a reflexive ensemble, however directly or indirectly. In the attack described above, the event involved a threat to one's flock (about which, more below). But it could range from finding the door of one's home ajar to receiving news of a death in the family, from realizing that one's hen laid an unusually large clutch to the faint memory of a propitious dream, from spilling broth on one's best blouse to learning about one's husband's reputation. The relation, or ground, between this sign and object could thus be iconically transparent or dreamily imagistic, indexically proximal or inferentially distal, lexically explicit or symbolically encrypted. In particular, women could learn of such an attack, and its attendant threat, through any number of signs—from the sight of a hawk's shadow to the scream of a neighbor's child, from the sudden presence of hens at the hearth to the excited barking of one's elderly dog.

More specifically, as I have established in this chapter, a woman's reflexive selfhood was at stake in the context of such an attack in a variety of ways. First, insofar as chickens were a key possession in her self-qua-ensemble, such an attack represented a threat to her selfhood in the most transparent way—that is, as a loss of one or more of her relatively alienable belongings, themselves a rich collection of potential use values and exchange values. Second, insofar as chickens (as well as their parts and products, through processes like barter circles and ritual slaughters) were a key means to mediate her relation to others (children and husband, in-laws and neighbors, god and community), a range of other relatively inalienable entities in her self-qua-ensemble was threatened at one or more degrees of remove. Third, chickens were themselves reflexive selves, and shared a number of properties with women. In this way, there was the opportunity for empathy—that is, fear for someone with whom one was both similar and intimate (Kockelman 2007b). Chickens were figured as reflexive selves who were not themselves capable of full reflectivity; women related to them as warden, caregiver, or representative. As we saw, women's children and chickens were frequently figured in similar terms, all of them, at key times, constituting a single unit of accountability. In other words, a woman was responsible for recognizing a threat to her chickens because they were less able to recognize it themselves. Given the fact that women were fully responsible for the loss of chickens, but shared the rights to the benefits provided by chickens, women could fear being held accountable for the loss, as much as fear the loss per se.

In short, a woman's self was threatened in a variety of more or less direct ways—and so just as multiple signs were in play (however explicit or implicit), multiple objects were at stake (however immediate or deferred). In this way, part of what is so crucial about such *affective unfoldings* is that they figured the boundaries and loci of selves in relation to the values and categories of communities.

As a function of these sign-object relations, a range of interpretants is then available. Such interpretants are themselves effects of such signs that are relevant in relation to such objects and thereby "make sense" only in relation to the selfhood of the interpreter. Moreover, these interpretants are also potential signs (and objects) themselves, with their own potentials to generate interpretive cascades (by the self and others). And they too can be more or less immediate. Loosely speaking, and building on Peirce's (1955b) typology (Kockelman 2005), there are affective interpretants, that is, relatively involuntary transformations in the state of one's body that may be felt by the one embodying them (and even perceived by others, if only indirectly). From an increase in metabolism (and the racing of one's pulse) to blushing (and the feeling of heat in one's cheeks), from a faint sense of déjà vu to the pleasure offered by arousal. There are energetic interpretants, which range from voluntary actions to involuntary behaviors. These included grabbing a machete and sprinting down a path, to clenching one's fist and interjecting, "ay dios." There are representational interpretants, that is, signs, be they public or private, that framed such events (and their causes and effects) in terms of relatively propositional contents. These could range from describing to one's daughters what happened to wishing one's flock was closer to home. And there are ultimate interpretants, or dispositional variants of any of these interpretants, qua habits to affectively, energetically, or representationally interpret in particular ways in more distal contexts. Indeed, much local behavior could be framed as retrospective modes of readiness for the next chicken hawk attack, qua "indices of anxiety" in the face of such replicated singularities—for example, remembering or recounting the last attack, trimming the underbrush, becoming restless as the afternoon wears on.

The fact that certain aspects of such semiotic unfoldings (for example, affective interpretants, in the strict sense, and uncontrolled energetic interpretants) are often framed as relatively unagentive, has some important consequences. From a semiotic stance, the interpretants per se (as incipient semiotic processes in their own right) might be framed as relatively difficult to control (as to when and where they are expressed), relatively difficult to compose (as to what sign is expressed and what it stands for), and relatively difficult to commit to (as to what effect the sign-object relation will have when expressed in such a time and place). They may be understood as more likely to reveal an authentic self (for they are less amenable to censure). One may be accorded less responsibility for their repercussions (as they are less likely to be "intended"). And emotion per se may be read as more natural, pancultural, or even cross species. Such points, and their caveats, are well-rehearsed. I stress them here only to make sure the reader does not project them *tout court* onto the foregoing analysis.

Moreover, just as a sign may be more or less transparently related to its object, an interpretant may be more or less transparently related to a sign-object relation. And just as there exists a range of more or less immediate interpretants (affective, energetic, representational, ultimate), there also exists a range of more or less overt interpretants. Relatively covert interpretants may arise for the simple reason that, as potential signs themselves, they are subject to one's own and others' subsequent interpretations (and the judgments these may entail). Freud, in a psycho-medical paradigm, Goffman, in a socio-interactional paradigm, and Foucault, in an institutional-historical paradigm, handled this in now canonical ways. Censoring agencies, and parasites more generally, whose presence may be internalized, lead to the recoding and rechanneling of such potential signs—giving rise to minimizations and maskings, condensations and lies, gestures and displacements, shifts in footing and slips of the tongue (as well as a host of hermeneutic techniques, or interpretive epistemes, for recovering the original sign-object relations—from psychoanalysis, through genealogy, to linguistic anthropology). Such censoring agencies may be real or imagined, internally imposed or externally applied, consciously undertaken or unconsciously executed. And they may be figured as any kind of generalized other—not just fathers, wardens, and dictators, but also unratified bystanders, ego ideals, and evaluative standards. Such issues are well-rehearsed. I mention them here to highlight the differences between such analyses and my own, as well as some possibilities for pushing this analysis further.

That said, the local ontology of poultry I presented in this chapter had all the bells and whistles of a Freudian unconscious, a Lacanian imaginary, or a Nietzchean allegory. However, we understood such a rich and ambiguous range of figurings, almost dreamlike in their texture and tension, not as the repercussion of deferred affect or sublimated desire, itself grounded in some universal psychodynamic subject. Rather, we understood these figurings as the only empirically tractable entryway into local understandings of self, alters, and objects (ontology); and thus local ways of framing reflexive modes of desire, affect, and accountability (selfhood); and thus local ways of grounding interpretations of sign-object relations (affect). In this way, the analysis necessarily wraps back onto itself, for the ontology with which we began was itself grounded in semiotic processes, semiological structures, and social relations that were themselves the collective products of signifying and interpreting selves (both human and nonhuman). And so as we have ended, so we may begin again.

To return to Wallace Stevens, anthropologists and critical theorists alike, as well as NGOs and ecotourists, have all too often been the "thin men of Haddam," focused as they are on cock fights and commodities, companion species and the agency of ants, cyborgs and *homo sacer*, spirits and shamans, symbols and shifters, self-narratives and spectacle, panopticons and penises, endangered avifauna and biodiversity. However, culture (language and mind) need not be approached always through its "golden birds," but sometimes simply through the signs (and squawks) of its nonindigenous domestic fowl.

CHAPTER 3

From Reciprocation to Replacement

GRADING USE VALUES, LABOR POWER, AND PERSONHOOD

Apples and Oranges, Coffee and Corn

Let me begin this chapter with a comparative utterance, which was spoken by a woman during an ethnographic interview on a canonical kind of anthropological topic—*awas*, which are the local equivalent of taboos.

> q'eq-q'eq li kape' chi-r-u li hal
> black-black Dm coffee Prep-E(3s)-RN Dm corncob
> "Coffee is very black in comparison to corncobs."

In this statement, the woman is assessing one entity's degree of blackness relative to another entity. To understand the importance of such an utterance, first note that to compare two substances in this way presumes that the two substances are comparable—and hence "commensurate" in one important sense. That is, *it is not that they have the same measure (though they might); it is that they can be measured with the same metric.* In this case, they may be characterized by the same predicate (black), and framed as having greater or lesser degrees of the quality referred to by this predicate (blackness).

While one might think that coffee and corncobs are the equivalent of apples and oranges, it turns out that there is a local ontology, itself sensible in the context of the area's history, where the comparison is warranted, if not demanded. In particular, the taboo in question was against drinking coffee during planting; coffee is much blacker than corncobs, and so if it is drunk while planting, the corncobs in one's milpa become very black (like coffee) and are inedible and unsellable.[1] Indeed, unlike classic examples of sympathetic magic (where there is a qualitative and causative relation between two substances), the issue here is that there is a quantitative relation as well; it is not just that one substance (coffee) shares a quality (blackness) with another substance (corn), such that it may affect it causally (by making it black); it is that it has a higher degree of that quality than the other. In other words, *it is not just sameness of qualities, but rather graded difference in quantities (of those qualities) that generates causality.*

Coffee, it should be remembered, was an important crop in Alta Verapaz since the late 1800s, when a wave of new European immigrants came in. There is a whole history waiting to be written here, one of forced labor, enclosure of collective lands, displacement from villages, fight, flight, liberal reforms, and what was arguably a second colonization, all of which was simultaneous with the writing of modern grammars and geographies of Mayan-speaking people, such as those produced by scholars like Otto Stoll and Karl Sapper. While that is not the purpose of this chapter, it should be noted that there are very good reasons to be wary of coffee if you are a Q'eqchi' speaker in Alta Verapaz, which make its drinking in the context of highly ritualistic and stereotypically Mayan practices like planting corn taboo. Indeed, it is arguably precisely the coupling of a cultural logic of taboo grounded in a political and economic history of colonization that allows corn and coffee—and thus apples and oranges—to be treated as commensurable in this way. And so figured in this comparative construction is not just a foundational topic in anthropology (sympathetic magic), but also a core concern of political economy in relation to cultural history.

But let us step back from these more anthropological and economic issues for a moment, and look at the particularities of the grammatical construction itself. First note that the construction turns on a preposition (*chi*) and a relational noun (-*u*); together these are usually used to indicate that one thing is in front of, before, or prior to another. (The relational noun comes from *uhej*, an inalienable possession that means face, or front surface.) The construction might best be translated as "coffee is very black in the face of, or in comparison to, corncobs." Indeed, it is tempting to translate it as *in confrontation with*—in part to capture the sense of a face or front surface, and, in part, to capture the inherently agonistic nature of comparison.

This framework may be tentatively formalized, and thereby generalized. Such a comparative construction may be understood to turn on the relation between a figure of comparison (Fc), a ground of comparison (Gc), and a quality in comparison (Qc). In this example, coffee is the figure, corncobs are the ground, and blackness is the quality. The comparison is itself made explicit via the adposition *chiru* (in front of, before), which also helps specify the direction of comparison (Dc). That is, the figure is understood to have a greater degree of the quality than the ground. And the reduplication of the adjective specifies a magnitude of comparison (Mc) in this direction. In particular, it does not just have a greater degree, but a much greater degree.

Crucially, while such relatively explicit comparative constructions are a staple item in grammars, in actual discourse they are relatively rare in comparison to constructions that are only implicitly comparative. For example, far more frequent are constructions like, "the coffee is very black" (*mas q'eq li kape'*), meaning the coffee is very black *in comparison to the average or typical member of the class of entities with which it is being compared* (say, cups of coffee the speaker is used to drinking). In such a construction, the ground of comparison and, indeed, the comparative relation itself, is relatively implicit, and so only indexically revealed by reference to the speech event, co-occurring text, or broader cultural presumptions. And, for this reason, its meaning is not only content-dependent, but also context-bound—and so may shift accordingly. For example, what counts as "very black" in the case of coffee may count as "barely black" in the case of coal; what counts as "many" in the case of roosters may count as only "a few" in the case of chickens; what counts as "cheap" for a tourist may count as "expensive" for a speaker of Q'eqchi'.[2]

Given the ubiquity of utterances containing comparative constructions of this implicit and contextually shifting kind (e.g., he is quite tall [for his age]; today will be quite hot [for a summer day in San Francisco]; this is not very heavy [for a shopping bag]; she is the best student [in the class]), one should get a sense of the necessarily agonistic and shifting nature of all experience—whereby entities, individuals, and events are both implicitly and explicitly *graded* in content-specific and context-bound ways.

That is, some action or utterance, gesture or affect, indicates *the degree to which* an entity or event presents a particular quality to the experience of an agent; where such an indication, however elusive or elliptical, plays a role in determining the entity's trajectory, the event's outcome, and/or the agent's relations.

Becoming Use Value

In his classic essay entitled *Grading: A Study in Semantics*, Edward Sapir ([1944] 1985) sought to bring attention to judgments like *this bag is very heavy* and *today is hotter than yesterday*, which he thought were presupposed by judgments involving measurable units and countable quantities, such as *this weighs fifty pounds* and *it's ninety-seven degrees outside*. In some sense, he was interested in quantity before it becomes explicitly quantified—what we will call *quantia* (by loose analogy with Peirce's notion of *qualia*, understood as semiotically relevant qualities prior to their embodiment in a substance or their characterization by a predicate). Taking his essay as a point of departure, one goal of this chapter is to demonstrate the radical importance of grading to all things anthropological. In particular, I will push past the semantics of grading, and detail its patterns of usage, focusing on the social relations, cultural values, and material processes that get expressed and elaborated through these patterns. As will be seen, while many scholars valorize qualitative research in opposition to quantitative research, ethnographic inquiry is necessarily quantia-tative if it is to be qualia-tative.

But this movement from quantification to gradation is just one of the tasks of this chapter. It should be understood as one key moment in a more general movement from modes of reciprocation to modes of *replacement*. Among speakers of Q'eqchi' living in the village of Chicacnab, replacement (*eeqaj*) refers to a range of practices which, loosely speaking, turn on the replacement of a use value rather than the exchange of one use value for another use value. Such activities include house building, civil and religious elections, soccer goals, vengeful actions, labor pools, loan returns, illness cures, adultery, and namesakes. In particular, all such activities involve the substitution of one entity for another entity, insofar as these entities have relatively similar degrees of shared qualities, and insofar as they hold a role in a necessary or obligatory position. For example, one man may substitute his labor for another man's labor insofar as men have similar degrees of strength and skill, and insofar as a position in a labor pool must be filled. And an effigy of a sick person may substitute for that person during a healing process insofar as they have inalienable possessions in common (such as hair and clothing), and insofar as a divinity requires one or the other as compensation. To put this in terms of deontic value, entities within certain domains *must* have a replacement (lest their role go unfulfilled, or their function stay unserved); and other entities *may* substitute for such entities (insofar as they are judged relatively equivalent in regards to their embodied qualia and quantia). While anthropologists, critical theorists, and social scientists of all persuasions have studied modes of reciprocation ad nauseam (from gift to commodity, and everything outside and in between), the literature on replacement is almost nonexistent "in comparison."

As a case in point, one of the most emblematic—and arguably problematic—equations of classical political economy is this: *one bolt of cloth is equal to three bushels of wheat.* Such an equation turns on utilities (wheat and cloth, traditionally understood as ensembles of desirable qualities), units (bushels and bolts), and numbers (three and one). In particular, two use values—each consisting of a particular number, unit, and utility—are equated insofar as they seem to have (more or less) the same exchange value. Such an equation goes back to Aristotle, who famously inquired into its condition of possibility, asking how is it that two radically different things can be equated in exchange, and what determines their relative proportion? And nineteenth-century economists—such as Smith, Marx, Jevons, and Marshall—were to give a range of interrelated answers, such as labor-commanded, marginal utility, and supply and demand. In this chapter, a much more basic (and much less often posed) question is put forth: not how is it that two distinct use values can have the same exchange value, but how is it that two distinct entities can have the same use value? In other words, what are the social, semiotic, and material processes whereby substances get utilized, unitized, and numericalized? Or, in the terms of the previous section, and so as not to privilege use value per se as a general category, what are the conditions for, and consequences of, "qualia-fying" and "quantia-fying," or *kinding* and *commensurating,* and thereby enclosing, little swatches of the world in this way?

While most critical theorists, such as Marx himself, were not particularly interested in such processes—relegating "the various uses of things," as well as "the establishment of socially-recognized standards of measure for the quantities of these useful objects," to "the work of history" (1967: 43)—they are a condition of possibility for political economy (and not just as it unfolds, but also how it is analyzed retrospectively). While historical metrologists and historians of science have analyzed the vicissitudes of weights and measures in relation to science, technology, and state building, the quotidian practices and cultural meanings of measurement have largely been ignored.[3] While linguistic anthropologists have documented numerical systems and noun classifiers in relation to cognition and culture, they have been focused on semantic categories rather than social processes or pragmatic functions.[4] While economic anthropologists have elaborated various modes of exchange, they have tended to treat the utilities, units, and numbers of the use values being exchanged as given—and hence not in need of interpretation.[5] While linguists like Sapir have long understood grading to turn on relatively ubiquitous lexical and grammatical processes, nonlinguistic practices of grading and pragmatic, as opposed to semantic, aspects of linguistic grading—involving modes of residence in the world and not just modes of representing the world—have received scarce attention. And while value itself has long been a key topic for anthropological research and critical theory more generally, use value itself has not been treated as problematic, or in need of theory.[6] Indeed, the emphasis on exchange value relative to use value probably has its roots in Aristotle who—in first distinguishing between "value in use" and "value in exchange" (2001a, 2001b)—only saw a need to discuss the latter at length.[7]

In the following section of this chapter, I describe the range of practices that are locally understood as involving replacement, or substitution. After that, I explicitly link stereotypically discursive practices of grading to stereotypically economic practices of replacing, and move from relatively explicit to relatively implicit modes of equivalence. I then focus on labor pooling, a particularly important mode of replacement insofar as the underlying utility is labor-power itself, as mapped onto various kinds of persons. Next, I further explore this relation between potentia and personhood, and explicitly link it to core ideas of Marx, Mauss, and Linton. I then examine linguistic practices whereby different kinds of persons are explicitly graded in regards to their ability to replace each other in labor pools. And I use these ethnographic, economic, and linguistic details to retheorize use value from the standpoint of replacement, discussing who and what can serve as replacements, the inherent utilities (or qualia) shared by such replacements, the units and numbers (or quantia) in which such utilities typically appear, and the nature of the necessity and obligation (or modality) that requires the replacement itself. I thereby show the intimate connection between so-called use value and value per se. I then discuss various temporal scales of historical importance, highlighting the exclusionary relation between replacement and colonial practices of labor extraction. And, in the final section, I summarize the various forms of equivalence that are in play in this chapter and introduce the notion of *equalia*, or equality that is (seemingly) prior to its political mobilization and mathematical formulation.

Modes of Replacement

A wide range of practices get framed in terms of replacement. As will be seen, such practices span so much of Q'eqchi' life that it is tempting to call replacement an exemplary instance of a social order: local practices for making certain activities, objects, and people relatively equivalent. (And, consequently, for making other activities, objects, and people relatively non-equivalent.) Indeed, if we consider economy to be the systematic provisioning of goods (Polanyi 1957), and if we consider that most classes of replacement have to do with the periodic renewal of some particular good, then replacement also seems to provide an exemplary instance of an economy being subsumed by a social order.

For example, a newly built house was called the replacement (*eeqaj*) of the owner's old house. It was equivalent to the old house in its ability to provide shelter, a necessary utility. Besides referring to houses for humans, replacement was also used to refer to houses for domestic animals, for example, chicken coops, turkey runs, and pig pens. Shelters for both human life and animal life under human care required replacements when they wore out. Roofs for human houses used to be rebuilt every five years or so, after the thatch had begun to rot and the rain had begun to leak through. And houses themselves used to be rebuilt, from the ground up, every ten years or so. As will be seen in chapter 4, however, there was a surge of house building during the late 1990s, due both to an influx of money from ecotourists, and to an expectation that there would be more ecotourists to house in the future. For this reason, many families came to have two houses, one built in the older style with a thatch roof, and the other built in a newer style with a tin roof. And so there were many new houses that did not originate as replacements for old houses. And there were many new houses with little use value outside of their ability to index their owners' lack-of-substitutability (or rather "irreplaceability"). As will be argued, the expertise and money required for building houses in the newer style undermined labor pooling—perhaps the most extensive form of replacement—in favor of cash payment.

A newly elected village mayor was called the replacement of the previous mayor. He was equivalent to the old mayor in his ability to fulfill a local political duty, itself a kind of status. Elections—the institutional means for choosing replacements—were held once a year, and any married men in the village could run. The mayor's main responsibility was to act as a political liaison between the village (*k'aleb'al* or *aldea*) and the town (*tenamit* or *cabecería*). In this capacity, a mayor helped institute top-down programs such as vaccinations and sanitation, and a mayor helped present village concerns to his immediate superior, the town mayor. For example, a long-term concern of villagers was to get a road built between the village and the town so that goods could be more easily bought and sold in intervillage markets. (And several mayors were elected on the promise that they would get the government to construct such a road.) In general, however, a mayor spent most of his time mediating village-internal disputes, including fights, arguments over the pillaging of unrestrained domestic animals, and water rights. (His authority in such disputes, however, ultimately rested in his ability to enlist the town mayor, who had legally enforced rights—to levy a fine, to make an arrest, or to mediate a property dispute.) In addition, the village mayor organized village-wide labor pools, for instance, to clean the trail to the nearest village, to build an additional room for the school, or to help a man rebuild his home after a mudslide destroyed it. Because of his position, a mayor tended to have close contacts with external institutions such as NGOS, churches, national and regional political organizations, anthropologists, and Proyecto Eco-Quetzal itself. And while mayors were originally chosen from among the older men in the village, younger men were being voted in more and more often, it was said, because they had a better command of Spanish, and a better understanding of more recent institutions (two forms of knowledge thought necessary to be an effective mayor). In this context a man as young as twenty-eight had been elected mayor, and men as young as twenty-five were starting to run for the office.

In the religious hierarchy, or *cofradía*, a newly elected married couple (*mertoom*) was called the replacement of the previous couple. They were equivalent to the old couple in their ability to fulfill a local religious obligation (and thus inhabit a particular kind of status). The cofradía in the village consisted of six couples, who were entrusted with the physical care of the church. Their weekly duties consisted of cleaning and decorating the church, and overseeing the spending of contributions. In addition, whenever the priest came to give mass (several times a year), they provided and prepared food for him and his entourage (usually slaughtering their own chickens for his meals). Each year a new couple was elected for a six-year tenure, during which time they annually moved up one position in the hierarchy. As will be discussed in chapter 4, household-internal tensions often arose because of men not wanting to join the cofradía (against the desires of their wives—for whom cofradía election was one of the only forms of replacement open), yet wanting to be elected mayor (even though they would normally be considered too young). Such a difference between husbands and wives in their desire to join the cofradía was probably related to the fact that other forms of village-internal recognition were only possible through village-external social relations—relations that were more accessible to men than women.

One man's vengeful action toward another man was called the replacement of the other man's prior insulting or harmful action. It was equivalent to this prior action in its ability to settle the score, which was presumed to be necessarily equal. In other words, this form of replacement was the local equivalent of "an eye for an eye" or "tit for tat." Nevertheless, while there were many stories of revenge or justice, the only cases I experienced were in situations in which two men were play-fighting or wrestling. If one got the better of the other—landing a well-placed blow or flipping the other on his back—there was usually encouragement from the spectators to "give him his replacement." Indeed, my first personal experience with substitution occurred after I was attacked by a dog (physically unscathed but psychologically scarred). Several men who heard about what happened fashioned me a whip out of a tree branch, and then told me to "give the dog a replacement for what it did" (*k'e reeqaj li k'aru xb'aanu*). Even the anthropologist could be encouraged to participate in the local system of replacement (at least in settling scores with animals).

One soccer team's tying goal was called the replacement of the other team's previous goal. It was equivalent to the last goal in its ability to even the score. Soccer games usually occurred after church on Sundays, weather permitting. (Boys, however, played after school during the week. And on market days there were often intervillage soccer games in town.) They took place in a large field, which had been made by men working together for the explicit purpose of constructing a site for playing soccer. Most men who played soccer were between fifteen and thirty years old. Teams were not fixed. Rather, they were drawn up differently each Sunday—either by "captains" taking turns picking men from a lineup, or on a "first-come first-serve" basis, as men straggled in from church, lunch, or labor. One might note, then, that in both soccer scores and vengeance tallies, replacement seemed to presuppose that the norm was for both sides to match scores—to have a tie, or come out even. But while soccer seemed to be modeled on vengeance, teams were nevertheless orientated toward winning rather than tying.

A man who slept with another man's wife was called "his replacement." He was equivalent to the husband proper in his ability to satisfy a marital commitment (sometimes phrased as a responsibility or right). While I never collected data on the frequency of adultery, insofar as men were often away from the village working on plantations, many men worried about their wives sleeping with other men in their absence. For this reason, a man's parents would often drop in on their daughter-in-law's house while their son was away—and thereby kept a silent watch to see where the woman went and who stopped by.

A man who took another man's place within a labor pool, or fulfilled another man's more solitary labor obligations, was called the latter man's replacement. He was equivalent to the man in his ability to perform a certain amount of work. Labor pooling usually occurred with arduous or time-consuming practices such as the clearing and planting of agricultural fields, and house building. But it could also occur with weeding and harvesting, as well as with less agriculturally relevant tasks, such as wood chopping and cow tending. It should be emphasized that to replace another person in a labor pool was not merely to return their labor; it was to take the place of a second person who had to return a third person's labor. Thus, if one man was obligated to work for a second man (because they were reciprocating within a labor pool), but could not make it because of sickness, he could send a third man as his "replacement." Or, in nonpooling contexts, if a man could not fulfill a daily household task as obligated by his role in the domestic mode of production (say, chopping wood), he could send his older son in his place. These issues will be developed at length in later sections.

The money returned to another as the settling of a loan was called the replacement of the originally loaned money. Loans were usually made among members of an extended family. For example, a man might lend his daughter-in-law money to buy household supplies while her husband was away working on a plantation. Or a married couple might lend the woman's brother money to buy cement for the foundation of his house. These loans were usually less than one hundred quetzals (about US$14, in 2000) and were paid back within six months, usually without interest. Loans were the only form of replacement in which economic value was the underlying utility and, consequently, in which the utility being replaced could come in any quantity—the unit being the Guatemalan national currency, the quetzal (and sometimes the American dollar), and the number varying. While this mode of replacement looked like money lending (M-M' or EV-EV'), in its classical guise, and thus a form of relatively negative reciprocity involving exchange value or quantity, it is probably best to think of it as replacement. That is, one was merely replacing the money with its functional equivalent, or substitute, sometime later. Thus, rather than think of loans as a place where exchange value (money or quantity) began to invade use value (utility or quality), it is probably best to think of loans as a place where exchange value got figured in terms of use value—or, indeed, as yet another site where the distinction makes little sense.

(Q'eqchi' speakers in the village of Chicacnab were also familiar with usury, or loans with nonkin and nonneighbors, that had to be repaid with interest [or M-M' proper]; and, as we saw in chapter 2, their term for interest was *ral tumin*, or "offspring of money." [Conversely, their term for capital was *xna' tumin*, or "mother of money."] And recall our discussion of chickens and kinship relations, where it was seen that *ral* was also used to refer to the offspring of domestic animals more generally.)

The process of replacement was even wide enough to include gifts, at least in a certain sense. In the following utterance, for example, a speaker explains that, if you give gifts, that is good—and god will give the gift's replacement back to you. In contrast, if you do not give gifts, you will be very poor.

1) wi nak-at-sihink, us, li qa-wa dios t-Ø-x-k'e r-eeqaj
Cond Pres-A(2s)-gift good Dm E(1p)-sustenance god Fut-A(3s)-E(3s)-give E(3s)-substitute
"If you give gifts, (that is) good, our lord will give you their replacement."
2) wi ink'a' nak-Ø-aa-si, ma, mas neeb'a-q-at cha'an-k-Ø
Cond Neg Pres-A(3s)-E(2s)-gift Part very poor-Fut-A(2s) say-Pres-A(3s)
"If you do not give gifts, you will be very poor, it is said."

As may be seen, there are two relatively parallel conditional constructions (lines 1 and 2), each representing a possible (and opposing) world. As may also be seen, while the if clauses of each construction are more or less alike aside from their valence (unmarked versus negative), the consequent clauses refer to different kinds of events that seem distinctly coupled: god giving a gift's replacement back to the giver, and the nongiver becoming very poor. While speakers routinely claimed that gifts did not involve replacement (essentially by definition; that is, if someone gives you back a gift's replacement, it's not a gift), this shows that a third actor—god—can replace the gift to the giver. And, as seen by the consequent clause of the second utterance, this replacement comes in the form of a more generalized wealth (or, conversely, its absence).

As mentioned in chapter 2, and as taken up at length in Kockelman (2010b), in cases where a person has suffered fright (*xiwajenaq*), as brought on by a moral breach such as forgetting to pray or deprecating maize, they could bury a replacement, or effigy, of themselves in the place where they were frightened. Only in this way would the person not fall ill, insofar as the agency that frightened them accepted the effigy as a replacement for the person's health. These effigies were iconic indices, consisting of tree sap, formed in the shape of a person, and mixed with the sick person's fingernails, hair, and clothing. A replacement that was formed of the sick person's inalienable possessions simultaneously acted as the pledge that brought about their cure, as well as an admission of their culpability.

In cases where a boy was given the name of his father, he would be considered his father's replacement. This was the one form of replacement that was not frequently practiced. This was because children named after their parents were thought likely to inherent their bad traits or negative personal tendencies. For instance, a penchant for alcohol or adultery, or a tendency for sloth, illness, anger, or even poverty. A name was intimately associated with the negative characteristics of a person—those personal qualities that could have an effect on their health and economic well-being. For this reason, namesaking was the only form of replacement that turned on a *negative* obligation—a man should *not* name his son after himself, insofar as the negative traits of one generation should not be renewed in the next generation.

Practices somewhat similar to replacement, and words somewhat similar to *eeqaj*, have been documented in other Mayan communities—albeit in a much more circumscribed fashion. For example, Carlsen and Prechtel (1991) argue that the Tzutujil word *k'ex* refers to the replacement of older persons with younger equivalents. They refer to this as "making the new out of the old" and "reincarnation," and they characterize it as "relating to the transfer, and hence continuity, of life" (26). And Mondloch (1980), working with the Mayan language Quiche, has discussed the use of the word *k'e?s* in relation to naming practices, describing it as a "social mechanism for replacing the ancestors" (9). Similar themes have been echoed by other Mayanists working in Highland Guatemala (Coggins 1989; Ruz Lluillier 1973; Warren 1989). While I have no data on the historical transformations of the word *eeqaj*, in meaning or in form, it may be the case that reincarnation—and the replacement of persons more generally—is the more originary and widespread usage. If so, it would indicate that the replacement of people—not only in namesaking, but also perhaps in civil-religious elections, such as mayor and cofradía—is the more basic process.

More generally, the replacement of persons relates to the idea of personage (*personnage*), first theorized by Maine ([1866] 2002: chap. 6) in the legal context of inheritable statuses (such as property rights), but made famous by Mauss ([1938] 1979: 11–17) in the religious context of ritual, wherein a finite number of roles, usually marked by names or masks, were inhabitable by members or clans of a bounded society, in the context of ritually replaying the reincarnation of ancestors (and see

Allen 1985, Kockelman 2010b). While replacement relates to use value in the classic sense (as used by Aristotle, as well as by Marx and other nineteenth-century political economists), it also relates to personhood in a more Maussian sense. Below, both these issues will come together in the context of labor pooling, where the underlying utility (or potentia) was a person's labor-power. Indeed, while the religious-cosmological interpretation of replacement offered by scholars such as Carlsen and Prechtel is important, it is also worthwhile to maintain a more worldly interpretation. As will be discussed below, for example, it has been suggested that labor pooling among the Q'eqchi'—which, as we just saw, involves one of the most extensive modes of replacement—may be a response both to pre-Hispanic forms of tribute taking, and to colonial forms of labor extraction.

Earthenware Griddles and Metal Griddles

It should be emphasized that there was a large number of other forms of replacement, turning on the equivalence of everyday objects of utility, rather than human actors and their activities per se. For example, after I knocked my coffee cup onto the floor, my host told her son to bring me "its replacement" (reeqaj). Or, when the gas in their lamp was all used up, a man suggested to his wife that they go get "its replacement." That is, the accidental loss or normal provisioning of a necessary item entailed a replacement. Such processes often involved the most stereotypic of use values. For instance, a bag of salt, a lantern's worth of oil, a set of batteries, or a pair of rubber boots. And such modes of replacement thereby seem to involve the most quotidian kinds of equivalence, similar quantities (e.g., numbers and units) of shared qualities (e.g., utilities). With this last mode of replacement in mind, let us turn to an example in which two seemingly substitutable goods were graded as nonequivalent in key respects:

1) li ch'iich' k'il moko mas ta li xam na-Ø-r-aj
Dm metal griddle Neg very Neg Dm fire Pres-A(3s)-E(3s)-want
"The metal griddle does not require a lot of fire (because the flame is very low)."
2) pero li ch'och' k'il, a'an naab'al li xam na-Ø-r-aj
but Dm earth griddle Pro(3s) much Dm fire Pres-A(3s)-E(3s)-want
"But the earthenware griddle, that requires a lot of fire."

3) pero moko na-Ø-k'atok ta li ch'och' k'il
but Neg Pres-A(3s)-burn Neg Dm earth griddle
"However the earthenware griddle does not burn (the tortillas)."
4) mas chaab'il li wa' na-Ø-x-k'e
very good Dm tortilla Pres-A(3s)-E(3s)-give
"Very good are the tortillas it makes."

Here my host, Angelina, was comparing two kinds of griddles (*k'il*) for me, those made out of metal (*ch'iich'*) and those made out of clay (*ch'och'*). She said that the metal griddle does not require a lot of fire, because the flame is very slow, whereas the earthenware griddle does require a lot of fire. Conversely, the tortillas made with the earthenware griddle are more delicious, and less likely to burn.

In short, even though metal griddles required less fuel for their functioning, earthenware griddles were preferred when one could justify the extra fuel needed to cook with them—for the tortillas they made were superior in taste and outcome. But not withstanding the qualitative superiority of earthenware griddles, in a context like the cloud forest, where the NGO was determined to protect the forest, and dry wood was scarce in any case, they tended to be used only on ceremonial occasions, when many families got together, and the fuel use could be justified by reference to the kind of event and the number of people. The use of an earthenware griddle usually indicated that a large festivity was at hand, or at least immanent.

Here, then, we have a tale of two relatively "substitutable goods" in the strict economic sense, use values with similar enough functions, in similar enough proportions, that one can be substituted for the other in a pinch. And, simultaneously, we have a tale of two relatively nonequivalent goods—for the griddles differ enough in their salient qualities as to be habitually differentiated in actual use. Indeed, we also have a contrast between a relatively new good (metallic griddles) and a relatively old good (earthenware griddles), itself mapping onto relatively mundane and celebratory occasions. And, concomitantly, we have an overdetermined tension between instrumental and existential values (say, fuel used versus taste achieved), and so there is also the foregrounding of a trade-off in a classic economic sense—when does the degree of taste achieved, for example, justify the amount of fuel used? Finally, it should be noted that many earthenware griddles were "irreplaceable" in our own vernacular sense. In particular, they were passed down through the generations, and thereby constituted quasi-inalienable possessions, and thus emblems of social relationality and mnemonics of family history. This meant that even a seemingly identical replacement could not make up for the affective singularity. In short, the two kinds of griddles could be compared by reference to many different dimensions, or qualities, and thereby judged as more or less equivalent relative to each.

With this difference in mind, let us turn to the kind of commensurability with which we opened this chapter; when two entities may be described by the same predicate, and differentially graded as a function of the degree to which they possessed the quality denoted by that predicate. Note first that, in contrast to our opening example about coffee and corn, this example about griddles contains no explicit grammatical comparison (via a relational noun like *chiru*, or "in confrontation with"); rather, discourse contrast, and parallelism more generally, makes the comparison implicit. In line (1), we learn that metallic griddles do not require a lot of fire—where, again, what counts as "a lot" is contextually determined as a function of the comparison class in question (e.g., something like, *fires used for cooking*). And, in line (2), we learn that earthenware griddles do require a lot of fire. That is, rather than explicitly comparing the amount of fire used by earthenware griddles and metallic griddles, each is implicitly compared to an average or typical amount of fuel use; and, insofar as these implicit comparisons are contextually co-occurrent, both kinds of griddles are thereby compared with each other. Finally, having set up such a contrast, other qualities predicated of the earthenware griddles (such as not burning tortillas, and making tasty tortillas) are understood as not applying to metallic griddles.

Crucially, this example also turns on poetic parallelism in a narrow sense, in that the word for metal (*ch'iich'*) is phonologically close to the word for earth (*ch'och'*), a similarity that is especially significant in overlapping compound constructions like *ch'och'k'il* and *ch'iich'k'il*. This can be called, following Jakobson (1990b), poetic parallelism, which, in an expanded sense (as the repetition of tokens of common types), is quasi-synonymous with grammatical analysis. Recall, for example, that signs that partake of the same paradigm are equivalent in a grammatical sense. And if grammars state such equivalences, poetry shows such equivalences. And so the elements conjoined in poetic parallelisms, no less than the constituents in grammatical paradigms, or form-classes more generally, are commensurable entities in yet another sense. There is thus a very good reason to call such forms of repetition poetic *meter*, and to see them as central to any study of measurement, or commensuration more broadly.

There is yet another kind of commensuration at work here, one that is Q'eqchi' specific, but has analogs in other places. In particular, as introduced in our discussion of the connotation of chickens (*kaxlan*) in chapter 2, the word *ch'iich'* is itself caught up in a range of other compound constructions, whereby it is added to a noun that usually refers to a relatively old and nonmetallic object in order to refer to a relatively new and metallic object, often in slightly humorous, ironic, or pedantic ways. For example, if *so'sol* means "vulture," *so'sol ch'iich'* can be used to refer to "airplanes"; and if *ulul* means "brains" *ulul ch'iich'* can be used to refer to "computers." Pairings of ch'iich' and non-ch'iich' entities, which is a kind of comparison through analogy, also renders a kind of commensuration; while the form or function might be similar (flight in the case of vultures and airplanes, thought in the case of brains and computers), the material, artificer, or origins are different.

Finally, in contrast to our opening example, which foregrounded how different grounds of comparison license different kinds of grades depending on a relatively normative standard (i.e., what counts as "very black" in the case of coffee is different from what counts as "very black" in the case of coal), we see here how changing historical circumstances transform normative standards; a new tool may make an old tool seem slower or less efficient, as well as make its products seem tastier or more authentic. That is, not only may the grade of an entity contextually shift as a function of its conventional ground of comparison (qua point of departure), conventional grounds of comparison may contextually shift as a function of collective history. For example, what counted as a very fast train or a risqué advertisement for my parents may count as a slow train or a very tame advertisement to me. Phrased another way, *just as figures may be graded in relation to conventional grounds on interactional timescales, conventional grounds may be regraded in relation to collective experience on historical timescales.*[8]

This is another reason practices involving grading should be considered tools as much as topics, radically sensitive to real-time practices as much as longue durée processes. And, as this example shows, in many contexts, entities with old grades and new grades can coexist around the same hearth fire, and thereby contrast with, comment on, and potentially confront each other.

Comparing Men, Boys, Women, and Money

Agricultural clearing was a key site in which men's activities were rendered relatively qualifiable and quantifiable as use values, as well as one of the last stands of labor pooling. It counts as a perfect example of comparison (qua confrontation). Suppose it was February, and a man had five *tarees* of land that he wanted to sow in the upcoming months (less than one-fourth hectare). Before he began to sow (and after he had burnt any remaining trees or cloud forest cover), he and four other men would clear the five-taree area, each man laboring alone throughout the day on his designated one-taree swatch (usually marked out ahead of time by the owner with *retaalil*, or boundary markers). The work would consist of clearing grass, weeds, small shrubs, and dead limbs from the ground so that the subsequent planting of seeds could proceed smoothly. The only tools used would be a machete and a *lokoch* (a stick in the shape of the number seven, usually made at the site from a tree branch). The lokoch would be used to pull the weeds together and then hold them while their roots were cut with the machete; to rake already cut weeds into a pile; and to dislodge rocks and sticks. All the men would work separately from each other, but engaged in the same relatively repetitive—or poetically metered—task: rake, hold, slice, sweep; rake, hold, slice, sweep; rake, hold, slice, sweep; and so on.

Such work groups were usually composed of a man's older sons, father, brothers-in-law, and close friends. These men would meet at the owner's house in the morning for breakfast and be at the work site by around seven o'clock. They would break only to sharpen their machetes, and to take drinks of coffee or juice brought to them by their host's wife or daughters. In addition, they would eat lunch together—usually tamales, but often more expensive, celebratory food like chicken. (This food would be prepared by the host's wife, usually working in conjunction with several other women—a point that we will return to below.) Work was usually finished by four o'clock in the afternoon. And the men would then return home to wash up, tend to their domestic tasks, and eat dinner with their families. On each successive day, all the same men would again work together, but on land belonging to a different member of the group—working in this way for five days in a row (excluding Sundays) until all the labor had been reciprocated, and each man's plot of land had been cleared. Each man had the tools, skills, strength, and social relations necessary to clear more or less the same area (one taree) in more or less the same amount of time (one day). And, as we saw above, if a man could not fulfill his obligation to the pool, he could always send a substitute in his place, another man who could carry out his obligation for him.

The most socially extended form of labor pooling was village-wide community service (*sa' komunil*). For example, every two or three years all the men in the village (some one hundred able-bodied adult males) would get together after church several Sundays in a row to clean and fix the trail that ran to the nearest town. Additionally, each year there was usually some construction activity taking place within the village that benefited all villagers. For example, villagers once constructed a multipurpose room next to the church. In this case, all the men worked four Sundays in a row, carrying heavy bags of cement from the town to the village, leveling the ground, building the foundation, and laying bricks. Another key place for village-wide labor pooling was community-based aid—for example, helping a family rebuild their house after a mudslide knocked it down. (In the wake of deforestation, lack of terracing, and limited land holdings, such disasters were almost an annual event during my field-work.) In such cases, the mayor would immediately organize a labor pool to salvage the remains of the unfortunate family's previous house and to construct them a new house. To do this, he would spend the evening (or early next morning) walking to every house in the village, spreading the news and requesting assistance. Usually, such houses could be erected with two days of continuous labor. Although no official tally was taken of who came and who stayed home, both the owner of the house and the mayor personally greeted each man who came in the morning, shaking their hands and thanking them. Reciprocation was duly noted, both at the personal level and the political level. And all the men working usually remembered who did or didn't come, and who worked hard or sat idle. In such community-wide labor pools the act of reciprocation—and thus the necessity of replacement—was instantaneous. If one could not make it to help, one would send along as one's replacement one's oldest son (or the paid oldest son of a family member), as well as an excuse—legal work in town, sickness (no replacement necessary), or prior commitment to a labor pool in another village (but this was infrequent insofar as labor pooling was usually village internal).

Once a boy was around fifteen years old, he could replace a man (who would usually be his father, but who could also be his uncle, brother, grandfather, or godfather). In particular, a boy of this age was said to finally possess enough strength (*metz'ew*) and skill (*na'leb'*) to be able to endure (*kuyuk*) the labor. Nevertheless, men would often complain if someone scheduled to work for them sent along a fifteen-year-old son—especially if the boy was either still too weak to carry his weight, or known to be lazy. Boys younger than fifteen would often tag along with their father to labor pools, working as best they could. However, such boys were not expected to contribute nearly as much labor as a man—indeed, they were not usually assigned a particular taree to cut (in the case of clearing) and instead spent the day clearing the irregular, hard-to-reach, or unassigned sections of the owner's field. And boys older than seven could help their father when he had to go into town on some errand while there was still clearing to be done. In such cases, they could work alone, or with their brothers, in fields close to home. And, in relatively light or unskilled work, such as harvesting, a young boy could replace his father—not in the sense that the boy was fulfilling his father's obligation to a labor pool, but in the sense that he was carrying out his father's usual domestic task.

Nonetheless, all people agreed that if a boy was sent to work in a man's place, and he was still not an adult, bad things could happen. For example, one boy sliced open his shin with his machete—some thought owing to his exhaustion, and others thought owing to his lack of skill. In any case, that very morning I had heard the boy's mother warning him not to cut himself. And several times throughout the day she mentioned that she was very worried about him. Replacement was a relatively charged issue; the stakes of sending someone too young to substitute could range from bodily injury to social insult.

The only man a woman could ever replace was her husband. But even this could occur only in a limited number of situations, most of which did not involve labor pools per se. For example, when her husband was away from the village working on a plantation, a woman could weed, chop firewood, harvest corn, or—more and more frequently over the course of my fieldwork—guide ecotourists. A woman could replace her husband in his solitary domestic tasks—not ones that he would do with other men, but rather ones that he was assigned either via his role in the domestic mode of production, or via his relation to the ecotourism project. (Note that this was similar to the way in which a young boy could replace his father in his domestic tasks.) However, men's replaceability with women was viewed differently depending on whether the viewer was a man or woman. For example, in interviews, men wouldn't mention these practices unless prompted and tended to say that women could not replace men. In contrast, women usually claimed that they could indeed be men's replacements and pointed to exactly these practices as proof. One reason that this was a relatively contentious issue was that there was no third party involved (as there was in the case of labor pools); it was *not* that a man had to reciprocate labor given to him by another man, and that his wife was fulfilling his obligation; rather, a woman was standing in for a man in his usual domestic duties. In other words, women could not replace men in their house-external labor pools (in the sense of standing in to fulfill their husbands' labor obligations to other men), but they could replace their husbands in their house-internal or NGO-related tasks.

One reason for the agreement between men and women regarding whether a man could be replaced with a woman was a shared assessment that women were not as strong as men. For example, with regard to a man's normal agricultural work, most men said that women did not have enough strength to replace them (*lix metz'ew moko tz'aqal ta*). And women usually endorsed this view about brute strength. In speaking about why she could not replace a man in labor pooling, a woman said, "I cannot endure (carrying) a post; we cannot endure it" (*moko ninkuy ta chaq li oqech, moko tqakuy ta*). Notice, then, that graded differences in strength (metz'ew) and endurance (kuyuk) were given as reasons for women's lack of substitutability for men (which, as will be shown below, were also used to figure the difference in value between dollars and quetzals). It should be stressed, however, that the bulk of men's labor did not involve carrying heavy objects, so that both men and women tended to focus on the least exemplary, but most difficult, form of men's labor when discussing their views about the physical inadequacies of women.

But this agreement between men and women did not extend to their respective assessments of what counted for women's work. This differential assessment is important, for whether or not one thought a woman was substitutable for a man had to do with how much work one thought a man or woman usually did, and what strength, skills, tools, and knowledge one thought this work required. In discussing whether a woman could be a man's replacement, one man said, "Women don't work, well they work I guess, but they only make tortillas, or perhaps sew bags or make baskets. Perhaps they collect water. Perhaps they sew. But that's the only work women do." Contrast this with one woman's account of her daily work:

> *Ay*, during one day! When the sun rises, I first light my gas. I start the fire. I put in firewood. After that I wash. I fill up water for the coffee. I wash the pans. Perhaps there is no cooked corn, so I start to wash corn. After I finish washing the corn, I start to grind the corn. After I finish grinding the corn, I wash my utensils. After I finish washing my utensils, I start to sweep the house. After I finish sweeping the house, I start to wash my children's clothing. After I finish washing my children's clothing, if I have something to weave, I start to weave. After I finish weaving, I begin to find some food for lunch. I cook the food. I again wash my corn for lunch. After I finish washing my corn for lunch, I fill up water for my coffee. After I finish filling up water for my coffee, I begin to season my food. After I finish doing that, I begin to grind corn until lunchtime arrives. When lunch has passed I don't rest. I wash my utensils again. After I finish that, I go out to look at my plants. When I finish that, with my thread I begin to weave. After I finish my weaving, I begin to wash corn for dinner. I search for food. I again put coffee on to heat up. After that comes dinner. If I don't have cooked corn, I begin to dekernel corn. I cook the corn until six o'clock arrives in the evening. This is what I do every day. I don't have a day of rest during the year. And don't forget my children and chickens [she laughs].

While women could not replace their husbands within labor pools, they could replace each other. In particular, when men were pooling their labor, their wives could pool their labor in order to feed the men; and in the context of such labor pools opportunities for replacement could arise. For example, as mentioned in the case of agricultural clearing, men were fed both breakfast and lunch at the host's house. In preparing these meals, several wives of the men would help the host's wife cook, making tortillas, preparing coffee, cooking beans, and so on. However, such cases of women's labor pooling were less extensive than men's. The other women would often work in their own homes and then bring the prepared food to the host's house. In addition, the women who helped the wife were typically the wives of the husband's closest relatives and so usually lived nearby—if they were not coresidents in the same housing cluster. In such contexts, one woman could send a friend, neighbor, relative, or elder daughter as her replacement (to fulfill her place in the pool); and, in this way, women could replace each other. And last, the cooking would last only through the morning—after that a woman returned to her usual domestic duties. In sum, while women were implicated in labor pooling, these activities were small in corporate scope (involving less extensive social relations: sisters, mothers, and mothers-in-law), were reciprocated on relatively short timescales, involved less social interaction and coordination, and in all cases took place in a dependent relation to men's exchange. For these reasons, the opportunities for women to replace other women were less frequent.

Such claims about domains of women's and men's work are articulated in local myths (Kockelman 2010b) and are well substantiated by other ethnographers working among speakers of Q'eqchi' (see Wilk 1991; R. Wilson 1995). Such claims also resonate with widespread arguments over the "public" and "private" quality of men's and women's respective social worlds vis-à-vis the "gendered allocation of labor" seemingly inherent to the domestic mode of production (see Du 2000; Hart 1989; Lamphere and Rosaldo 1974; Sacks 1974; Sahlins 1972; Sanday 1974; Yanagisako 1987; among others).

Rather than focusing on gendered domains, I want to use Strathern's (1988) notion of symmetric and asymmetric social relations. As she points out, there are minimally two forms of activity, namely, *collective* activities, in which "persons come together on the basis of shared characteristics. What they hold in common is regarded as the rationale of their concerted action. This is usually group affiliation or gender" (48); and *particular* activities, in which "interaction proceeds on the basis of and in reference to the particularity of an inherent difference between the parties" (49). In this latter case, what is shared between two members is only the relation itself—and thus it is difficult to concretize what they have in common. As Strathern points out, a division of labor between husband and wife is concomitant with a set of particular relations. In particular, it is "constituted on dependency relations between nonequals, by contrast with those constructions of clanship where members are seen as replicating one another, a possibility that allows enumeration and the measurement of respective strengths" (282). In other words, collective relations—such as those underlying labor pooling—are, or at least seem to be, more easily quantifiable than particular relations.

One way to understand the process of gendering a person is thus to focus on the types of social relations in which they are implicated insofar as such social relations allow for the equivalence (or commensurability) of the person with respect to other persons. And one can understand male and female gender, or public and private domains, as turning on the kind of social relation one is maximally implicated in, insofar as this social relation conditions and constrains one's potential for equivalence with others. In other words, a seemingly gendered division of measurement correlates with a seemingly sexual division of labor; the nonequivalence of the sexes (via physical size) is articulated, while the gendering of equivalence (via social relations) is elided. And so modes of replacement regimented gender divisions as much as reflected them.

Money could also replace men by means of paid assistance in labor pooling. If a man could not fulfill his labor obligation, and if he could not find a man to replace him, he could pay another man to work for him. Similarly, if a man did not want to engage in labor pooling, he could pay others to help him, and thereby opt out of accruing labor debt in the first place. Such a paid man was called a *moos*, from the Spanish word *mozo*, which referred to servants (such as waiters, porters, and farmhands). During most of my fieldwork, the going rate of moos labor for one day's work was fifteen quetzals (about two dollars), in addition to breakfast and lunch. Men told me that they arrived at this price by halving the daily wage paid to them at plantations (where the work was longer, more difficult, and came with the semblance of room and board—a place on the floor to sleep, and unseasoned beans and tough tortillas to eat).

While payment could theoretically come with any price, and labor in any amount, most men resisted working for half days, quarter days, and the like. That is to say, even though one could potentially work for any sum of money within fifteen quetzals (or indeed any area of land within one taree), most men were still paying their helpers, just as they were still replacing each other, in one-day-sized lumps (and, when relevant, in one-taree-sized swatches). This was probably for a number of inter-related reasons, including the fact that labor time was allocated in one-day intervals (which mapped onto areas of land and endurances of men) rather than half days or hours. Men were usually paid for an amount of work rather than a period of time. Given the current techniques and units of measurement, it was difficult to quantify smaller amounts. Thus, not only the underlying utility (strength, skill, knowledge), but also the units of this utility, constrained the forms replacement could take. Moreover, payment may have originated on plantations, in which labor was usually paid in terms of the quantity of bananas or coffee beans collected in a one day period, rather than the amount of time one engaged in some particular task. In sum, money could replace men in certain cases, but only at the level of moos, that is, one man's daily labor for one lump sum of money. Setting aside the kinds of transformations described in chapter 4, the fineness of the calculation usually went no further.

Potentia and Personhood

Marx famously defined *labor-power* as "the aggregate of those mental and physical capabilities existing in a human being, which he exercises whenever he produces a use value of any description" (1967: 164). As just seen, the substitutability of certain kinds of people in the context of labor pools turned on their having particular capacities in common, as ultimately evinced in the relatively equivalent results of their actual labor (as the exercise of this power). For Marx, and other classical political economists like Ricardo, labor-power was the ur-utility; that is, when exercised, it not only produced almost all other use values (cleared fields, chopped wood, harvested corn, warmed tortillas, and so forth); it also—under capitalist conditions of production—created economic value (as expressed in the price of a commodity). Indeed, as understood by such theorists, it was precisely because most commodities were ultimately effects of similar causes that they were commensurable (Marx 1967: 97; and see Smith [1776] 1976: 41). That is, however different their actual qualities and quantities as use values, their value could be adequately measured by one and the same commodity (namely money, itself as a stand-in for abstract labor time) insofar as they originated in one and the same cause (labor-power, and its exercise).

Marx's original definition, turning on a distinction between labor-power, on the one hand, and its exercise, on the other, maps onto a distinction found in Maine ([1866] 2002: 170) and Linton (1936: 187–88), and echoed in Mauss ([1938] 1979: 11–17). In particular, as classically understood, a *status* is a collection of rights and responsibilities (attendant on occupying some position within the social fabric); and a *role* is the enactment of a status (actually exercising these rights and responsibilities). As seen, key modes of replacement turned on various social statuses, not just mayor and cofradía member, or healthy person and named person, but also male and female, as well as adult and child. That is, the system of replacement both presupposed and produced various modalities of personhood: in the idiom of Maine and Linton, statuses (and those who can inhabit them); and, in the idiom of Mauss, masks (and those who can wear them).[9]

While these kinds of distinctions (labor-power and its exercise, status and role) relate to an essence-appearance distinction, which is itself related to a rather problematic metaphysics (though one the Q'eqchi' are quite amenable to, through the trope of containers and contents),[10] they may be locally understood in terms of the institution of replacement. In particular, replacement shows the continuity between the "utility" being substituted in the context of labor pooling (e.g., mental and physical capabilities, or creative potentia more generally), and the "utility" being substituted in the context of civil-religious elections, naming practices and illness cures (e.g., rights and responsibilities, or personae more generally). Though not necessarily the source of the relative commensurability of all commodities, the practices involving replacement were a condition for the equivalence of entities in—and often across—otherwise disparate domains. Through the lens of replacement, then, we may move from use value proper (e.g., things like houses and salt), through labor-power (qua productive abilities), to personhood (qua social distinctions). To return to some of the concerns of chapter 2, the practices involving replacement project and reflect a local ontology of people and things (as well as many other kinds of entities, both outside and in between), and the processes that (re)produce them.

Sufficiency, Subjectivity, and Substitutability

Crucially, the entities and individuals caught up in replacement did not have to be equivalent per se (qua perfect replacements), they merely had to be equivalent "enough" (*tz'aqal*). For example, one man said that if a boy is twelve years old, that is "not yet enough" (*maji' tz'aqal*); but if he is fourteen, fifteen, sixteen, or seventeen, that is "enough for substitution" (*tz'aqal cho'q li eeqaj*). Here we get a graded series of ages and learn that age twelve is not yet sufficient for substitution, but fourteen (and up) is enough. (As we saw above, there was indeed often a gray area, depending on the difficulty of the task and the maturity of the boy.) As a related example, a man said that a twelve-year-old "will not yet be able to endure" (*maji' tkuy*) carrying a bag of cement; whereas a boy who has already completed fifteen years is "more than able enough to endure the weight" (*naru tz'aqal chik tkuy li aal*). And compare these examples with the discussion above about women's relative strength and endurance, which was said to be "not enough" in comparison to men. In these ways, the word *tz'aqal* usually indicated that some quantity of some quality was (or, more often was *not*) sufficient for some desired or required end. And the qualities in question were usually strength (metz'ew), endurance (kuyuk), knowledge (na'om), or reason (na'leb'). From such discursive practices, we see how lexical practices of grading can both reflect and regiment more stereotypically economic processes of replacement. We see again how graders are shifters; that is, what counts as "old enough" in the case of labor pools may count as "not old enough" in the case of civil-religious elections. And we see how things were shaking up with the advent of tasks particular to ecotourism (such as hosting and guiding tourists); indeed, it may have been because of the ontological uncertainty brought on by this transition that replacement so often arose as a topic.

To put some of these concerns in the terms of the previous section, to understand the relatively replaceability of individuals belonging to the same kind, attention to their qualities was not enough; they also had to be graded—and, indeed, to "make the grade"—in regards to their quantities of those qualities. The word *tz'aqal* ("sufficient" or "enough") derives from the word *tz'aq*, which refers to price. For example, to ask how much something costs, one says, "jo' nimal lix tz'aq," or "how large is its price." And the verb *tz'aqalok*, which in turn derives from it, means "to be sufficient" or "to have enough." In this role it was often used to state that one didn't have enough money to buy something (e.g., "ink'a' natz'aqalok li qatumin," or "our money is not sufficient"). This is yet another instance where the difference between use value and exchange value is elided (or, rather, nonsensical). That is, just as one may not have enough strength or know-how to substitute for a certain person in a task, one may not have enough money to buy a certain good in the store. Indeed, in this latter function, utterances could involve both kinds of constructions (tz'aq and tz'aqal) at the same time:

> pero moko tz'aqal ta in-tumin r-e li-x tz'aq
> but Neg sufficient Neg E(1s)-money E(3s)-Dat Dm-E(3s) price
> "But my money was not sufficient for its price" (i.e., I didn't have
>   enough money to buy it).

Finally, the word *tz'aqal* could be used as an adverb or adjective to mean something like "really," "real," "genuine," or "true," as may be seen in the following kinds of examples:

> 1) tz'aqal yaal tawi' li na-o-x-ye ut mare ink'a' yaal
> sufficient true Pos Dm Pres-A(3s)-E(3s)-say and perhaps Neg true
> "Could what he says be really true (tz'aqal yaal), or perhaps it is not
>   true."
> 2) naq wi raj tz'aqal in-na', moko x-Ø-x-numsi ta raj li aatin a'an
> Comp if COUNTERFACT real E(1s)-mother Neg Perf-A(3s)-E(3s)-pass
>   Neg COUNTERFACT Dm word Pro(3s
> "If she were my real mother (tz'aqal inna'), she would not have passed
>   on those words."

These latter kinds of usage are frequent enough that some compound constructions have relatively fixed meanings (Sam Juárez et al. 1997: 379–80). For example, there are constructions like, *tz'aqal wa* (*tortilla legítima*, or "genuine tortilla"), *tz'aqal plaat* (*mera plata*, or "pure silver"), *tz'aqal b'isleb'* (*medida exacta o cabal*, or "an exact or sufficient measure"), *tz'aqal t'uj ixq* (*mujer virgen*, "virginal woman"), and *tz'aqal winq* (*hombre de palabra cabal o maduro*, or "mature, a man of his word").

In short, the word for price (*tz'aq*) was caught up in a set of lexical and grammatical processes that directly linked it to constructions that meant not only "sufficient" or "enough," but also "authentic," "real," "true," "pure," and "exact." And the grader *tz'aqal* (enough, sufficient) was habitually used to grade people in regards to their ability (capacity, or power) to replace others in a labor pool, just like a certain amount of money could be graded in regards to its ability to be exchanged for a good (given the price of the latter). What other ontologies separate out as use value, exchange value, and semantic value (or "truth value"), got bundled together through a frequent trope as much as a pervasive institution. In the next section, these relations among seemingly different kinds of values, powers, and properties will be more systematically explored.

Entities, Qualities, Quantities, Necessities

In short, replacement may turn on (1) replacing a person in some kind of office, for example, mayor, cofradia, namesake; (2) settling some kind of score, for example, revenge, soccer goals, loans, labor pool, illness cures; and (3) replenishing a worn out or used up good, for example, houses, batteries, and use values more generally. It should now be apparent that replacement was a kind of generalized practice that was grounded in several presuppositions: what types of entities existed in the world (qua kinds); what types of qualities these entities shared (qua indices); what kinds of quantities (or numbers and units) these qualities appeared in; and what kinds of modality (or obligation and necessity) required the replacement of such quantities of quality. In other words, presupposed by the relatively heterogeneous ensemble of practices involving replacement was a local ontology of entification, qualification, quantification, and obligation.

For example, notice that the entities being replacements could be adult male for adult male (labor pooling and mayor election), father for son (namesaking), married couple for married couple (cofradía election), goal for goal (soccer), house for house (house building), sum of money for sum of money (loans), violent action for violent action (vengeance), and effigy for sick person (illness cures). And notice that the social relations and temporal frames underlying the replacement of such entities ranged from the intrapersonal (in the case of illness cures) to the intercommunal (in the case of soccer goals), and from a single day (in the case of labor pooling) to a whole generation (in the case of namesaking). In other words, replacement linked radically distinct material, social, and temporal frames—indeed, it helped constitute such frames.

Nonetheless, it should be emphasized that it was men, not women, who were implicated in most of these forms of replacement; for example, soccer was a sport played by men; namesakes were usually discussed only in the context of father and son; vengeful actions were carried out between men; adultery was usually understood as a man sleeping with another man's wife, not a woman sleeping with another woman's husband; only men could be village mayor; and, as seen in the previous section, it was mainly men—as adult, male persons—who could take part in labor pools. Replacement primarily involved men—materially, socially, and temporally. Only in cases of illness cures (usually undertaken by women), cofradía elections (involving women as much as men), and labor pooling (in which a woman prepared food for the men assisting her husband) were women explicitly brought into relations of replacement. Quite importantly, then, if replacement was a local institution whereby certain entities were rendered equivalent in regards to their use value (or qualities and quantities), it was also a system whereby other entities were rendered nonequivalent (in particular, men and women). It was a system of exclusion as much as inclusion.

Moreover, the practical replaceability of such entities rested on their equivalence with respect to certain relatively abstract properties (qua underlying kinds, capacities, or utilities). In other words, if equivalence was a condition for replacement as a practice, replacement was a sign of equivalence as a property. So along what kinds of dimensions were the underlying properties of equivalence determined? Recall that adult males were equivalent not only in their capacity to labor and hold the rights and responsibilities of mayor, but also in their capacity to have sex (and in producing and parenting children more generally). Thus, they could substitute for each other in the context of labor pooling, mayoral elections, and adultery. Men had skills, knowledge (social and practical), strength, and semen in common—all seemingly abstract, intangible, or unquantifiable properties. Similarly, married couples were able to fulfill the gendered labor obligations of cofradía service insofar as their respective strengths, skills, and knowledge could be coordinated: the women cooking, decorating, and cleaning, and the men building, buying, and collecting. That is, they had the strength and skill to undertake the rights and responsibilities that were accorded members of the cofradía. In the case of namesaking, consanguineally related kin were equivalent in their capacity to have certain attributes—name, personality, health, and economic well-being. Or, moving from Mauss to Maine, a namesake, or child more generally, could inherit the property rights of a parent, and thereby take on their legal persona. Similarly, illness cures required the equivalence of a kind of iconic-indexical value—in particular, the inalienable possessions held in common by a person and the person's substitute (clothing, hair, and name), or person-internal part-whole relations. Finally, loans were equivalent with regard to their economic value—their price, calculated in terms of local currency. Vengeful acts were equivalent with regard to their retributive value—a calculus of blows and insults. And soccer goals were equivalent with respect to their contribution to the score.

Aside from soccer, vengeance, and loans, all these underlying qualities turned on embodied equivalences (often male body equivalences): skill, knowledge, strength, semen, and various other inalienable possessions. And notice how this set of embodied equivalences belonged to a larger set of substances that primarily turned on relatively commonsense notions of value—namely score, money, and justice. In short, just as reciprocation (in a market) can commensurate across different use values (insofar as they have the same exchange value), replacement can commensurate across different substances (insofar as they have the same use value).

Perhaps then we should think either of such substances as values in themselves, or of such values as substances in themselves. Such a view would seem to be corroborated by Q'eqchi' notions of economic value. In particular, as we saw, economic strength was phrased in exactly the same terms as physical strength: "the dollar is very strong in comparison to (or *in confrontation with*) the quetzal" (*mas li metz'ew li dolar chiru li q'uq*). Indeed, speakers would go so far as to speak about economic strength as human endurance, saying: "the dollar lasts in comparison to the quetzal" (*naxkuy li dolar chiru li q'uq*). In other words, the underlying value of money was phrased in exactly the same terms as the underlying strength or endurance of men. This means that exchange value was articulated in terms of use value—or rather that the difference was not great to begin with. And this means that although strength, skill, inalienable possessions, and knowledge were not explicitly treated as values, they were covertly treated as values insofar as they were part of the same system of replacement as score, justice, and money. For this reason, all these qualities should perhaps be considered values in themselves—a point we will return to.

Notice that while this equivalence in quality could be based in an abstract substance or value, replaceable entities nevertheless came in integer units of number, or fixed units of tenure. That is to say, there were no half goals, half men, or half couples. And there were no half years, half days, or half generations. In other words, replacement required *units* to be replaced: units that usually came in basic temporal, substantive, or social quantities that were unable to be further divided; and units that mapped onto seemingly natural entities or time spans (a male body or a married couple, a day or a generation). Recall our discussion of Whorfian projection, as a mode of enclosure, in the introduction. Replacement was itself naturalized. That is, unlike stereotypic commodities that often have units such as pounds and pats, or bushels and bolts, the units replaced were usually *self-segmenting* (Lucy 1992: 58). Hence, rather than add a substanceless form (e.g., liter or bushel) to a formless substance (e.g., water or wheat), the entities caught up in replacement seemed to involve an inherently formed substance—be it a type of person or a type of thing (e.g., a house or mayor, a married couple, or a soccer goal). Such self-segmentation meant that what replacement rendered equivalent and nonequivalent usually appeared to be naturally rather than socially derived.

Only in the case of loans could a replaceable entity be divided more thoroughly, that is, any sum of money for any sum of money—where the units were usually identical (quetzals, but more and more often dollars), and the numbers were different. As money began to enter into these relations in place of replacement—especially in the case of house building, when people began to pay for labor rather than pool it—seemingly natural and quantized units of duration, quantity, skill, and strength were (and more often were not) broken up into abstract and minutely divisible pieces. Indeed, as will be shown in chapter 4, houses, the labor involved in their construction, and the inhabitance that went on inside them, began to lose their quantized and quasi-naturalized boundaries—and thereby came to be more and more easily mapped onto money. That is, in contexts where one could exchange such use values for money, the seemingly motivated numbers, units, and utilities of replaceable entities could be rendered in terms of the seemingly unmotivated numbers, units, and utilities of national currencies. The exact equivalence of replaceable entities could transform into the commensurable difference of run-of-the-mill commodities.

And last, notice that replacement indexed a mode of obligation, or condition of necessity. That is, houses *must* be rebuilt; loans *must* be paid; scores *must* be settled; labor *must* be returned; and so on. These forms of deontic modality were a matter of course; they were relatively tacit requirements that nobody would ever dispute or even discuss. Indeed, like the units themselves, many of these needs were presupposed, and ultimately naturalized, by the domestic mode of production and its conditions of renewal—for example, replacing a house, raising children, sowing maize, partaking in cofradía service, and electing mayors. Compare this mode of obligation with that discussed by Mauss in the case of (reciprocal) gift giving, that is, the obligation to give, receive, and reciprocate ([1950] 1990: 13). Compare it with the mode of obligation underlying Weber's conception of the Protestant ethic ([1930] 1992: 51); namely, the duty to increase one's capital. Compare it with the mode of obligation underlying contract, that while one freely volunteers to transact, one is legally obligated to fulfill the terms of the transaction. And compare it with the mode of obligation underlying religious and ethical values, or existential value more generally; in particular, that thou shall not covet thy neighbor's goods; that thou shall turn the other cheek; and so on. In contrast, the key obligation underlying replacement was nothing other than the systematic provisioning of social life—not only including so-called bare life, in its productive and reproductive forms, but also including so-called political life, in its civil and religious forms.

In short, the many forms of replacement mapped onto the local expression of economy in the classical sense of Aristotle (and Polanyi), but now generalized to include both persons and things (as products), and both reproduction and production (as processes). It was an economy in which human capability was gauged in terms of social obligation, itself framed as economic necessity and naturalized in terms of the periodic renewal of local forms of social life: wherein the underlying value was not exchange, but use (in a radically extended sense); and wherein the ultimate end was not riches, or even "reciprocation," but rather replenishment.

"The Most Prophetic Pointer Ever Made in the Realm of Social Science"

Needless to say, what passes as a local cultural order may have its origins in a colonial imposition. And what passes as a natural process of renewal may have its origins in the novel demands of capital. For this reason, it is important to keep in mind the following five timescales on which such worlded ontologies and ontologized worlds were likely to transform: the possibility of pre-Hispanic tribute economies; five hundred years since the Spanish conquest; 125 years of a coffee-plantation economy (in confrontation with a much older and far more entrenched corn economy); replacement as a practice with a depth of several decades, as presented in the previous two sections; and ongoing events with a timescale on the order of ten years, as will be documented in chapter 4. Against such a historical backdrop, Wilk (1991) has suggested that labor pooling—perhaps the most extensive form of replacement—may be a response both to pre-Hispanic forms of tribute taking, and to colonial forms of labor extraction.

> The colonial government continued and intensified the pre-Hispanic practice of taking tribute in labor and services as well as commodities. Through independence into the coffee era, it was common practice for church, government, and capitalist forcibly to recruit labor teams from Kekchi communities. And the communities themselves were artificial entities created by the colonial regime. I *suspect* that this was the environment in which the Kekchi pattern of exchange labor originated, in an era when the subsistence economy was subject to unprecedented stress. People were forced to live in villages, commute to their farms, and produce more surplus. All this increased their need for labor at a time when they were subject to being taken away from their fields without warning for weeks and months at a time. The continuance of individual farm units would have been close to impossible, and the village itself must have become a corporate unit crucial to survival (Wolf 1957). The organization of communal labor-exchange groups would ensure at least the subsistence needs of individual households, even if the men in those households were dragged off to carry a priest's baggage for a week at corn-planting time. The communal labor organization [itself built on replacement, as argued in this chapter] was therefore an adaptation to predatory capitalism. (202, italics and bracketed insertion mine)

If Wilk is correct in suggesting that communal labor bears an intimate relation to predatory capitalism, then replacement—and the social order in which it is implicated—appears rather suspect. Long ago Aristotle made a distinction between "the art of household management" and "the art of wealth-getting" (2001b)—a distinction that Polanyi (1957) would later call "the most prophetic pointer ever made in the realm of social science" (53). In particular, Aristotle distinguished between a natural art of acquisition, in which "the amount of property which is needed for a good life is not unlimited" (2001b) and an unnatural art of acquisition, in which "riches and property have no limit" (2001b). As is well known, Polanyi understood the introduction of market systems to involve exactly this shift from the natural motive of subsistence to the unnatural motive of gain (1957: 41). How, then, might replacement as a local social order relate to money making in the guise of an external and insatiable labor market?

As summarized in the previous section, replacement seems to have much more to do with house holding than money making—and thus to the economy as the systematic provisioning of social life, and to production orientated toward replenishment rather than wealth. But in considering the historical origins of labor exchange from Wilk's vantage, replacement seems to bear an integral relation to money making insofar as one of its most extensive forms—labor pooling—is directly opposed to it. In other words, house holding, an economy based on replacement and subsistence vis-à-vis its practice of labor pooling, may be said to bear an intimate relation to money making, an economy based on extraction and gain, insofar as the former partially arose in response to the latter.

Money making and house holding seem to be two distinct forms of economy, which are mutually implicated only by the following two relations of exclusion, as classically formulated. First, money making is dependent on house holding in the sense that there is a global export economy that cannot afford to fulfill the subsistence needs of the workers whose labor it seasonally requires (see Cambranes 1985). And second, the local subsistence economy has set up barriers against the market, sometimes couched as a "moral economy," such that the circulation of certain goods must be kept village internal (see Wilk 1991; M. R. Wilson 1995).[11] One might then say that the money making (in the guise of a global export economy) relates to house holding (in the guise of the local system of replacement) as a vanquished antagonist encamped within sight of the city: significant but no longer—or perhaps just not yet again—in force.

Qualia, Quantia, and Equalia

In one of his earliest, and perhaps most transformative essays, Peirce ([1867] 1992) analyzed judgments such as *The stove is black*. In such a judgment, a qualia (in this case, "blackness") is being put into relation with a substance (such as "the stove"). As he would put it, a relatively mediate term relates to a relatively immediate term. And, as linguists might put it, a focus relates to a topic, a predicate relates to a subject, or an adjective relates to a noun phrase. (Those are not identical terms; they just happen to align in this sentence.) More generally, a figure relates to a ground. While I didn't find any judgments as to the blackness of stoves in my fieldwork, I did find judgments as to the blackness of corn and coffee, and I did find judgments as to the quality of metal and earthenware griddles. So close enough. And it was partially through such judgments, as figures, that I grounded the foregoing analysis.

For present purposes, note three important results of this analysis. First, such a mediate-immediate relation emerges (as figure) only in relation to another mediate-immediate relation (as ground). That is, to judge the stove's blackness makes sense only in relation to the relative blackness of the class of entities to which it is being compared. Notwithstanding the importance of qualia to the anthropological endeavor, especially as seen through the important work of Munn (1992), and the many scholars who followed in her tracks (Keane 2003; Chumley and Harkness 2013; Manning 2012; among others), quantia, which turns on a relation between two relations, is prior to qualia. And ethnography, notwithstanding how often it is framed as a mode of qualitative analysis (as opposed to quantitative analysis), is a radically quantia-tative discipline (even if it is not traditionally recognized as such).

Second, to analyze local modes of qualia and quantia necessarily presupposes—and often helps produce—various modes of *equalia*, which might best be defined as equality prior to its explicit mathematical formulation or political mobilization. In particular, in the course of this analysis, about a dozen modes of equalia were repeatedly deployed—all of which have their equivalents (or, rather, equalia-valents) in other contexts: not just grading per se, but also translation and paraphrase, reciprocation and replacement, conversion and metaphor, analogy and displacement, poetic meter and metalanguage, habit and justice, and much else besides. And, more generally, such frames of equivalence could turn on signs of the same object, tokens of the same type, instances of the same individual, interpretants of the same sign-object relation, and so on, and so forth. In each case, two entities (which are deemed more or less different) relate to another entity (which is deemed more or less the same).

As seen most clearly in the case of labor pooling, when one kind of person was judged unable to replace another, the key issue was usually not "equivalence" so much as lack of equivalence—a failure to make the grade, so to speak. In particular, all the modes of equalia that were deployed in this chapter are double-edged for three key reasons. They establish equivalence as often as they merely evince it. They may be used to establish and evince lack of equivalence as much as equivalence. And both of these processes not only apply directly to the entities being judged; they also apply indirectly to the agents doing the judging. We will take up these issues at length in chapter 4.

Finally, it should be argued that such frames of equivalence are not just presupposed by "translation" and "transaction," in their conventional senses; they are also central to the methodologies of two key (and not unproblematic) projects in our discipline, which are themselves often figured as modes of commensuration, best understood in terms of (coordinate) *transformations*. First, there is ethnography as a central project in cultural anthropology, understood as making sense of seemingly strange or even senseless practices by reframing them in terms of local beliefs and values. And second, there is linguistic relativity as a central project in linguistic anthropology, understood as showing that while all languages are capable of touching the same worlds, their speakers often feel those worlds in very different ways.

CHAPTER 4

From Measurement to Meaning

STANDARDIZING AND CERTIFYING HOMES
AND THEIR INHABITANCE

High-Quality but Uninhabitable Homes

Several of us were seated around Don Mauricio and Doña Rosa's hearth. We had been invited over to see their new home. The roof was made with sheet metal rather than thatch; and the walls were made with precisely hewn boards rather than rough-cut logs. Although we had been inside the house for only twenty minutes, the smoke—unable to escape through the roof and walls— had proved unbearable; so we all hung back, squatting on our haunches as far from the fire as space would allow. Don Mauricio, eyes bloodshot but beaming, asked, "Chaab'il, pe' yaal," or "Quality, isn't it?" And glumly, though in harmony, we assented, "Hehe', chaab'il," or "Quality indeed."

An uncomfortable place to be, and a discomforting situation to understand, here is where I begin this chapter, at Doña Rosa and Don Mauricio's high-quality but uninhabitable home. This couple was not unique in having built a home that was bad for their health. Six other couples in the village had recently built metal-roofed and tight-walled houses around hearth fires. All these families hosted ecotourists sent to them by Proyecto Eco-Quetzal, the NGO dedicated to preserving the cloud forest that surrounded this community. And like twenty-two of the eighty families in this village who were receiving ecotourists, they had been encouraged by the NGO to change the architecture and inhabitance of their homes in order to be better hosts. But whereas most of these villagers had one metal-roofed home to house ecotourists, and one thatch-roofed home to house themselves and their hearths, these six families had built two metal-roofed homes with relatively disastrous results.

In this chapter, I examine the conditions of possibility for the construction of such high-quality and uninhabitable homes—such expensive and unhealthy belongings. Building on the analysis of replacement undertaken in chapter 3, I seek to answer two interrelated questions. First, what happened to local values when pressures existed for people, objects, and activities to change from being "equivalent" (via the local system of replacement, and so more or less the same) to being "commensurate" (via the money-making opportunities initiated by ecotourism, and so measurably different)? And second, how did local ontologies, and the values embedded therein, enable and constrain the recoding of such values and the rechanneling of such pressures?

Chapter 3 focused on processes of grading in relation to modes of replacement. This chapter, by way of contrast, focuses on processes of measurement in relation to modes of reciprocation (such as labor pooling and, in particular, cash payment). To be sure, as seen in chapter 3, and as will be further developed in what follows, grading and measurement, like replacement and reciprocation, are intimately connected, and overlap in so many ways, that to even distinguish them as such is already artifice. But as distinct tensions, experienced as ensembles of distinctive commitments, categories, and modes of conduct, they are usefully opposed.

In particular, as a function of their participation in the NGO's ecotourism project, with its focus on capacitating villagers to engage in various modes of immaterial labor, I show how tourist-taking villagers began to drop out of the local system of replacement—giving up labor pooling in favor of cash payment, and constructing houses with no local equivalent. And I show how, and to what degree, new modes of labor and measurement made villagers and their homes newly commensurate. I argue that this pressure to move from equivalency to commensurability was facilitated by the NGO's interventions, which helped to produce not only "irreplaceable" persons (via new modes of immaterial labor in which only certain villagers were capacitated to engage), but also signs of these persons' irreplaceability (via the awards and certificates villagers were given and the new and highly visible houses in which they were encouraged to live). I also argue that the NGO's strategies and techniques inadvertently reso- nated with this system of replacement, rather than displaced it. That is, whereas replacement was once a condition for local values (constituting, as it were, the systematic provisioning of social life), irreplaceability (as opposed to commensurability per se) became, for those villagers impli- cated in the ecotourism project, a value in itself.

I detail the techniques used by the NGO to capacitate villagers, and transform village homes, in order to better host and house ecotourists (taking up where chapter 1 left off). I relate labor pooling—perhaps the most extensive form of replacement—to local modes of measurement and coordination (taking up where chapter 3 left off). I then detail changes in this system of replacement, and in these modalities of measurement and coordination, as a function of villagers' interactions with the NGO's eco- tourism project—paying particular attention to the loss of labor pooling and the advent of serial house building. Finally, I show how all this relates to my core concerns in chapter 2, regarding selfhood, affect, and value.

Capacitation and Commensuration

When Peace Corps volunteers began reassessing the ecotourism program in 1997, they noted that a number of elements had to be in place for the program to run smoothly: a reliable means of communication between the village and the project; a village-based organization in charge of eco- tourism; a system of rotation for tourist-taking villagers; courses inform- ing villagers of the desires and needs of tourists; courses training villagers to better host and guide tourists; and meetings dedicated to deciding and articulating the responsibilities of the village and project (PC 1997a). To carry out such a relatively encompassing intervention, itself a particularly insidious mode of enclosure, meetings were held in Chicacnab (approxi- mately seven times per year) in which villagers and project members en- gaged in daylong training sessions.

In April 1997, twenty-seven villagers from twelve participating fami- lies met with project members in a villager's home for a "reunion" that lasted five hours (PC 1997a). During this meeting, a committee of tourism was formed, consisting of three male heads of household who would be in charge of making sure the village end of the program worked smoothly. A system of rotation was established for families and guides, so that certain villagers weren't receiving more tourists or income than others. A walkie-talkie system was initiated, so that there would be reliable two-way communication between the NGO and the community for day-to-day operations as well as emergencies. In addition, the Peace Corps volunteers explained to villagers how they would benefit from the ecotourism program, stressing incentives such as increased economic income, cultural interchange, business opportunities as artisans, and the opportunity to learn how to care for their natural environment so that it would become an international attraction. For their part, the villagers asked the NGO to help them secure potable water, in addition to loans for the construction of toilets, private rooms, and showers to be used by tourists. The first meeting was designed to put a social organization and a system of communication in place, in addition to articulating the opportunities for villagers and the responsibilities of the NGO. Subsequent meetings (held, on average, once a month, eight times per year) would focus on capacitating villagers to host tourists, and imposing finer and finer standards on this capacitation.

During a subsequent meeting (PC 1997b), the Peace Corps volunteers presented information to the villagers (in Spanish, and then translated into Q'eqchi') about the desires and habits of tourists. They explained where the tourists would come from, what kinds of clothes they would wear, and that they would probably not speak any Spanish. They said that the tourists had no cloud forests in their own countries, nor the same kinds of plants and animals. The tourists would be coming to the village for a variety of reasons, including exploration, photography, observation of the wilderness, and education about medicinal plants. The volunteers stated that the tourists wanted to learn any information and history that villagers had about the forest and its inhabitants. And they also stated that tourists were coming for culture; that is, they wanted to know about local life and customs, and they wanted to see villagers working in the fields and kitchen, to hear and learn words from the Q'eqchi' language, and to participate in ceremonies and celebrations. In short, the volunteers spent a lot of their time teaching villagers about tourist culture, couched as desires and habits qua rights, as it would intersect with Q'eqchi' culture, itself couched as service and spectacle qua responsibilities.

Phrased in analytic terms that were carefully defined in earlier chapters, a new set of social relations was to come into existence; villagers were being capacitated to inhabit the reciprocal social statuses, or embody the labor-powers, such relations presupposed (such as being a host in relation to a guest); and the statuses-qua-powers themselves turned on modality (e.g., rights and responsibilities, norms and rules) as much as meaning (e.g., signification, objectification, and interpretation).

In particular, along with this articulation of the basic desires and habits of tourists as strangers, the volunteers also stressed their more pressing needs and demands as guests. These basic needs were usually listed as material objects and housing arrangements that villagers were required to provide as hosts—for example, a clean place for tourists to sleep; their own bed; space without animals; candles, water, and a blanket. In addition to having such material amenities, the villagers would also have to engage in certain social practices to be good hosts. For example, the volunteers explained to women how to prepare food hygienically, stressing the cleaning of utensils, the boiling of water, the cooking of food, the washing of hands, and the shooing of domestic animals from the hearth fire. And they explained to men how they must guide tourists, stressing where to pick them up, how to answer their questions, how often they should rest, how fast they should walk, and what to point out as interesting (e.g., medicinal plants, the names of local taxa, and the footprints of animals). Thus, not only were villagers taught to recognize and accommodate the desires and habits of tourists; they were also required to have material objects and engage in linguistic practices that would ensure the comfort, interest, and safety of tourists.

The volunteers also emphasized the communicative needs of tourists and tried to train villagers to speak and understand some Spanish and English. For example, at one meeting the volunteers provided a list of phrases for villagers to say and understand. These phrases turned on a number of basic speech acts—for example, identification ("what is your name"; "my name is"); greeting ("how are you"; "well, thank you"); parting ("goodbye"); ingratiating ("please"); apologizing ("I am sorry"); evaluating ("the food is good"); desiring ("I want to rest"); and referring, or sharing attention more generally ("quetzal"; "monkey"; "forest"). Through the pair-part structures of discursive moves (offer-acceptance, question-answer, assessment-agreement, point-look, and so forth), and through a vocabulary of basic objects and activities of interest, the NGO provided villagers with a kind of pidgin language of ecotourism.

To couch this in the terms of chapter 1 and chapter 3, the NGO focused on fostering new modes of semiotic and social competence, a kind of power that was to be exercised by villagers (or "performed") when intersubjectively interacting with ecotourists. The performance of this competence, as a mode of immaterial labor, was embodied in pair-part structures, qua semiotic practices, which were ultimately measured, standardized, and priced. And, as will be seen below, an individual's possession of this power would be certified and emblematized by the project, and so made semiotically consequential to both a local and a global public. To protect a variety of life-forms, the project attempted to impose a new form-of-life, and the enclosure of this form-of-life (qua capture) would be simultaneous with its creation.

The NGO Gauges and Grades Its Own Interventions

Six months after the first meeting, the Peace Corps volunteers could say that, because of their interventions, villagers were beginning to understand the economic advantage of tourism and the desires of tourists and had thus changed their behavior accordingly. They saw many indices of such changes. For example, the volunteers noted that village women were beginning to ask for classes to learn how to cook for tourists. And many families had begun to improve their latrines and beds, were constructing private rooms for tourists, and were buying necessary utensils such as forks and spoons. Such changes indicated to the Peace Corps volunteers that villagers were becoming "personally involved" in making tourists comfortable. The volunteers noted that when they asked "what [villagers] thought tourists most wanted to see, . . . [the] immediate response was 'li k'iche' (the forest) and 'li q'uq' (the quetzal)." Such "immediate responses" indicated that villagers now understood what tourists wanted. The volunteers noted that, "on the basis of receiving eight tourists in his home last year, a community leader decided to cut no more of his forest." In other words, such a decision indicated that the program was actually working, that is, that such economic incentives were contributing to the conservation of the cloud forest. And last, the volunteers noted that "there are more than twenty families now participating in the program" (PC 1997b). The increased number of families participating in the ecotourism program indicated to the volunteers the project's local legitimacy. All these processes, then, were signs of the NGO's success, at least to the Peace Corps volunteers, given their own ontology (qua causal under-standings of the ramifications of particular interventions).

Other interventions initiated by the project also seemed to be taking effect. The volunteers found that "the idea of tourists and the understand-ing of their needs and wants has started a positive ripple effect in PEQ's other areas of emphasis." The NGO had long proposed gardens "as both a means of diversifying and improving the family diet and as a potential source of income," but very few families had been interested. As a func-tion of recent interventions, however, "every host family has asked for help with establishing a garden to provide better food *for the tourists*" (emphasis in original). Similar effects had "occurred with issues such as improving the latrines, providing furniture, shooing the livestock away from the cooking fires, washing hands before preparing food, planting fruit trees, and having all the family learn some key phrases in Spanish" (PC 1997b). "Ripples" of understanding others—that is, villagers' under-standing of tourists' wants and needs—moved out from the ecotourism program to other areas of intervention. To the volunteers, then, it seemed that domain-specific desire had been analogically transposed, or onto-logically ported, to other areas of social life.

But there were incipient problems. Peace Corps volunteers had noted a hitch with the system of rotation by September 1997. Owing to their normal economic pursuits (maize agriculture, plantation labor, etc.), men were not always home when their turn came to take tourists. Competition among other villagers to attend to the tourists and "the income they rep-resent" (*los ingresos que ellos representan*) ensued. The volunteers decided not to do anything about these problems, since "we believe that this is a community-based problem, and that if they are not able to take the re-sponsibility to be honest, there is nothing we can do." Here, then, we have two of the limits of intervention, as understood by the NGO—namely, the personal sincerity of villagers and conflicts with more quotidian demands of subsistence. In addition, the volunteers said that men who worked as guides for tourists were worried that they would be the object of thieves and assassins. Because of this, they were wary of picking up the tourists in other villages. Indeed, at one meeting these men told the volunteers that "what they want is a large, 'brave' guard with a pistol to accompany the tourists [and guides] to Chicacnab" (PC 1997b). Here, then, we have another limit of intervention, as interpreted through the NGO's causal ontology—fear of the repercussions of jealousy brought on by the economic success of the ecotourism program and its participants.

Standardization, Certification, Internalization

Despite such potential problems, the training continued, slowly ratcheting up the standards for how villagers should coordinate their objects, actions, and utterances with tourists. Indeed, by the end of 1999, actual measurements were given for the sizes of rooms and beds, and lists were compiled for the kind, size, and quantity of required tourist amenities. One such list had the following specifications: private room (minimum of two meters by two meters); a large bed (one meter by two meters); a small table with water container and wash basin, soap, and candle; a typical decoration; a rope to hang clothing; a clean toilet; a place to wash; a table with chair, candle, and complete table setting (plates and silverware); sugar and chili served separately. If villagers had all these items, in the right quantities and with the appropriate dimensions, they were authorized to charge ten quetzals (about US$1.50 at the time) for lodging, which was double the previous price (PC 1999). Such upgraded standards—turning on size, number, and item—went hand in hand with higher prices. Use values were remade in the image of exchange value; qualia and quantia became ensembles of quantified qualities. And such a standardized ensemble of use values could be expected to secure a stable exchange value.

Besides delimiting finer standards for the tourist-related material objects owned by families, the NGO also delimited finer standards for the social and semiotic practices involved in guiding and hosting tourists. One set of standards included the following specifications for a guide: be punctual; introduce yourself; walk with tourists on the trail, no more than five paces ahead of slowest tourist; wait for group to keep group together; take at least two five-minute breaks; talk with tourists four times during the hike (using speech acts like, *how are you, where are you from, do you have any questions, how do you like the forest*); show and explain points of interest (such as agricultural practices, or life and culture in forest); and even "explain how the families' lives are different with ecotourism, other changes that have resulted from involvement with PEQ, and why these changes are important" (PC 1999). Besides having to take into account pace length, pause duration, and speech-act coordination, a guide had to be able to express the general effects and importance of the program itself—that is, a trailside discourse on the manner in which ecotourism has positively affected local modes of village life. In other words, a villager was required to perform an internalization of the underlying moral value and projected outcome of the project's intervention.

Finally, after highlighting the early successes and failures of the project's interventions, and as a function of these standards, the volunteers presented families with certificates showing that they had been capacitated in certain skills, and explicating to readers the price-to-service calibration. In villagers' homes one could find diplomas indicating the owner's passing of various examinations. "Project Eco-Quetzal and the Peace Corps give the present diploma to [name of owner], for having satisfactorily completed the kitchen examination offered in Chicacnab, Alta Verapaz." Similarly, one could find signs listing the price-to-service relation.

> "Proyecto Eco-Quetzal, adventures in the cloud forest. Authorized price for hospitality: 10 quetzals per night per person. Guest House: [name of owner]. This price includes: a bedroom separate from the main room of the house equipped with: a bed, a mattress, a small table with water, a wash basin and a candle, a rope to hang clothing. A clean toilet outside with good access to it. A place to take an eco-shower closed with wood or plastic with a table, water and a wash basin. A table to have meals with a chair, plates, silverware, and a candle."

The private space of a family's home became a public site for demonstrating the family's success in meeting the NGO's standards. And the ecotourism intervention was not only creating the conditions of possibility for tourist-taking villagers to be nonsubstitutable with non-tourist-taking villagers (in terms of the modes of production and valuation in which they engaged, and as evinced by the fact that only some villagers were certified); it was also producing signs of these villagers' nonsubstitutability (the displayed certificates themselves). The conditions of possibility were in place for *irreplaceability* to become a value.

In sum, capacitating families for the modes of interaction involved in ecotourism was perhaps the NGO's most insidious mode of governance. Whereas the NGO's other interventions were wide in scope, the ecotourism program was profound in depth. All aspects of a family's private, domestic life were touched—including hygiene habits, household arrangements, use values of new and old objects, cooking techniques, communication practices, and guiding skills. Villagers were capacitated in communicative, affective, and bodily modes of comportment whereby they could coordinate their interactions with ecotourists, and calibrate their reciprocal role inhabitance. These modes of coordination and calibration, and the signs, objects, and activities that underlay them, were made more precise and articulable over the duration of the project's intervention. Such finer and finer standards were motivated by tests and competitions and emblematized with attendant prizes and certificates. And these standards and emblems were tied to permission (who could be involved in such interactions) as much as price (what one could make through such interactions). The conditions and consequences of these modes of commensuration are so important they will be the focus of the rest of this chapter—but to understand their importance, we need to back up a little.

Techniques of Measurements

In chapter 3, I described two key forms of labor pooling among men, village-wide labor exchange and the clearing of individually owned agricultural plots. I focused on the extent to which boys and women could replace men, women could replace each other, and money could replace men. And I showed how the system of replacement constrained further commensuration; that is, entities could typically only be replaced in all or nothing units, rather than in any proportional quantity of a shared quality. Finally, using Strathern's distinction between collective and particular activities (1988), I showed how such constraints were implicated in processes of gendering persons. I now pick up where that section left off, returning to one particularly important mode of replacement—labor pooling, but now reexamined in relation to measurement in order to show the mediating role such a form of replacement had in the uptake and influence of ecotourism. As will be seen, techniques of measurement were modes of residence in the world, as much as ways of representing it.

In the case of agricultural clearing (*k'alek*), a man's bodily frame was the lowest common denominator of measurement. A length, one *b'aar*, was the distance between a man's heart and hand. This length, repeated twenty-five times in one direction and then twenty-five times in a perpendicular direction, yielded an area of one *taree*, which was the amount of land one man could clear in one day. Basic units of strength, length, area, and time were not only expressed in terms of each other but also directly mapped onto the adult male body. In addition, by means of this commensurability and embodiment, the units themselves were rendered relatively natural (corresponding the distinctions "in the world") and basic (being the smallest unit out of which all other units were typically derived).

Contrast this with a woman's bodily frame. Her body could not reach a man's measure insofar as the length of her heart to her hand was less than a man's. For this reason, when women measured rope (with which to measure the length of objects in the world), unlike men who pulled the rope across their chest (measuring out two b'aars at a stretch), they put it over the head in order to add in the necessary length (having, as it were, a head-to-hand measure). Only in this way did women bring their measure up to a man's. Indeed, to see a woman measuring off lengths of rope was to see a woman with a stretch of rope running from the hand of one outstretched arm, over her head, to the hand of the other outstretched arm. It was an ungainly position—and one woman told me she felt ashamed (*yoo inxutaan*) to be seen measuring in this way. Notice, then, that when seen from the perspective of measurement's relation to bodily form, women's bodies were unnatural, nonbasic, and incommensurate—indeed, in certain cases, shameful. Insofar, then, as women could be compared to men, their bodies showed up as a relation of "less than" a man's body, and thus not just nonequivalent, but also "insufficient" (*moko tz'aqal ta*).

While the b'aar was the standard unit for measuring length, it could be both divided into smaller units and multiplied into larger units. In particular, one b'aar was divisible into approximately thirty-two inches. Twenty-five b'aars times twenty-five b'aars made one taree. Sixteen tarees made one *manzaan*. And sixty-four mazaans made one *caballería* (equal to about forty-five hectares). It should be said, however, that of all the units within this system of measurement, the b'aar and taree were the ones most frequently used by villagers. This was for several reasons. First, agriculture was the key occupation of men. Just as units of measure were given in terms of the male body, objects of measure prototypically pertained to men's tasks. Moreover, most families owned less than one manzaan of land. This meant that most of men's day-to-day measurements required units of area on the scale of one taree. And finally, although there were three standardized systems of measurement currently used around the village (b'aar, foot, and meter), they were relegated to distinct spheres of activity—two of which were relatively novel. In particular, while the b'aar was used for agricultural work, the foot (or more frequently the inch, or *pulgada*) was mainly used in the construction of new houses, and the meter was confined to some government and NGO-sponsored projects. Feet and meters—and their associated units—had only recently become widespread systems of measurement.

But perhaps the real reason for the relative infrequency of units of length other than the b'aar was that only a few techniques of measurement actually involved a ruler. Indeed, so far I have been assuming that the key techniques of measurement were ruler-to-object (for example, a man using his arm span as a ruler to measure off a length of rope) and ruler-to-ruler (for example, a man making notches every 2.5 cm on a stick so that he could use it to measure off inches). However, these were only the most stereotypical techniques of measurement. Three other techniques were far more frequent. We might call them object-to-task, object-to-object, and object-to-intuition. As an example of an object-to-task technique of measurement, take house building. In this context, one notched a board for cutting by putting it where it would eventually go and noting how much was still in excess. Or, similarly, a man could put on a pair of pants he had just bought secondhand in the market, and his wife would cut off the legs at the right length for him. House building can also be used as an example of an object-to-object technique, wherein men would cut one post of a certain length, and then use it as a jig to cut the remaining posts. And to understand the prevalence of object-to-intuition techniques of measurement, note that most tasks did not require precision work (e.g., a man building a chicken coop or an outhouse), or men and women's embodied intuition were already precise (e.g., a man gauging the size of his neighbor's cornfield, or a woman cutting a length of cloth). Indeed, as we saw in chapter 3, practices of grading (using constructions such as *bigger, smaller, as big as, big enough, too big, just right*, and so forth) could serve very similar functions and were usually more than sufficiently precise for the task at hand: grounds for comparison, or "points of departure," could be both widespread and context-specific.

One technique of measurement was directly related to changes in local life induced by the ecotourism project, demonstrating how the NGO helped foster social relations between villagers and village-external institutions. One man spent several days measuring out the contour lines of a small valley behind his house, in order to learn the techniques necessary for terracing agricultural fields. Such terracing had been called for by a national relief group in the wake of erosion and mudslides caused by severe rains and denuded soils. (Mudslides were a serious problem; upward of one house per year was destroyed by them, in addition to many tarees of milpa.) In this context, the man was practicing to become the "promoter" between this group and his village. He would spend his mornings deciphering their booklet, which consisted of about fifteen overly photocopied pages written in Spanish, but interspersed with lots of pictures. And then he would set out to practice the techniques he saw displayed therein. Besides stressing the danger of hurricanes, this booklet also demonstrated how to build the equipment used to level ground such that one could terrace fields and thereby minimize erosion and mudslides. Following their directions, this man built a small A-frame with a plumb line down the middle—what he called a *jayalinkil* or "directional." He used this to measure off contour lines, separated from each other by one-meter lengths. Nonetheless, after each painstaking pass around the valley, using this A-frame to make a contour (taking upward of thirty minutes per pass), he would always finish by second-guessing the results. In particular, he would use his sight and intuition to eyeball a more steady contour (which, as far as I could tell, was much more even anyway). While he had built an A-frame in terms of a metric dimension, and while he had used this relatively advanced tool to stake out contour lines of one-meter length, the end result was as if he had just used his "embodied intuition" for what ground seemed relatively level, and what distance seemed relatively like one meter. (And, as the man might well have guessed, the use of a meter was perfectly arbitrary—one b'aar or yard could have been used instead.)

While the booklet and the job were provided by the Guatemalan government, the NGO sent someone to assess this man's ability, to see if they should have him teach other men in the village how to terrace their fields. In other words, a nongovernmental organization decided to assess, improve, and redeploy a government-directed activity, insofar as it thought the government was not directing the activity effectively. Another interesting aspect of this interaction is that, in order to get capacitated by the project in this way, the man gave up his soccer playing one Sunday afternoon and his labor pooling for a whole week (paying off his brother-in-law to replace him)—even though teaching terracing to other men was not paying. The man was acting for neither cash, nor use value, but externally recognized expertise. He gave up his role in the local system of replacement in order to earn an externally recognized sign of his own irreplaceability. New techniques and systems of measurement were introduced by men who were simultaneously implicated in the ecotourism project and dropping out of the local system of replacement. In particular, notice how this man was at the intersection of two systems of measurement, village external and metric, and village internal and intuitive—and he opted for the latter, while displaying his work as if it were based on the former. In sum, this single event shows the complex relation between irreplaceability as a value, a system of measurement becoming metric (as a technique of measurement becomes intuitive), the NGO's redirection of government action, and a local man's response to external intervention.

Grading Homes

Each year the project held several contests in which tourist-taking villagers competed for prizes. One contest sought to determine who had the best house for hosting ecotourists. First-, second-, and third-place winners were awarded cash prizes of five hundred, four hundred, and three hundred quetzals apiece (equal, in range, from US$75 to US$50). In addition, the winners were given a certificate showing their name, the date, and a list of the criteria on which their houses had been judged. The explicit rationale behind such contests was to motivate villagers by rewards rather than sanctions, in order to get them and their houses to meet the project's requirements for accepting ecotourists. In this case, members of the project visited all twenty-two of the ecotourist-taking houses in the village, in order to grade the owners on the quality of their homes for hosting ecotourists. Such grading practices, themselves somewhere between elementary school examination and hotel assessment (e.g., one to five gold stars), were also modes of quantia-fication in the terms of chapter 3. Villagers were graded on whether or not, and to what extent, they had tourist-related items in their homes—for example, a sponge mattress for tourists to sleep on; large candles, so that tourists could read and dress at night; a thermos, in which soup and coffee could be kept hot for tourists; a small room, separated with a partition from the rest of the house, in which tourists could dress, sleep, and safely store their backpacks; utensils needed by tourists for eating, such as a spoon and a fork; a covered place to bathe, so that villagers could not see tourists in the nude; and a covered latrine, so that local children could not watch tourists using the toilet.

The week before this contest, villagers were trying to find ways to meet (and sometimes to go beyond) the project's criteria, and thereby "make the grade." Some were out buying plastic sheeting to use as walls for bathrooms, showers, and bedrooms. Others were cutting wood to make little tables and beds for their tourist rooms. One man bought a tiny padlock to put on the door to his tourist room and said he would give his ecotourists the key. In this way, he said, they would be certain that children would not be going through their backpacks when they were away on hikes. Flowers were collected and stuck in jars to be placed in tourists' rooms. A colorful sheet was strung over one bed as a kind of canopy. And some couples arrayed various local crafts on the walls of their tourist rooms, which they would try to sell to tourists during their stay—for example, knit bags, wood carvings, weavings, baskets, and hammocks. Indeed, some families went overboard in their enthusiasm. For example, one highly optimistic couple planned to buy a Coleman lantern to illuminate their house, a purchase that was going to cost them four hundred quetzals. Many additions were not explicitly due to the project's criteria but rather were suggested by the villagers themselves.

None of these objects would usually be found in a local home. The result of such a contest was not only to differentiate (by making more or less prize-worthy) one villager's home from another villager's home. It also caused a reassessment of what belonged in a home—in this case, objects with use values appropriate to ecotourists but not to villagers. Most of these additional objects would be used by ecotourists at most once a month, for one or two nights, at best. During the rest of the month, villagers simply closed the door to their tourist rooms so that their children would not dirty the mattress or break the thermos (the two most expensive of the newly required items). Houses were being externally and monetarily ranked as a function of the possessions that they held (and the economic value of those possessions), without taking into account the use value of those possessions (either locally or by ecotourists). And just as new needs were potentially being created via such objects (in particular, sleeping on a mattress rather than a board, holding hot coffee in a thermos while setting off to work, and having a sleeping quarter partitioned off from the rest of the house), these same objects were simultaneously kept off limits. This provided a particularly nasty bind for children, for whom such objects seem to offer the most enchantments and on whom there were the most restrictions. Whole sections of the house became standing reserve, on display but just out of reach, useful but not to be used by us.

That said, it should be emphasized that I benefited greatly from the changes in housing brought about by ecotourism. For example, when I first arrived in the village, most houses hadn't yet changed. So while I had my own bed, it was next to the family's two other beds. For this reason, I had to change clothing in my sleeping bag. I had to keep to the family's hours (going to sleep around nine, and waking at five). And I had no place to go to get away from the family (and they had no place to get away from me). But with the additional house they would build, and with all the tourist-related amenities with which it was filled, I became quite comfortable. There was a mattress beneath my sleeping bag, a thermos to keep my oatmeal and coffee hot, a sheet above my bed to keep the condensation from dripping off the metal roof onto my head, and the relative privacy of a separate room. It addition, it was easy to settle on a price. I just paid a sum similar to what the ecotourists paid. And if villagers ever questioned what I was doing in the village, my activities could always be interpreted in terms of an ecotourist who just happened to stay for an extended period of time. (Although villagers who knew me realized I was more interested in chickens than in quetzals and just as interested in grammatical categories as in cloud forests.) Ecotourism was not just an object of my research, but its very condition.

Grading People

Besides using contests to rank villagers' houses as better or worse depending on the objects in them, the project gave villagers certificates showing they were qualified to fill certain roles required by ecotourism. While these certificates were formally similar to the ones given to the winners of contests, they indicated the possessor's recent acquisition of novel abilities. And insofar as possession of such a certificate was necessary to accept ecotourists, such certificates connected newly acquired skills (and productive propensities more generally) to future income. As per the discussion above, the skills themselves involved learning what a tourist needed, expected, and wanted. For example, one certificate showed that a man had been certified to guide ecotourists. Such men had to be able to say and understand certain phrases in Spanish (*what is your name, are you tired, there is a quetzal*); to walk slowly, making sure to stop often for rests; to point out sites of interest to tourists (caves, nearby villages, milpa, and the biological station); and to know and point out various species of trees and birds. Indeed, as was shown in chapter 1, the path to the village was often a visitor's most extended exposure to the cloud forest, and thus one of the main attractions for ecotourists. The trail between the town and village—for Q'eqchi', a rather bothersome route to be quickly traversed, and for whom it would have been best turned into a road—came to be treated by tourist-taking men as a point of interest for others.

Women received certificates showing that they knew how to host and feed ecotourists in their homes. Again, a minimal command of Spanish was required (*where are you from, are you hungry, here is your food*), as well as an understanding of what food tourists did and did not like, and what choices one should offer them—in particular, chili or no chili in their soup, and sugar or no sugar in their coffee. In addition, women were trained in a number of sanitary practices—for instance, cleaning all bowls and cups with boiling water; serving only coffee or soup made with boiled water; washing hands with soap before cooking and serving food; and having a container to hold boiled water for tourists to drink. The negative effects of one's own cooking practices were flagged, and women's cooking techniques were changed accordingly (or at least ostensibly), turning traditional cooking practices into potential health risks, and traditional hosting practices into purchased services (and, of course, making many intimate features of one's life known to the furthest reaches of the world).

Such certificates were really assessing a person's ability to engage in novel forms of interaction, involving distinct and coupled roles. The guide's role and the host's role were not accessible to all villagers—only those who were implicated in the ecotourism project. The roles of the ecotourist and guide, or the ecotourist and the host, were nonreversible; that is, one could take into account another's role, but never actually inhabit it oneself. The roles were relatively thematized and standardized, and hence relatively self-conscious and rule-like, so villagers could list what behaviors such a role entailed. Such roles were precisely calibrated to price (i.e., how much a villager should make when interacting with a tourist in the appropriate way). And the underlying goal was shared only insofar as it was a payment for services, or the upholding of a prearranged contract—and sometimes, perhaps, a relatively abstract notion like protecting the cloud forests. As one lost various roles in which one's activities overlapped with other villagers, one gained various roles in which one's activities overlapped with ecotourists—a nation-spanning coordination of novel forms of selfhood and subjectivity.

Semiotically speaking, the certificates for contest winners and role capacitation were externally authorized emblems of standardized difference. They indicated an individual's or family's possession of novel skills, objects, values, social relations, and modes of coordination. They were generally displayed on the wall of a family's tin-roofed home. They ensured that both villagers and ecotourists could see the individual or married couple as possessing a range of objects, and inhabiting a range of roles, that were not equally valued or distributed among villagers. In other words, these signs served just as much to alert ecotourists to their hosts' qualifications as to alert other villagers to their owners' uniqueness. They showed that tourist-taking villagers could be differentiated, and that their differences could be tied to their income—what they won by having changed their house, or what they could earn by being capacitated to inhabit new roles. And they showed that certain roles were worth having, along with the novel forms of coordination that they entailed. In effect, they said that those villagers who took tourists were not replaceable with those villagers who did not take tourists. The project was thus helping to produce not only nonreplaceable persons, but also signs of these persons' nonreplaceability. These signs might therefore be thought of as a permanent disclosure of novel forms of personhood—articulated and intersubjectively recognized proof of their owner's ability to engage in new ways of being with others in the world.

The NGO, then, did not just produce new signs (emblems) and objects (people) per se; they also produced widely distributed grounds for interpretation, as well as semiotic agents with the capacity to interpret in such ways (Kockelman 2012a, 2013a). Ontologized worlds were concomitant with worlded ontologies, and both were precipitates of an enclosing practice (or, as we will now see, at least in impulse, if not achievement).

Gender Hierarchies and Age Grades

Although the project provided women with new opportunities for non-replaceability in the ways just described, there was often a house-internal trade-off in that these women's younger relatives had to fill in and perform their usual domestic tasks. In particular, while young women had probably always complained about their mothers-in-law, when the project offered opportunities for women to learn marketable skills, they complained even more—for they had to make up for the mother-in-law's foregone domestic labor when she was out being trained and certified by the project.

For example, one woman's mother-in-law would go into town several times a week to learn how to weave from the project. After learning this new craft, she devoted all her time to weaving with other women, or selling her newly woven textiles in the market. The young woman, however, had to stay at home to take care of her mother-in-law's domestic duties in addition to her own. "I stayed at home. I coarse-ground maize (for tortillas). I swept. I washed clothes. I made tortillas. I looked after the chickens. I looked after the cow. My mother[-in-law] didn't look after them. She would leave each day to work for the project, and she didn't return until after five each afternoon. I had to do all the work. By myself I did all the work." She seemed especially exasperated (*titz'k*) because she herself made no money filling in for her mother-in-law while her mother-in-law was off either making money or learning how to make money. "She went off to work with the project. She was paid every month. But around here, not a cent. I didn't have a cent. I wasn't allowed to make money because of all my work. Because of all that, I left the house. I got fed up (*xintitz'*). I got sick of working (*xintitz' chi k'anjelak*). I left." In sum, while various activities of the project were designed to help women become independent of their husbands by training them to inhabit money-earning roles, the burden of an older woman's new economic independence often fell on her daughters and daughters-in-law.

Last, as men had more and more opportunities to engage in non-replaceable and village-external work, they began to opt out of other forms of village-internal replacement—often to the chagrin of their wives. For example, many men no longer wanted to join the cofradía, which was one of the only forms of replacement open to women. As discussed in

chapter 3, for example, this recalcitrance among men to join the cofradía was a relatively recent phenomenon. While other positions—for example, mayor or promoter—attracted younger and younger men, cofradía positions seemed to be less and less attractive to these same men. In
addition, older women were more likely to be trained and certified by the
project (both because they were considered bastions of tradition and because they found it easier to get away from their domestic chores in the
ways just described), and thus the cofradía was the only form of replacement and village-external recognition available to younger women. Thus,
such differences in a husband's and a wife's desire to join the cofradía was
related to the fact that most other forms of village-internal recognition
were possible only through village-external social relations—relations
that were more accessible to men than to women. Changes in the social
life and nonreplaceability of tourist-taking villagers was a function of their
gender and age. And the conflicts that arose because of these changes
were not only village-wide but also family internal.

Precision and Decoration of Homes, Parasites and Hosts

To return to our opening example, many tourist-taking families began
building houses with walls made from precisely hewed and painted
boards, instead of rough-hewed and unadorned logs. These boards (*tabla*)
came in sizes of approximately one inch by fifteen inches by ten feet.
Rather than being cut with an ax or handsaw (as in the case of old-style
houses), they were cut with a chainsaw using a jig. In addition, they were
typically beveled on each end, and they overlapped with the boards above
and below them. (In contrast, older-style houses were constructed using
flat-edged boards of varying size.) Because of this beveling, and because
of this standardization of size, wind could not enter a house, and heat
could not so easily escape. Indeed, people would point to the tightness
of a house's walls when characterizing its "quality" (*chaab'ilal*), itself a
pervasive kind of meta-qualia (insofar as it was applicable, as a predicate,
to a wide range of objects that otherwise had few sensuous qualities in
common, indicating that the object in question would last, or perform,
much better than the typical member of its class in regards to what it
was designed to do). And, given the harsh winds, cold temperatures, and
slanting rains of the cloud forest, this beveling significantly contributed
to the comfort of sleeping in such a house—and thus seemed worth the

price of the chainsaw and expert that it required. (For those homes without tightly constructed walls, villagers often put sheets of brightly colored plastic on the inside walls—both for decoration and to keep the wind out.) Such precision required that chainsaw-owning men have a tape measure (to produce standard sizes using inches), a taut line (to produce straight lines), and a jig (for beveling edges). New styles of houses went hand in hand not only with new materials, instruments, and skills, but also with new limits of precision—involving both new techniques and new systems of measurement.

Not only were the walls of homes more precisely constructed; they were also decorated. In particular, many houses were being painted. They were usually given only one coat, arranged with two different colors, white and red, blue and white, or red and blue. And the fronts of houses, which could be seen from the widest vantage, were painted with the most care and elaboration, while the backs of houses were either left untouched, or painted lightly and haphazardly. Several women remarked that not only were they the ones who encouraged their husbands to paint their homes, but they were also the ones who paid for the paint (using the money generated from their care of chickens). Along with precision came decoration, and along with decoration came a differentiation of family members' contribution to the home—a differentiation easily quantifiable in terms of cash and readily thematizable by owners. But perhaps most importantly, the outsides of these precisely hewed and painted walls were now standing as emblems of the nonreplaceability of their owners, just like the certificates and prizes displayed inside.

In part, this was for the simple reason that the houses of tourist-taking villagers were no longer being built as replacements for old houses. Rather, they were being constructed either as additional houses, or as nonequivalent replacements for old houses. In either case, they were not replacements per se. Indeed, as per the analysis in chapter 3, such houses were not necessitated by a natural (or at least naturalized) process of renewal. They were encouraged by an externally fostered expectation that they would be useful for someone—usually ecotourists. And such houses were not composed of a shared substance coming in a similar quantity, or proportional quantities of similar qualities. Instead, they had new walls— both constructed with better materials and decorated for public display. And, as a function of these novel architectural patterns and material properties, the labor that went into the construction of such houses required novel and nonequally accessible roles, such that some of the men who built such houses had to have differentiated levels of expertise. For this reason, such houses were no longer constructed using labor pools of mutually replaceable men.

In sum, not only was the inhabitance of such houses distinct, as per the discussion offered in the last section, and not only was the architecture of such houses distinct, as per the foregoing discussion, but the very mode of coordination underlying the construction of such houses was distinct, as was the explicit ontological categorization of the houses themselves (insofar as they were not considered "replacements").

The nonreplaceability of such houses with traditional houses (vis-à-vis these distinctions in their purpose, inhabitance, architecture, and construction) was concomitant with the nonreplaceability of their owners with other villagers. And for this reason, houses could be considered both the embodiment and the announcement of their owners' differential access to skills, tools, resources, and social relations (or power, competence, and kindedness per se). What the project helped to bring about in the interiors of homes with its certificates and prizes, villagers did to the outsides of their homes with their architecture and construction. Given that homes were also treated as their owners' inalienable possessions (Kockelman 2010b; and recall the discussion of selfhood in chapter 2), in addition to being the social skin of the domestic mode of production, such an inhabited announcement of nonreplaceability was a stark statement about changes in local modes of personhood. New modes of nonequivalence were made possible by novel forms of commodification and rechanneled by the local ontology of replacement. And this ontology was itself—as per the arguments at the end of chapter 3—the precipitate of a relation of long duration in regards to both Q'eqchi' customs (qua replacement of the ancestors) and global capital (qua labor quotas for coffee export).

But this nonreplaceability of houses not only reflected the nonreplaceability of their owners (via the loss of labor pooling); it also reflected the nonreplaceability of men who were not directly related to the ecotourism project. Let me explain. Given that a key requirement of the project was that a family could adequately host ecotourists, there was a flurry of building—either renovation (for example, building an enclosed room as part of an old house so that tourists had a private place to sleep), or full-scale construction (for example, building an additional metal-roofed house to host tourists). To this end, many tourist-taking villagers hired chainsaw-owning men to cut them wood. One man, for example, paid such a man ten quetzals for half a day's work cutting wood from his own trees. This was an important and novel transaction for several reasons. Whereas he usually hired men from the same pool with which he used to exchange labor, with woodcutting, this man hired whichever of the seven chainsaw-owning men in the village were free. In contrast to labor pools, then, he had no particular loyalty to any one man or any group of men. Such a transaction distributed money earned from ecotourism to other men in the village—but only to those who owned chainsaws, who were exactly the men whose activities the project wanted to curtail. This chainsaw-owning man was paid to work for a unit of time on a less-than-one-day scale. Thus, even though this was still based on task achievement rather than mere time allotted, it still broke with the usual practice of paying for labor in one-day lump sums. And such a novel role shows how nonreplaceability affected men who were *not* implicated in the ecotourism project. In other words, it shows how effects propagated out into regions not only not targeted by the project but inversely targeted by the project. Indeed, in 1999 there were only two chainsaw-owning men, whereas by 2001 there were seven such men—and the mayor himself, who also hosted ecotourists, told me that he too was planning to buy one.

Let me take up this point in greater detail. Through the money brought into the village by ecotourists, a key possession became a chainsaw. And this was true even though chainsaws were directly opposed to the project's own goals of preserving old-growth cloud forests. In other words, chainsaw-owning men made their money cutting wood for those who made their money hosting tourists. As we saw in chapter 1, these men became implicated in the ecotourism project as "notorious individuals" who were thought to be the key destroyers of the cloud forest (a category that also included hunters). Indeed, with the money they made, these men did not engage in seasonal plantation labor, and most would not engage in what they considered more difficult, less-skilled work—such as agricultural clearing. Chainsaws were becoming the key index of nonreplaceability among non-tourist-taking villagers—a form of labor that was economically and semiotically parasitic on the success of ecotourism. Given that this was a form of labor that was not directly based on social relations, in which any amount of work was possible, in which measurable precision was required (tape measures and adequately straight lines), and in which labor was paid rather than pooled, the parasite resembled the host (who happened to resemble the guest).

From Contract to Status

Not only did new houses have walls made with precisely hewed and painted boards; their roofs were made with metal. Unlike thatch roofing, which lasted only five or so years, metal roofing could last upward of ten years. And unlike thatch, which had to be painstakingly collected, sheets of metal could be purchased in town. However, metal roofing cost between eighteen and thirty-four quetzals per piece, and an average house required around twenty-five pieces. The roof alone raised the cost of a house considerably. Moreover, after being purchased in town, metal sheeting had to be arduously carried into the village, whereas thatch could be collected from around the village. The real problem with metal roofing, however, was not the cost so much as the fact that smoke could not escape. Given that a hearth fire (used for heating, cooking, and light) was kept burning some ten hours per day, to remain inside a metal-roofed house was unbearable. Thus, while one was paying five times the price of a thatch-roofed house in order to live in a metal-roofed house, its livability decreased considerably. For this reason, a metal-roofed house was a useful option only if one retained a thatch-roofed house for cooking and boarding family members. And most families who had two houses kept one thatch-roofed house for dwelling and one metal-roofed house for storage, ceremonies, and boarding extended relatives and ecotourists. Like the metallic and earthenware griddles discussed in chapter 3, such distinct types of housing confronted each other—and not just in regards to their differential quantities of shared qualities, but also in regards to their incommensurable qualities. The fact that six tourist-taking families (out of twenty-two such families) came to have two metal-roofed homes each indicated that something was semiotically suspect about such houses.

Over the course of my stay with one family, their household arrangements changed three times. Between 1997 and 1999, they had a single thatch-roofed house, filled with two children, an occasional ecotourist, and a seasonal anthropologist. (And before that they lived in an old thatch-roofed house on the husband's father's property.) In 2000, they built a metal-roofed house, which remained empty for almost five months. In 2001, they got rid of their thatch house and built another metal roofed house in its place (and the wife gave birth to a third child). And when I arrived again in 2002, they were were discussing tearing off the roof to build again with thatch, or making significant changes to the roof (akin to a chimney). And all the while they complained mightily; for one home was too smoky, while the other was too cold. The woman developed a hacking cough, and guests came less often and stayed for shorter periods of time. Such an addition was dramatically counterproductive, causing not only the curtailing of social relations, but also serious risks to health.[1]

This could happen because men (affected by nonreplaceability more than women) did not spend ten hours a day inside their homes near the hearth fire. The ill effects of breathing smoke were much worse for women and young children. Had women had more of a say in house building, I suspect, metal roofs wouldn't have been built except for houses without hearth fires. At the beginning of the movement toward metal roofs, women existed on very uneasy terms with such houses. One woman told me of her lost sleep due to her baby's raspy breathing at night. And other women pointed out that, inside the first house to ever have a metal roof over a hearth fire, the children were always sick. (And, indeed, in church services you could locate the kids because they spent the service clearing their throats and sniffling.)

In sum, metal roofs were really advantageous only if one had two homes, one in the old style with a thatch roof, and the other in the new style with a metal roof. That some villagers had moved to two metal-roofed homes was an indication of a revaluation—not just that these villagers were nonreplaceable (as per the project's certificates and prizes, and as per the architecture and construction of their homes), but that nonreplaceability had become a value in itself.

In particular, Veblen's (1991) classic claims about pecuniary emulation may be reframed as follows: any sign of one's means to produce one kind of value (e.g., livelihood or cash), may parasitically become a second kind of value (e.g., distinction or status)—and thus be sought after, in addition to, or even at the expense of, the first kind of value for which it originally stood. This is especially likely if the sign is highly public and nonperishable. And this is especially evident if the second kind of value leads to non-pecuniary, if not seemingly "irrational," strivings.

So how can we understand and argue for such a secondary valuation in the case of nonreplaceability? First, as seen by the foregoing discussion, nonreplaceability was certainly a local means for attaining the first kind of values; that is, having new roles, modes of coordination, and social relations was not only conditioned by one's implication in the ecotourism project; it was also required for a villager to engage in novel forms of income earning. Houses built in the new style were certainly good instances of nonperishable and public signs of one's nonreplaceability. And these houses were clearly at the limits of use value, as classically understood, in at least two respects. To villagers, such houses were virtually uninhabitable because of hearth-fire smoke that could not escape; and to the project itself, such houses were contributing to the very destruction of the cloud forest that its interventions were designed to stop. They were "bads" as much as "goods."

In some sense, the ecotourism project was too successful. Rather than removing the local system of replacement, it inadvertently resonated with it. And, in resonating with the local system of replacement, key values that villagers vied for were altered—an alteration most easily demonstrated by the creation of high-quality but uninhabitable homes; expensive but unhealthy (in)alienable possessions.

Long ago William James wrote of the self as an ensemble of all that one may call one's own. Revisiting some of the claims offered in chapters 2 and 3, and drawing on James, we might frame the self as an ensemble of social statuses, mental states, and material substances (or, rather, projected propensities more generally), the indices that evince these (which include items of possession, inalienable and alienable, as well as actions and affects), and the interpretants (by selves, others, and alters) that both recognize and regiment such index-propensity relations. Such an ensemble of semiotic processes (and semiological structures and social relations) may be more or less reflexively coherent; that is, just as desires can be directed at expanding the self and staving off its contraction (or, more generally, simply caring for the ensemble's constituents), affective unfoldings are the embodied register of this expansion and contraction (or, better, key indices of the vicissitudes of care).

In this expanded sense, value turns on securing the recognizing and regimenting interpretants of temporally, spatially, and socially distal others toward one's capacities and propensities (or "powers" more generally) as evinced in and generated by one's indices. Selfhood is thus a ground of motivation as much as meaning.

From this framing, one can see the radical entangling of three classic theories of value. Roughly speaking, Veblen's focus on pecuniary emulation (and theories of distinction more generally) foregrounded signs. Marx's focus on capitalist production, and abstract labor time as the source of value, focused on objects (in the semiotic sense); and Malinowski's focus on circulation foregrounded interpretants. While all these components are, by necessity, interrelated by virtue of being part of a semiotic process, desires are often directed at a single component: (1) gaining greater and greater propensities; (2) expressing more and more emblematic indices; and (3) securing more and more widely distributed interpretants (of such index-propensity relations).[2] While we just foregrounded the most Veblenesque aspect of a novel practice (an overemphasis on signs of status), the other two components—and much else besides—were hard at work as well.[3]

Value and Meaning Revisited

I have used the terms *meaning* and *value* in various, overlapping ways throughout this book. There are the signs, objects, and interpretants of semiotic processes; and, concomitantly, the qualities, causalities, and conventionalities of semiotic grounds (Kockelman 2005, 2012a, 2015).

There are the use values (functions), exchange values (prices), truth values (concepts), and deontic-values (norms) that help organize our worlds; and, concomitantly, the institutions, infrastructure, and interactions that enable the sharing and stabilization (as well as isolation and perturbation) of such values (Kockelman 2010a).

There are the goods (actions, entities, outcomes, etc.) that are striven for (as objects of desire and interest); and, concomitantly, the evaluative standards (instrumental, affective, existential, etc.) that allow striving agents to grade such goods as to their relative desirability (Kockelman 2010c).

There are the forms of property and modes of belonging that one fiercely holds onto (from body parts to kinship relations, from homes to hearths, from inalienable possession to alienable wealth); and, concomitantly, the forms of reflexive care (affect, desire, and accountability) that constitute the selfhood of the one who holds so fiercely (Kockelman 2007b).

There are the relatively finite and fought-over resources of the world (not just concrete entities like coal, air, and water, but more generally time, energy, information, order, etc.); and, concomitantly, the forms of affect, action, and thought that orient to them (Kockelman 2006).

There are the indices, individuals, agents, and kinds of ontologized worlds; and, concomitantly, the embodied, embedded, and enminded assumptions of worlded ontologies (Kockelman 2013a, 2013b).

And, perhaps most abstractly, there are the relations between relations that underlie ensembles of entities and events (semiological structures, semiotic processes, social relations, parasitic practices, and so forth); and, concomitantly, the conditions and consequences of such forms of inter-relationality (Kockelman 2011).

All these frames are particular ways of understanding meaning and value; they thereby enclose such notions as much as they disclose them, and do so in ways that may be considered negative (e.g., reification) as much as positive (e.g., explication). Each of these understandings of meaning and value overlaps with the others, but sometimes only tenuously; that is, while they all bear a family resemblance to each other, there are often intellectual generations and scholarly lineages that separate them, so that not only the kind of meaning or value portrayed, but also the conventions of portrayal per se, have changed. But that said, across the frames, there is a commonality of complementary concerns—somewhere at the intersection of what entities stand for, and what agents strive for.

For the sake of explication, each of the frames has been articulated in terms of two complementary facets (e.g., semiotic process versus semiotic ground, evaluated good versus evaluative standard, ontologized world versus worlded ontology), where each facet relates to the other (in potentially reversible ways, depending on the frame), as figure to ground, precipitate to process, or relata to relations. All such frames and facets are more or less useful as analytic lenses, depending on the stance of the analysts and actors in question. And all arguably exist, however differently figured, and however faintly realized, in any context for any collectivity at any era of history.

Finally, members of different collectivities in part constitute a collectivity not just because they have such meanings and values (more or less) in common with, and in contrast to, members of other collectivities, but because they are (by degrees) reflexively aware of their contrastive commonality. And, of course, only a few of these collectivities are "cultures" as traditionally understood. On the one hand, some values and meanings seem to have a hold on very many members of our species (as well as members of other species), whatever their culture or creed. On the other hand, collectivities are, in some sense, constituted by their shared holdings. And given that there are not only different kinds of values and meanings to hold, but also so many ways of framing the values and meanings so held, there are many different kinds of crisscrossing, overlapping, undercutting, overpowering, and constantly transforming collectivities. And so where one draws such boundaries in shared meanings and values is, in part, a function of scale; and, concomitantly, the scale chosen (presumed, projected) is, in part, a function of such values and meanings.

Understood as such, one key sense of "commensurate" is the degree to which the meanings and values of two or more collectivities may be rendered in terms of each other, such that each is understandable from the standpoint of the "other." And one key sense of "portable" is the degree to which particular values or meanings can be presupposed (carried, found, made, imposed, taken for granted) across collectivities, such that it will be treated as valuable or meaningful wherever it "goes." Portability and commensurability are thus scale-dependent, as much as source-dependent, phenomena. Finally, as should be apparent, such issues bedevil the frameworks used by analysts as much as the frameworks used by the actors so analyzed, so that, at best, such mutually entangled frameworks are merely "patches" that seem—however small the scope, and brief the span—to "work."

With this review, and these revisions, in mind, we may now turn back to the title of the previous section, "From Contract to Status." This title is an inversion of Henry Sumner Maine's ([1866] 2002) classic claim— that one key way to understand what makes us modern was a move from social statuses that one is born into (male and female, Dinka and Nuer, master and slave) to social statuses that one has bought into (in particular, property rights and responsibilities acquired through market transactions). For Maine, not only was there a transition from ascribed statuses to achieved statuses as such, but the permission-granting and obligation-bearing body went from a corporate entity (family, lineage, tribe, etc.) to the biological individual (in particular, the adult man or woman); the kind of deontic modality that grounded it went from particular tradition to universal law; and the kind of social relations you were typically entangled in went from family and neighbor to stranger (Kockelman 2007a). Many other oppositions and transitions are related to Maine's insights—from *Gemeinschaft* and *Gesellshaft* in Tönnies to concrete and abstract domination in Marx, from symbolic capital and capital in Bourdieu, to gift and commodity in Mauss, from "the Great Transformation" narratives of Polanyi to "the Great Commensuration" narratives of modern sociologists (Espeland and Stevens 1998), themselves tightly coupled to, if not coterminous with, the often reactionary and romantic "radical incommensurability" narratives of much of anthropology.

Maine's insights were themselves grounded in earlier distinctions, like quantity versus quality, or money making versus house holding in Aristotle. And they often licensed a series of further dichotomies, from the local and the global, through the private and the public, to the context dependent and context-free. And, of course, most folks would say that— at best—such distinctions are but two poles of a continuum, any actual social formation involves each of them (and much else besides), and all of us are always already implicated in both of them to various degrees. The point here is not to argue for them, or against them, or even to problematize them—but merely to note the radical hold they have on the sociological imaginary. In particular, I want to stress how the foregoing account of meaning and value (qua summary of some of this monograph's arguments), like the ethnographic and historical details of the many little transformations underway in the village of Chicacnab (as detailed in each core chapter), runs heavy and roughshod over such simplistic distinctions. I may thereby highlight the small, fragile, and fleeting scales (and often fledgling collectivities, composed of actors and analysts alike, caught up in chickens as much as quetzals, and confronted by chicken hawks as much as chainsaws) where complementary as much as contradictory tensions seem to arise.

An Epilogue of Sorts

In time, Project Eco-Quetzal would itself be graded. In her thesis on resource conservation, Miller (2008) evaluated the design and management of four community-based ecotourism projects in Guatemala using Hip-well's (2007) six criteria: "(1) tourism activities must be small enough to be managed solely by the community without outside support; (2) a broad representation of community members must be actively involved in the project; (3) the project must benefit the community as a whole; (4) the project must improve the quality of life for community members across the board; (5) it must result in increased awareness of conservation values; and (6) it should facilitate the maintenance or enhancement of the local culture" (Miller 2008: iii).

From Miller's standpoint (and see Argueta 2014), Project Eco-Quetzal did not improve life for locals and did not maintain a small scale and so was "unsatisfactory" in regards to criteria 1 and 4. In particular, vil-lagers reported not earning enough money from tourism to make a sig-nificant change in their lives (a small number of benefits were distributed across too many participants), and many of the villagers she interviewed resented the NGO for overmanaging the ecotourism project (instead of handing it over to the community). That said, Project Eco-Quetzal was graded "satisfactory" in every other respect except criterion 6 ("maintains or enhances culture"), in regards to which Miller said that there wasn't enough information to decide. In any case, Miller was undertaking her work just prior to 2008, right before PEQ would report a 40 percent de-crease in the number of tourists from previous years.

My point here is not to laud or decry the results, fixate on the irony, support or critique the criteria themselves, highlight the recursive nature of grading, or hint that such issues were soon to become moot. It is merely to return to the NGO's own ontology—the kinds of categories and com-mitments they would have used to judge the success of their own inter-ventions, and how they were so judged.

Conclusion

PATHS, PORTABILITY, AND PARASITES

Going Awry, Leading Astray

Let me begin by provisionally characterizing *equivalence* in a seemingly narrow way. An origin is equivalent to a destination in the context of a path that connects them. While this characterization no doubt stretches the conventional meaning of the word *equivalence*, it is meant to capture the idea that relatively different variables can (seem to) have relatively similar values. In particular, while the two places (origin and destination) are relatively different according to one criterion (e.g., one is over here, and one is over there, so to speak), they are relatively similar according to another criterion (wherever one can go from the destination, one can also go from the origin, insofar as the path connects them). That is, while their "location" may be more or less different, the possibilities of travel that they afford, and thus the possible future places they each avail, are more or less the same.[1]

To make this characterization more concrete, we may return to the village of Chicacnab. Such a place may be figured as a destination (and, indeed, to tourists, as a "destination"), itself reachable by a well-trod path through the cloud forest, a path that originates in another place—the town of Caquipek. Caquipek, in turn, can itself be figured as a destination that can be reached by other "paths" (one of which is a road) from other places. And so it goes . . . all the way back (and sometimes forth) to places where tourists (as well as anthropologists, biologists, Peace Corps volunteers, soldiers, and colonists, not to mention chickens, Coca Cola, guns, dollars, cartoons, and democracy) come from—not just New York, London, Paris, and Berlin, but also Santa Fe, Palo Alto, Hyde Park, and New Haven. You can even get to Rome. Through a network of ever-changing paths, one place is simultaneously and sequentially linked to many others—in a space of fantasy as much as actuality or necessity, be it encoded on a map, embedded throughout a terrain, or embodied in a traveler.

To be sure, even if all places are possible, insofar as all roads eventually lead there, many places are radically improbable. Indeed, even if you (the tourist) make it all the way to Caquipek, you might have to stop there. It may have recently rained, and so the path is too muddy. You may have worn the wrong shoes, or your pack may be too heavy. Your guide may not arrive, or have sent a feckless son in his place. And even if you eventually start up the path, you may never get to the destination. There are guard dogs, ambiguous way markers, downed trees, and crappy maps—and even the occasional beautiful bird that might distract you. Or, backing up to a previous path, the road to Caquipek may not have been well maintained, you might have missed the bus, not have had enough coins to pay the fare, or have been set on by thieves. You may have gotten off too early, having misunderstood a sign, or lost your map, or been unable to hear the call over the noise of the engine, the cries of children, and the clucks of chickens. And, of course, travelers, as much as the paths they take, are transformed by their travels. You may not want to continue on once you arrive or may have come to have further destinations in mind. In some sense, and perhaps most generally, every place along the path is itself a potential origin, leading—by other paths—to other destinations. Framed another way, the essence of a path (or text) is arguably all the ways it may go awry, and thereby lead a traveler (or reader) astray . . .

And where were we going with this argument, anyway? Equivalence, itself understood in terms of paths, themselves understood in terms of ways of going awry. That is, an origin is (more or less) equivalent to a destination in the context of a path that connects them (given the similarity of places they avail), where any path is best figured in terms of all the ways it can go awry or lead astray. As will now be made clear, not only does a "path" constitute a particularly generalizable metaphor (insofar as many other equivalence-oriented processes may be seen in its light); metaphors themselves constitute particularly important paths. In particular, most domains can be connected to many others (time and money, texts and journeys, chickens and children, corn and coffee) so long as there exists a metaphor, trope, ground, or ontology more generally, that finds, as much as imposes, a connection. And thus, if a person or thing, utterance or idea, qualia or quiddity, affect or effect, can make it to Chicacnab, there are many other transformations it can undergo, many other modes of equalia it can be caught up in, and thus many other journeys it may undertake.

Frame, Failure, Function

Let me offer some overlapping examples of such undergoings and undertakings, most of which were ethnographically detailed and analytically elaborated in various parts of this book. A sign, or signifier, is (more or less) equivalent to an object, or signified, in the context of a code (that connects them). A speaker (or signer more generally) is equivalent to an addressee (or interpreter more generally) in the context of a channel. Labor power and means of production (what is worked on as well as what is worked with) are equivalent to finished products in the context of a production (or reproduction) process. A commodity (say, labor) is equivalent to a certain amount of money (say, wage) in the context of a market, or an economic order more generally. A domain is equivalent to a range in the context of a function. An input is equivalent to an output in the context of an algorithm. One or more premises is equivalent to a conclusion in the context of a logic (and a set of background assumptions). A cause is equivalent to an effect in the context of a field of forces. Something virtual is equivalent to something real by reference to one or more shared "virtues." A concrete domain is equivalent to an abstract domain in the context of a metaphor. A text in one language is equivalent to a text in another language in the context of a translation. One tool is equivalent to another in reference to a shared function. One chord voicing is equivalent to another in the context of a musical composition. One token is equivalent to another token in the context of a type, or mode of typification (which includes aesthetic patterns). Two substances are equivalent in the context of shared qualia (and even more equivalent in the context of shared quantia of such qualia), for example, height and weight, desirability and price, pain or beauty, suffering or cruelty. Relatedly, two courses of action are more or less equivalent in light of the values to which they orient; or two values (say, commodities) are more or less equivalent in light of the actions (involving both labor power and means of production) they incorporate. One form of energy is equivalent to another form of energy in the context of a mode of conversion. A circumstance is equivalent to a behavior in the context of a norm. An affordance (say, the slipperiness of mud) is equivalent to the action that heeds it (say, walking carefully) in the context of a habit. A punishment (or reward) is equivalent to a crime (or service) in the context of an international law or a local custom. To go back to our original metaphor, a path does not have to move through space; it can also move through time. Storage is thus a form of transportation; that is, the possibilities available to an actor in the present are equivalent to the possibilities available to an actor in the future, presuming they he or she can "wait" (without undue deterioration). Perhaps most generally, an interpretant is (more or less) equivalent to a sign in the context of an object (that they both relate to) and an agent (that can either perceive or project such an inter-relation). And, perhaps most village-specifically, one entity is (more or less) equivalent to another insofar as it embodies the same potentia to exhibit particular quantia of particular qualia (and can thereby "replace" it). We could go on.

In each case, one entity (event, individual, process, system, content, sign, practice, qualia, thing, medium, person, assemblage, etc.) can be more or less transformed into (replaced with, exchanged for, interpreted by, etc.) another entity in the right context, such that if such a context (logic, code, habit, norm, virtue, channel, custom, composition, algorithm, imaginary, etc.) exists, the entities in question are more or less equivalent. That is, *some of what avails itself to the second (destination) avails itself to the first (origin) in the context of the third (path).*

Given these metaphorical extensions of our initial characterization, I will use the terms *origin*, *destination*, and *path* in an expanded sense in order to include each term (first, second, third) in the foregoing examples. Every such path (in a particular frame, and to a certain degree) delimits a landscape (the relata come into being through the relation), facilitates a passage (one relata can be transformed into the other or replaced with the other), and forestalls a loss (the first relatum, by being transformed into the second relatum, can undergo subsequent transformations that would otherwise be unavailable to it). Crucially, some of these paths are figments of imagination, and some are only figured out through interactions; some are hardened into infrastructure, and some are watched by institutions.

To be sure, the "functioning" of such thirds is still best understood in terms of their propensity to "fail," but now in a very generalized sense: all the little ways they can go awry, and thus be of "novel avail" as much as of "no avail." There are slips of the tongue as much as slips on the path; there are transaction costs as well as noisy channels; there are bad translations and faulty calculations; there are misidentifications and atypical tokens; there is friction and scrambling, pirates and exploits, tolls and trolls, enemies and parasites (Kockelman 2010a). Bridges can be out as much as burnt. Goods can spoil, messages can degrade, and reputations can wither. There may be no "substitute," and individuals can become "irreplaceable." Our algorithms may have bugs; our laws may be misapplied. Actors embody dangerous habits, and middle-men extract unfair prices. There are incommensurable substances and misplaced assumptions, nongradable qualia, and impossible-to-reckon quantia. And, of course, metaphors themselves can be overused as well as inaptly applied, mixed as much as forced.

Topologies of (and in) Transformation

It is worth stressing the "topology" (itself a kind of ontology) of the foregoing metaphor. There is an ensemble of "places" (or relata), and an ensemble of "paths" (or relations). Most places are simultaneously frameable as an origin or a destination and so may point not only forward to "subsequent" places (qua destinations), but also backward to "prior" places (qua origins). Most places are connected to many other places, as origin or destination, and thus have many possible "roots" and many possible "fruits." Many seemingly short paths can be "expanded," revealing a series of sequential paths within them. Conversely, many seemingly long paths can be "condensed," eliding the sequential paths within them. Some paths are relatively reversible, and some go in only one direction. Some sequential paths involve "conversion" (from one kind of third into another—cause to norm to channel to code to metaphor to algorithm); others involve "conveyance" (path to path, cause to cause, code to code, function to function). And any place, however tempting it is to enclose, is best understood in terms of the paths that flow through it.

Relatedly, of all the possible paths leading from or to a place, only a few may be profiled, or even be profilable, at a particular time, or by a particular actor. The horizons of agents are never commensurate with the worldlines of entities. Such a topology can be used to describe an ontologized world (here are the ensembles of possible and necessary, or permissible and obligatory transformations), or a worlded ontology (here are an actor's assumptions, be they embodied or embedded, encoded or enminded, about such an ensemble). Indeed, it may even be used to describe an actor's journey through a world, and the relative worth of particular journeys; that is, here is the set of transformations an actor has undergone or will undergo, could have undergone or can undergo, should not have undergone or should undergo (Kockelman 2010c). In all these ways, the topology itself is reflexively frame dependent, where the frame in play often depends on the place (within a frame) of the actor doing the framing.

The point, then, in going through all these modes of thirdness (grounds, paths, relations), and ways of framing the functioning and failing of thirdness, is not just to inundate the reader with new modes of equivalence in addition to "translation" and "transaction" proper. It is also to indicate that there is a kind of logic at work that can, given the right framing, judge any two entities, events, or experiences equivalent (or, crucially, nonequivalent). This foregrounds the point that equivalence and nonequivalence exist only within particular interpretive frames, as grounded in particular ontologies. Concomitantly, it foregrounds the point that multiple frames of interpretation exist, as well as do multiple grounds for interpretation, any of which may be called on at a given moment, in the name of difference as well as similarity, to undertake a specific action or motivate a particular transformation, if not secure a specific advantage or rationalize a particular relation.

Such otherwise disparate paths, and framings of paths, are equivalent in that they each foreground the relation between variation and invariance. Needless to say, the usual sorts of issues arise, as came up again and again in this book. For example, what is preserved is only more or less preserved (indeed, a value is often dramatically transformed); and what is changed may be minimally changed (for example, the origin and destination may be perfect copies, if not identically positioned). And, more generally, agents can judge equivalence categorically, by degree, or through quantification—and thus not just change frames but also adjust scales within a frame. The paths in question can be stated, as much as shown, and are thus as likely to be evinced in relatively tacit practices as espoused in relatively explicit pronouncements. Sometimes travelers create the paths they travel along; sometimes they travel along already existing and well-worn trails. There is thus conformativity as much as transformativity. Depending on the relative overlap (or lack of overlap) between a given agent's horizon (of equivalence space) and a given entity's world line (through equivalence space), agents have different degrees of power (over the entity) and knowledge (about the entity), and thus differential abilities to understand or intervene in the transformations that entities (events, individuals, processes, practices, ideas, etc.) will undergo. Finally, and perhaps most crucially, not only may the paths in question involve movement across and within already established systems (as in translation proper); they may also help to undermine the notion of a relatively bounded or stable system, as well as serve as a key condition for the emergence or disappearance of such a system.

Such paths, so far as they are shared, reflexively oriented to, and presumable across contexts, by members of one or more collectivities, constitute infrastructure (or institution, or interaction, or imaginary) in the most general sense. They can be distributed and regimented in any number of ways (norms or laws, causally or conventionally, function like a code or like a channel, be grounded in a habit or an equation, etc.). They can thus be "harder" or "softer," more or less difficult to circumvent, relatively "subjective," "objective," or "intersubjective," more or less predictable in effect or explicable in mechanism, more or less prone to failure. And so they can be more or less enclosed (or enclosing) in any of the senses enumerated in the introduction.

As we also saw throughout this volume, processes and practices that distribute (modify, erase, build) such thirds (as infrastructure, institution, interaction, or imaginary) are as important as the thirds themselves. And so the key relations that were examined were those that had as their destination relations between other origins and destinations, and thus processes that figured as much as reconfigured grounds for relations. That is, some of the most important paths have relatively reflexive relations to themselves (Kockelman 2010a, 2013a). For example, not only do some paths have other paths as their destination, but some paths get where they're going only as a function of where they begin. Not only do many paths have as their destinations the origins of new paths, but some paths get where they're going only as a function of having already been.

Some Paths to and through Chicacnab

To be sure, as this book has shown, such "paths" are very different as to their analytic details, not to mention their historical conditions and ethnographic particulars. And thus all the actions, processes, constructions, and events described in these pages—and, indeed, described in any ethnography—turned on complex ensembles of the foregoing kinds of thirds: codes, channels, norms, laws, habits, functions, compositions, conversions, interpretations, metaphors, productions, types, identities, fields, and, of course, paths in their original sense.

Villagers, by and large, followed their own paths, or followed others' paths in their own ways. And so each of the core ethnographic chapters in this book was devoted to tracing out their paths in and across a variety of domains: the hosting of tourists, the husbandry of poultry, replacement and grading, and commoditization and commensuration. For example, something as seemingly simple as poultry husbandry was, in some sense, an ensemble of paths that women urged chickens to travel. (Though, to be sure, chickens—as well as chicken hawks—often had their own travel plans.) From the reproduction of poultry (eggs to chickens and back again) to illness cures that projected equivalences onto chickens and women in relation to chicks and children. From barter circles to commodity chains, and thus from woman-chicken-woman (W-C-W') to commodity-money-commodity (C-M-C'), and beyond. From event to affect, from interaction to ontologies, from alterity to identity. There was also the institution of replacement itself, which delimited a complex ensemble of transformations: husband to lover, sick person to effigy, tit for tat, ingoing mayor for outgoing mayor, and even new for old battery. There was graded equivalence: coffee for corn, your labor capacity for my own, metal griddles for earthenware griddles. And there were all the more stereotypic modes of transaction and translation that villagers have always been subject to, however often they are transformed: Spanish and Q'eqchi', *b'aar* and meter, the dollar and the quetzal, even quetzals and chickens.

Not only were the practices of villagers aptly framed in such terms, but so were the activities of the NGO (who, like villagers, spent as much of its time creating new "paths" as conforming to old ones). The NGO not only followed its own and others' paths but was also devoted to setting up a space of paths for others to travel—villagers as much as tourists, things as much as people, messages as much as money, birds as much as humans. They matched codes, they established channels, they trained workers, they set prices, they created norms, they figured values, they directed habits, they established identities, they identified types, they composed art (or at least advertisement), and they even maintained trails. By means of such modes of governance, such ways of conducting conduct, they hoped that such actions, collective as much as individual, which would otherwise run along other paths, would thereby lead to a particular "place"—one more highly valued in their ontology. And, on their way to this destination, in their attempt to bring about this end, they were beset with objections (and hastened by allies) from all sides—often precisely the copresence of one or more alternate spaces of relations, traversed by tourists and villagers alike, chickens as much as quetzals. Framed another way, in their attempts to build such paths, however successfully or unsuccessfully, the NGO presupposed an ensemble of paths, however judiciously or erroneously. And the paths they managed to build went awry in any number of ways.

Portability Revisited

How does all this relate to portability (a particular qualia, however complex), which was loosely characterized in the introduction as the degree (a particular quantia, however difficult to measure) to which the meaningfulness and means-ends-fullness of a medium seems to be applicable to many contents and applicable in many contexts (and thus applicable across many scales)?

Clearly, our very definition of equivalence itself presupposes a certain kind of portability, that is, transportability from one position to another position in a seemingly abstract (but oh-so-concrete) space of relations. In other words, paths (codes, channels, laws, habits, norms, metaphors, types, equations, etc.) exhibit portability by their very definition. Moreover, the kind of interpretive framework such a characterization enabled was meant to be portable in another sense: while deeply grounded in the ethnographic and historical details of a particular place and time, the concepts and commitments at play (at least at one degree of remove from their actual instantiation) are widely applicable. But these two overarching senses of portability hardly exhaust the possibilities. For particular paths might be judged more or less portable, as a function of various parameters, from the standpoint of many different perspectives.

Marx, for example, defined the universal equivalent as the one commodity that can be used to express (or measure) the value of all other commodities. To serve as the universal equivalent was one defining feature of "money." Such a capacity was closely related to a second key function of money: that it constitutes a means of exchange, insofar as it may serve as an intermediary between any two commodities (C-M-C'). Such functions (capacities or features), in a relatively generalized sense, constitute two important senses of portability. But money is a medium, and media are always as material as they are meaningful. And, as one often told story goes (however imaginary or incorrect), certain media often play the role of money because they are "portable" in a variety of other senses. For example, typically as a function of their material properties, they are relatively storable (portable through time), transportable (portable across space), recognizable and alienable (portable across persons), and divisible (portable across scales). Finally, perhaps more important than any of these narrow definitions of portability, is their inherent reflexivity; that is, the relative portability of particular values is one of the reasons they are so valuable (which, in turn, contributes to their relative portability). Notice, then, how notions like "abstract" or "commensurate" barely begin to describe the actual factors that contribute to these kinds of portability.

And, just to show how portable such notions are, particular languages (or ways of mediating language) often have similar affordances projected onto them. For example, while it is often argued that languages are "formally complete" (Sapir [1923] 1985), in the sense that anything sayable in one is more or less sayable in another (with no end of caveats, as every anthropologist knows), certain languages often serve as "universal equivalents." That is, during certain histories, and over certain geographies, utterances encoded using their categories are readily used, however infelicitously, to translate (measure or render) the meaning of utterances from other languages. Think, for instance, of standardized English or Imperial Latin. (And, to be sure, there are many stereotypes about certain languages that make speakers believe they are better than others in such a capacity.) Certain languages, insofar as they are widely spoken, also serve as a key means of interchange; that is, not C-M-C', but Q'eqchi'-Nahuatl-Spanish, or Russian-French-English, or any lingua franca more generally

(Errington 2001). And certain mediatizations of language (say, written as opposed to verbal, or digitized as opposed to written) seem to exhibit the other kinds of portability as well, including storability, recognizability, transportability, and so forth. And, finally, certain languages are reflexively valued precisely because of the portability of their "values." (Indeed, if you want to port these notions even further afield, simply replace natural language with artificial language, or languages with formats, or formats with weights and measures, or weights and measures with codes and laws.)

Such are two widespread, and heavily entangled, stereotypes of money and language. Another important sense of portability is tightly coupled to these last two, namely, the capacity to be removed from one context and inserted in another context, all the while retaining a certain degree of intelligibility (functionality, value, etc.) across contexts. When applied to texts, Goffman (1981) called this process "excerptibility," itself necessarily paired with its converse, "insertability." And linguistic anthropologists, using terms like "entextualization" and "contextualization," have done particularly important work by understanding such phenomena not as a property (of texts and contexts per se), but rather as a process that helps to delimit what counts as "text" and "context" in the first place (Silverstein and Urban 1996).

Under the heading of enclosure, the introduction offered a synthetic look at a wide range of classic work with similar stakes and aims, itself undertaken to understand a much wider set of domains—for example, frames, closure, rails, interresment, materiality, privatization, networks, objectivity, discipline, measurement, commodization, and on and on. As we saw in this book, all such processes of enclosure work not just by minimizing the contexts necessary for interpretation, or widely distributing such contexts (in the habits of actors as much as through the workings of infrastructure), but also by packaging such "contexts" with such "contents" (e.g., "batteries included"). And we noted the tight coupling between such modes of enclosure proper and disclosure per se. That is, forms knowledge and power (and profit, whatever the value captured) are both condition for and consequence of various modes of enclosure. And, through such linkages, we figured the perils and pearls of various modernities (plus or minus their particular prefixes, e.g., *pre-*, *post-*, *para-*, and *epi-*). Indeed, framed in the "abstract," such modernities always seem to show up as scale-free modes of sociality, their values radically portable (or so it seems), and portability, in turn, their key value.

Overtakings and Undertakings

All that said, portability is not necessarily interesting in itself, but only insofar as it arose in the context of my field site. Proyecto Eco-Quetzal, in particular, was caught up in portability (and its lack) in a number of important ways. First, NGOs themselves seem to be the most portable of institutions. In particular, they have sprung up everywhere, engaged in every kind of intervention, for just about every kind of reason. The NGO was also trying to make its own interventions portable. It was trying to figure out how to make community-based ecotourism work in one place, such that its interventions could then be moved to other places. And to do this, the NGO had to port not just people (such as ecotourists) into other contexts, but also ideas, things, utterances, interactions, and commodities. And, more generally, they not only had to create the conditions of possibility for such portability (by creating, maintaining, and redirecting a network of paths, so to speak); they also had to find a way to capture some of the consequences of the activities that could then proceed along such paths. In short, they had to train people, set up environments, translate codes, channel interactions, create functions, establish force fields, regiment interpretations, maintain trails, and so on and so forth, such that certain kinds of activities with particular contents and effects could occur out of their normal contexts, or seemingly novel activities could occur in already existing contexts.

And finally, in doing so, the NGO was confronted on all sides by what seemed to be (at least to them) the least portable of entities and events, people and things, processes and practices. Not just "immaterial labor" in a village with no connecting road, but also (what appeared to be) an isolated and impenetrable language, a minimally marketed economy, and a community of inward-looking and isolated inhabitants. And, indeed, not only the NGO was so confronted. For note how much of anthropology's imaginary (like Heidegger's and most other romantics', and not just the sinister and silly, but also the serious) rests in *nonportability* as a value. Think, for example, of the value anthropologists put on the following notions: the qualitative, contextualized, rooted, grounded, ephemeral, auroric, irreplaceable, singular, concrete, dependent, incommensurate, uncopiable, faint, and fragile. Portability, then, is a "local term" par excellence—not just in my field site, but also for my discipline.

Of course, as much as anthropologists profess to love it, they are never faithful. For the very book you have in your hands (itself an instance of what is one of the most decisively portable media ever made) is filled with a content that is designed to be portable across contexts in all the foregoing ways and also, thereby, designed to transport the lives of villagers to distal places—to make such lives available for "understanding" to be sure, with the understanding that understanding is itself an overtaking as much as an undertaking, a mode of enclosure as much as disclosure, a parasite as much as a path.

NOTES

Introduction: Enclosure and Disclosure

1. Much has been written about Alta Verapaz and the Q'eqchi' Maya. On the history of Alta Verapaz, see King (1974), Sapper (1985), and M. R. Wilson (1972); and see Wilk (1991) for a particularly important critical revisioning. On liberal reforms and German colonialism, see Cambranes (1985) and Wagner (1996). On the northward migration, see Adams (1965), Carter (1969), Howard (1975), Grandia (2009, 2012); Kockelman (1999b); Pedroni (1991); Saa Vidal (1979); Schwartz (1990); Wilk (1991). On the civil war, and its relation to Alta Verapaz, see Carmack (1988), IWGIA (1978), and R. Wilson (1995). On the distribution of speakers of Q'eqchi' and their dialects, see Kaufman (1974), Romero (2008, 2012), and Stewart (1980). And for an in-depth look at the language through the lens of grammatical categories and discourse practices, as a means to understand social relations and modes of subjectivity, see Kockelman (2010b).

Chapter 1: NGOs, Ecotourists, and Endangered Avifauna

1. All sources for this section in PQ 1990.

2. Harvey (1996) has noted that all ecological projects are simultaneously political-economic projects and vice versa. Escobar (1995) has discussed how the discourses and practices of sustainable development depoliticize economic and ecological issues. And see the important early work by Orlove and Brush (1996), as well as recent work by West (2006) and Cepek (2012).

3. Needless to say, the project's advertisement of such values resonates with well-known anthropological accounts of what attracts tourists (Bruner 1991; Graburn 1989; MacCannel 1976; Stronza 2001; Turner and Turner 1978; among others). In

the Guatemalan case, see the particularly important work of Little (2000, 2004), with a particular emphasis on the logic and conundrums of performance.

4. It might be likened to a form of *governance*, understood as a process whereby the possible actions of formally free individuals are enabled and constrained (Burchell 1991; Foucault 1991).

5. While there is no consensus on just what an NGO is (Elyachar 2005; Fisher 1997; Gilbert 2001; Kockelman 2002), many definitions turn on their putative (and often erroneous) distinction from state-like forms of power. See, for example, Doane (2001); Ferguson (1990); Fisher (1997); Gilbert (2002); Hardt and Negri (2000); Sassen (1996); and Trouillot (2001); among many others. Leaving aside such large-scale definitional and philosophical questions, the general strategy in this chapter is to focus on the micropractices of governance that the project undertakes as an NGO—its strategies, techniques, and tensions; its genealogy, impulse, and achievement. Phrased another way, at issue here is not what an NGO is in an abstract or analytic sense, but rather what one NGO did in an ethnographic and historical sense. In some sense, we are looking at the particulars of what often seems to be the most portable of institutions.

6. Some might say that the NGO's scope, logic, and ethos was unabashedly neoliberal as a mode of governance (Burchell 1991; Foucault 1991, inter alia). *To be sure* (Kockelman 2002, 2006), but that is not my concern here.

7. See, for example, Hardt and Negri (2000), and especially Lazzarato (1996) and Virno and Hardt (1996).

8. The dependence of tourism on a service economy, and thus on modes of immaterial labor, is often noted (Brislin et al. 1986; Nash 1989; Reisinger 1997; among others).

9. See the collection of essays in the volume edited by Enfield and Levinson (2006) for a good summary of key voices and claims in this tradition, and see the monograph by Enfield (2009) for an approach to interaction that takes cognition as seriously as culture, gesture as much as symbol, Peirce as much as Grice.

10. Commensuration is usually defined as a process whereby otherwise distinct entities are rendered comparable by reference to proportional quantities of a shared quality (Aristotle 2001a; Espeland and Stevens 1998; Marx 1967; among others). Kockelman (2002, 2006) reviews some highlights in this literature, with a particular focus on all the work it takes to make seemingly disparate domains commensurate. There are, as will be seen in later chapters, many other ways to think about the relation between action, desire, value, failure, function, causality, accountability, and incommensurability, but this particular framing of such relatively classic relations should be enough for now.

Chapter 3: From Reciprocation to Replacement

1. This is an exemplary instance of a semiotic ground licensing a semiotic process (Kockelman 2015); that is, insofar as an interpreting agent presumes such an iconic-indexical relation, however "symbolic" (or conventional) it may seem to be to an observer, the cause (drinking coffee) may be read as a sign of the effect (barren milpa), or vice versa.

2. We might use these ideas to reformulate Jakobson's (1990a) framework for describing grammatical categories as follows. The figure of comparison (Fc) may be understood as a "narrated entity" (En); and the ground of comparison (Gc) may be understood as a "reference entity" (Er). A reference entity may be constituted by another narrated entity (as in our opening example), or it may be constituted by some entity in the speech event (e.g., "this is larger [than that]"), or by some more conventional entity (e.g., "this is bigger [than the average or typical member of the class of entities with which it is being compared]"). As such, a reference entity loosely corresponds to what Sapir ([1945] 1985) called a "point of departure." Just as aspect may be understood as a grammatical category that indicates the relation between a narrated event and a reference event, grade may therefore be understood as a grammatical category that indicates the relation between a narrated entity and a reference entity. Compare, for example, "I don't like you anymore" (end of narrated event prior to reference event) with "I don't have anymore" (extent of narrated entity no more than reference entity). (Tense, by the way, is usually best understood as a relation between a reference event and the speech event.) Kockelman (2010b) reformulates a range of grammatical categories in a three-term, as opposed to a two-term, system: not only tense and aspect (linking speech events and narrated events through reference events), but also mood, status, and evidentials (linking speech events and narrated events through deontic, commitment, and source events).

3. Classic work includes Alder (2002: 325–346), Galison (2003: 84–155), Heilbron (1990), Kula (1986: 161–266), Schaffer (1997), and Zupko (1990: 113–75).

4. Classic work includes Greenberg (1990), Lucy (1992: 23–84), and Whorf (1956).

5. For example, in the classic work of Malinowski ([1922] 1984: 146–94), Polanyi (1957: 43–55), and Sahlins (1972: 191–96). Key exceptions include Ballestero (2014), Crump (1990), Guyer (2004), Guyer et al. (2010), Lave (1988), Peebles (2010), Rotman (1993), and Verran (2001).

6. Classic works include Munn (1992) and Turner (1984); also see the important work of Appadurai (1986), Cepek (2012), and Graeber (2002).

7. Aristotle's key writings on the economy (2001a, 2001b) may be found in the Politics (book I) and the Nicomachean Ethics (book V.5). And see Meikle (1995) for careful and inspired exegesis.

8. And so grading is inherently temporal—not only evincing deep structural relations to grammatical categories such as aspect, but also evincing deep cultural ties to history.

9. Kockelman (2012a, 2013a) carefully retheorizes such simplistic distinctions. For present purposes, the point is not to commit to such categories per se, but rather to show some of the ways a wide range of influential theories resonated with each other.

10. See Kockelman (2010b).

11. For another approach to market-oriented versus subsistence-oriented production, see Dove (2011).

Chapter 4: From Measurement to Meaning

1. In Chicacnab, around 2000, there were about eighty distinct extended families, twenty of whom hosted ecotourists. Between 1998 and 2001, ten tourist-taking families built metal-roofed houses; and between 2000 and 2001, five of these were the second metal-roofed houses that these families possessed. Among non-tourist-taking families, there was less house building (only eleven out of sixty families built extra homes). And only four families had metal-roofed homes—but these were not newly built—rather, they belonged to families in the village center that ran small stores. In other words, while 50 percent of tourist-taking families had recently built houses and while 25 percent of tourist-taking families came to have two metal-roofed houses, less than 20 percent of non-tourist-taking families had built houses, and no non-tourist-taking villagers had recently converted to having two metal-roofed homes.

   Some men tried to fix the smoke issues by building "risers" (twelve-to-twenty-four-inch additions to their house so that the smoke had a space to go out); but many of the houses that had these risers still collected smoke. Subsequently, many of these villagers ended up rebuilding with thatch, in part because they needed cash and so had to sell the sheet metal. By 2008, and just before the radical drop in tourism throughout Guatemala, almost all villagers were taking ecotourists, and these sorts of issues had resolved themselves, in part, by villagers maintaining one thatch-roof home, and, in part, by villagers changing the architecture of metal-roofed homes. This decade, and especially the last five years (post–global financial crisis), deserves a monograph in itself.

2. Recall that such signs of status were themselves really indices of the capacities necessary to contract felicitously, themselves grounded in irreplaceability, itself the converse of replacement, itself mediated by labor quotas as much as a putative pre-conquest Mayan culture, and so it goes.

3. As always, the point of such ideal typical formulations is not to make a claim (e.g., formulation as hypothesis), but rather to foreground the discrepancies between the formulation and the facts in the field (i.e., formulation as reflexive attempt to see failures in the formulation itself).

Conclusion: Paths, Portability, and Parasites

1. As should be evident from the foregoing chapters, and especially obvious in the sections that follow, I have tried to mobilize a number of unruly allies in this monograph—in particular, Serres ([1980] 2007) on parasites and Peirce (1955a, 1955c, [1867] 1992) on thirdness. Kockelman (2010a, 2013a) spells out these interrelations in detail. Elyachar's work on phatic labor, communicative infrastructures, dispossession, neoliberalism, and NGOs is particularly relevant (2005, 2010, 2011, 2012a, 2012b), as is Maurer's work on equivalence, the pragmatics of money, credit and debt, and financial infrastructure more generally (2005, 2006, 2012a, 2012b, and Maurer et. al 2013). See also von Schnitzler on infrastructure and commensuration (2008, 2013) and Larkin on infrastructure and piracy (2004, 2008). Kockelman (1999a, 1999b) introduces the path/bridge/code/channel/infrastructure/interaction metaphor, through a particular reading of Frege, Wittgenstein, Heidegger, Jakobson, and tree-sap collection, in full.

REFERENCES

Adams, R. N. 1965. *Migraciones Internas en Guatemala: Expansión Agraria de los Indígenas Kekchíes hacia el Petén*. Guatemala City: Centro Editorial José de Pineda Ibarra.

Alder, K. 2002. *The Measure of All Things*. New York: Free Press.

Allen, N. J. 1985. "The Category of the Person in Mauss." In *The Category of the Person: Anthropology, Philosophy, History*, edited by M. Carrithers, S. Collins, and S. Lukes, 26–45. Cambridge: Cambridge University Press.

Anscombe, G. E. M. [1957] 1976. *Intention*. 2nd ed. Ithaca, NY: Cornell University Press.

Appadurai, Arjun, ed. 1986. *The Social Life of Things*. Cambridge: Cambridge University Press.

Arendt, Hannah. 1998. *The Human Condition*. Chicago: University of Chicago Press.

Argueta, Christina M. 2014. "Mending Guatemala's Tourism Industry through Private Regulation." *New York University Law Review* 89: 1381–418.

Aristotle. 2001a. "Nicomachean Ethics." In *The Collected Works of Aristotle*, edited by Richard McKeon, 1010–12. New York: The Modern Library.

Aristotle. 2001b. "Politics." In *The Collected Works of Aristotle*, edited by Richard McKeon, 1027–46. New York: The Modern Library.

Averill, James R. 1985. "The Social Construction of Emotion: With Special Reference to Love." In *The Social Construction of the Person*, edited by Kenneth J. Gergen and Keith E. Davis, 89–109. New York: Springer.

Bacon, Francis. [1620] 2000. *The New Organon*. Cambridge: Cambridge University Press.

Bacon, Francis. [1627] 2002. "New Atlantis." In *Francis Bacon: The Major Works*, edited by Brian Vickers, 238–79. Oxford: Oxford University Press.

Bakhtin, M. M. 1990. *Art and Answerability*, edited by Michael Holquist and Vadim Liapunov. Austin: University of Texas Press.

Ballestero, Andrea. 2014. "What's in a Percentage? Calculation as the Poetic Translation of Human Rights." *Indiana Journal of Global Legal Studies* 21 (1): 27–53.

Berlin, Brent. 1992. *Ethnobiological Classification: Principles of Categorization of Plants and Animals in Traditional Societies*. Princeton, NJ: Princeton University Press.

Boas, Franz. 1911. Introduction. In *Handbook of American Indian Languages*, 1–83. Bureau of American Ethnology, Bulletin 40:1. Washington, DC: Government Printing Office.

Boas, Franz. [1910] 1989. "Psychological Problems in Anthropology." In *Franz Boas Reader*, edited by George W. Stocking Jr., 243–54. Chicago: Midway Reprints.

Brislin, R., K. Cushner, C. Craig, and M. Yong. 1986. *Intercultural Interactions: A Practical Guide*. New York: Sage.

Bruner, Edward M. 1991. "Transformation of Self in Tourism." *Annals of Tourism Research* 18: 238–50.

Bulmer, Ralph. 1967. "Why Is the Cassowary Not a Bird?" *Man* 2: 5–25.

Burchell, Graham. 1991. *Peculiar Interests: Civil Society and Governing "The System of Natural Liberty."* In *The Foucault Effect: Studies in Governmentality*, edited by Graham Burchell, Colin Gordon, and Peter Miller, 119–50. Chicago: University of Chicago Press.

Callon, Michel. 1986. "Some Elements of a Sociology of Translation: Domestication of the Scallops and the Fishermen of St Briuc Bay." In *Power, Action and Belief: A New Sociology of Knowledge*, edited by John Law, 196–233. London: Routledge and Kegan Paul.

Cambranes, J. C. 1985. *Café y Campesinos: Los Orígenes de la Economía de Plantación Moderna en Guatemala, 1853–1897*. Madrid: Editorial Catriel.

Carlsen, R. S., and M. Prechtel. 1991. "The Flowering of the Dead: An Interpretation of Highland Maya Culture." *Man* 26 (1): 23–42.

Carmack, Robert M. 1988. *Harvest of Violence*. Norman: University of Oklahoma Press.

Carter, W. E. 1969. *New Lands and Old Traditions: Kekchi Cultivators in the Guatemalan Lowlands*. Latin American Monographs 6. Gainesville: University of Florida Press.

Cepek, Michael. 2012. *A Future for Amazonia*. Austin: University of Texas Press.

Chumley, Lily Hope, and Nicholas Harkness, eds. 2013. "Qualia." *Anthropological Theory* 13 (1): 3–128.

Coggins, C. 1989. "Classic Maya Metaphors of Death and Life." *Res* 16: 65–84.

Colapietro, P. 1986. *Peirce's Approach to the Self: A Semiotic Perspective on Human Subjectivity*. Albany: State University of New York Press.

Conklin, Harold. 1954. "The Relation of Hanunoo Agriculture to Their Plant World." PhD diss., Yale University.

Crump, Thomas. 1990. *The Anthropology of Numbers*. Cambridge: Cambridge University Press.

Deleuze, Gilles. 2003. *Francis Bacon: The Logic of Sensation*. London: Continuum Press.

Doane, Molly. 2001. "A Distant Jaguar: The Civil Society Project in Chimalapas." *Critique of Anthropology* 21 (4): 361–82.

Dove, Michael R. 2011. *The Banana Tree at the Gate: The History of Marginal Peoples and Global Markets in Borneo*. New Haven, CT: Yale University Press.

Du, Shanshan. 2000. "'Husband and Wife Do It Together': Sex/Gender Allocation of Labor among the Qhawqhat Lahu of Lancang, Southwest China." *American Anthropologist* 102 (3): 520–37.

Ekman, Paul, and Richard J. Davidson, eds. 1994. *The Nature of Emotions: Fundamental Questions*. New York: Oxford University Press.

Elyachar, Julia. 2005. *Markets of Dispossession*. Durham, NC: Duke University Press.

Elyachar, Julia. 2010. "Phatic Labor, Infrastructure, and the Question of Empowerment in Cairo." *American Ethnologist* 37 (3): 452–64.

Elyachar, Julia. 2011. "The Political Economy of Movement and Gesture in Cairo." *Journal of the Royal Anthropological Institute (Incorporating Man)* 17 (2): 82–99.

Elyachar, Julia. 2012a. "Before (and after) Neo-liberalism: Tacit Knowledge, Secrets of the Trade, and the Public Sector in Egypt." *Cultural Anthropology* 27 (1): 76–96.

Elyachar, Julia. 2012b. "Next Practices: Infrastructure, Public Goods, and the State from the Bottom of the Pyramid." *Public Culture* 24 (1): 109–29.

Enfield, Nicholas. 2009. *Anatomy of Meaning*. Cambridge: Cambridge University Press.

Enfield, Nicholas. 2013. *Relational Thinking*. Oxford: Oxford University Press.

Enfield, Nicholas, and Stephen Levinson, eds. 2006. *Roots of Human Sociality*. New York: Berg.

Errington, Joseph. 2001. "Colonial Linguistics." *Annual Review of Anthropology* 30: 19–31.

Escobar, Arturo. 1995. *Encountering Development: The Making and Unmaking of the Third World*. Princeton, NJ: Princeton University Press.

Espeland, Wendy Nelson, and Mitchell L. Stevens. 1998. "Commensuration as a Social Process." *Annual Review of Sociology* 24: 313–43.

Evans-Pritchard, Edward E. 1940. *The Nuer: A Description of the Modes of Livelihood and Political Institutions of a Nilotic People*. Oxford: Clarendon.

Ferguson, James. 1990. *The Anti-politics Machine: "Development," Depoliticization and Bureaucratic Power in Lesotho*. Cambridge: Cambridge University Press.

Fisher, William F. 1997. "Doing Good? The Politics and Antipolitics of NGO Practices." *Annual Review of Anthropology* 26: 439–64.

Foucault, Michel. 1991. "Governmentality." In *The Foucault Effect: Studies in Governmentality*, edited by Graham Burchell, Colin Gordon, and Peter Miller, 87–104. Chicago: University of Chicago Press.

Foucault, Michel. 1997. "Technologies of the Self." In *Ethics: Subjectivity and Truth*, edited by Paul Rabinow, 223–52. New York: New Press.

Frank, Robert H. 1988. *Passions within Reason: The Strategic Role of the Emotions*. New York: W. W. Norton.

Fustel de Coulanges, Numa Denis. [1873] 1955. *The Ancient City*. New York: Anchor Books.

Galison, P. 2003. *Einstein's Clocks and Poincare's Maps: Empires of Time*. New York: W. W. Norton.

GEF. 2000. Preliminary draft of a grant to the Global Environmental Fund of the United Nations Development Project.

Gibson, James. 1986. *The Ecological Approach to Visual Perception*. Boston: Houghton Mifflin.

Gilbert, Andrew. 2001. "Protean States: Shifting Grounds of Governmentality in Discourses on NGOs." M.A. thesis, University of Chicago.

Gilbert, Andrew. 2002. "Foreign Aid and Refugee Return: Theorizing State Power and NGO Governmentality in a Liminal Bosnia." PhD diss. proposal, University of Chicago.

Goffman, Erving. 1981. *Forms of Talk*. Philadelphia: University of Pennsylvania Press.

Graburn, Nelson H. H. 1989. "Tourism: The Sacred Journey." In *Hosts and Guests: The Anthropology of Tourism*, edited by Valene E. Smith, 21–36. Philadelphia: University of Pennsylvania Press.

Graeber, David. 2002. *Toward an Anthropological Theory of Value*. New York: Palgrave.

Grandia, Liza. 2009. *Tz'aptz'ooq'eb': El Despojo Recurrente al Pueblo Q'eqchi'*. Guatemala City: AVANSCO.

Grandia, Liza. 2012. *Enclosed: Conservation, Cattle, and Commerce among the Q'eqchi' Maya Lowlanders*. Seattle: University of Washington Press.

Greenberg, J. H. 1990. "Numeral Classifiers and Substantival Number: Problems in the Genesis of a Linguistic Type," "Studies in Numerical Systems, I: Double Numeral Systems," "Dynamic Aspects of Word Order in the Numeral Classifier," "Generalizations about Numeral Systems." In *On Language*, edited by K. Denning and S. Kemmer, 166–93, 194–206, 227–40, 271–309. Stanford, CA: Stanford University Press.

Griffiths, Paul E. 1997. *What Emotions Really Are*. Chicago: University of Chicago Press.

Guyer, Jane. 2004. *Marginal Gains*. Chicago: University of Chicago Press.

Guyer, Jane, et al. 2010. "Introduction: Number as Inventive Frontier." *Anthropological Theory* 10 (1): 36–61.

Hacking, I. 1995. *Rewriting the Soul: Multiple Personalities and the Sciences of Memory*. Princeton, NJ: Princeton University Press.

Hardt, Michael, and Antonio Negri. 2000. *Empire*. Cambridge, MA: Harvard University Press.

Hart, Keith. 1989. "The Sexual Division of Labor." In *Women and the Sexual Division of Labor in the Caribbean*, edited by Keith Hart, 9–28. Kingston, Jamaica: The Consortium Graduate School of the Social Sciences.

Harvey, D. 1989. *The Condition of Postmodernity: An Enquiry into the Origins of Cultural Change*. Oxford: Blackwell.

Harvey, D. 1996. *Justice, Nature, and the Geography of Difference*. Malden, MA: Blackwell.

Harvey, D. 2005. *A Brief History of Neoliberalism*. Oxford: Oxford University Press.

Heilbron, J. L. 1990. "The Measure of Enlightenment." In *The Quantifying Spirit in the Eighteenth Century*, edited by T. Frangsmyr, J. L. Heilbron, and R. E. Rider, 207–42. Berkeley: University of California Press.

Hill, Jane H., and Bruce Mannheim. 1992. "Language and World View." *Annual Review of Anthropology* 21: 381–406.

Hipwell, W. 2007. "Taiwan Aboriginal Ecotourism: Tanayiku Natural Ecology Park." *Annals of Tourism Research* 34: 876–97.

Howard, M. C. 1975. *Ethnicity in Southern Belize: The Kekchi and the Mopan*. Museum Brief 21. Columbia: Curators of the University of Missouri.

IWGIA. 1978. *Guatemala 1978: The Massacre at Panzos*. International Work Group for Indigenous Affairs 33. Copenhagen: IWGIA.

Jakobson, Roman. 1990a. "Shifters and Verbal Categories." In *On Language*, edited by Linda R. Waugh and Monique Monville-Burston, 386–92. Cambridge, MA: Harvard University Press.

Jakobson, Roman. 1990b. "The Speech Event and the Functions of Language." In *On Language*, edited by Linda R. Waugh and Monique Monville-Burston, 69–70. Cambridge, MA: Harvard University Press.

James, William. 1975. "The Experience of Time." In *The Human Experience of Time: The Development of Its Philosophical Meaning*, edited by Charles M. Sherover, 367–86. New York: New York University Press.

James, William. 1985. "The Self." In *Psychology: The Briefer Course*, 43–83. Notre Dame, IN: University of Notre Dame Press.

Kaufman, William. 1974. *Idiomas de Mesoamérica*. Guatemala: Seminario de Integración Social.

Keane, Webb. 2003. "Semiotics and the Social Analysis of Material Things." *Language and Communication* 23: 409–25.

Keil, Frank C. 1989. *Concepts, Kinds, and Cognitive Development*. Cambridge, MA: MIT Press.

King, A. R. 1974. *Coban and the Verapaz: History and Cultural Process in Northern Guatemala*. Middle American Research Institute Publication 37. New Orleans: Tulane University Press.

Kockelman, Paul. 1999a. "Poetic Function and Logical Form, Ideal Languages and Forms of Life." *Chicago Anthropology Exchange* 29: 34–50.

Kockelman, Paul. 1999b. "Shifting Liaisons and Lasting Salience: The Collection of Copal among the Q'eqchi'-Maya." In *Research in Economic Anthropology*, edited by B. Issac, 20, 163–94. Greenwich, CT: JAI.

Kockelman, Paul. 2002. "Minding Language and Measuring Labor: Stance and Subjectivity under Neoliberal Globalization." PhD diss., University of Chicago.

Kockelman, Paul. 2003. "The Meaning of Interjections in Q'eqchi'-Maya: From Emotive Reaction to Social and Discursive Action." *Current Anthropology* 44 (4): 467–90.

Kockelman, Paul. 2005. "The Semiotic Stance." *Semiotica* 157: 233–304.

Kockelman, Paul. 2006. "A Semiotic Ontology of the Commodity. *Journal of Linguistic Anthropology* 16 (1): 76–102.

Kockelman, Paul. 2007a. "From Status to Contract Revisited: Value, Temporality, Circulation, and Subjectivity." *Anthropological Theory* 7 (2): 151–76.

Kockelman, Paul. 2007b. "Inalienable Possessions and Personhood in a Mayan Community." *Language in Society* 36: 343–69.

Kockelman, Paul. 2010a. "Enemies, Parasites, and Noise: How to Take Up Residence in a System without Becoming a Term in It." *Journal of Linguistic Anthropology* 20 (2): 406–21.

Kockelman, Paul. 2010b. *Language, Culture, and Mind: Natural Constructions and Social Kinds*. Cambridge: Cambridge University Press.

Kockelman, Paul. 2010c. "Value Is Life under an Interpretation." *Anthropology Theory* 19 (1): 149–62.

Kockelman, Paul. 2011. "Biosemiosis, Technocognition, and Sociogenesis: Selection and Significance in a Multiverse of Sieving and Serendipity." *Current Anthropology* 52 (5): 711–39.

Kockelman, Paul. 2012a. "The Ground, the Ground, the Ground: Why Archeology Is So 'Hard.'" *Yearbook of Comparative Literature* 58: 176–83.

Kockelman, Paul. 2012b. "Nth Nature." *Yearbook of Comparative Literature* 58: 176–83.

Kockelman, Paul. 2013a. *Agent, Person, Subject, Self: A Theory of Ontology, Interaction, and Infrastructure*. Oxford: Oxford University Press.

Kockelman, Paul. 2013b. "Information Is the Enclosure of Meaning: Cybernetics, Semiotics, and Alternative Theories of Information." *Language and Communication* 33: 115–27.

Kockelman, Paul. 2013c. "The Anthropology of an Equation: Sieves, Spam Filters, Agentive Algorithms, and Ontologies of Transformation." *HAU: Journal of Ethnographic Theory* 3 (3): 33–61.

Kockelman, Paul. 2015. "Four Theories of Things: Aristotle, Marx, Heidegger, and Peirce." *Signs in Society* 3 (2): 153–92.

Kockelman, Paul, and Anya Bernstein. 2013. "Semiotic Technologies, Temporal Reckoning, and the Portability of Value." *Anthropology Theory* 12 (3): 320–48.

Kula, Witold. 1986. *Measures and Men.* Princeton, NJ: University of Princeton Press.

Lamphere, Louise, and Michelle Zimbalist Rosaldo, eds. 1974. *Women, Culture, and Society.* Stanford, CA: Stanford University Press.

Larkin, Brian. 2004. "Degraded Images, Distorted Sounds: Nigerian Video and the Infrastructure of Piracy." *Public Culture* 16 (4): 289–314.

Larkin, Brian. 2008. *Signal and Noise: Media, Infrastructure and Urban Culture in Nigeria.* Durham, NC: Duke University Press.

Latour, Bruno. 1988. *The Pasteurization of France.* Translated by Alan Sheridan and John Law. Cambridge, MA: Harvard University Press.

Lave, Jean. 1988. *Cognition in Practice: Mind, Mathematics and Culture in Everyday Life.* Cambridge: Cambridge University Press.

Lazzarato, Maurizio. 1996. "Immaterial Labor." In *Radical Thought in Italy,* edited by Paolo Virno and Michael Hardt, 133–47. Minneapolis: University of Minnesota Press.

Leach, Edmund. 1964. "Anthropological Aspects of Language: Animal Categories and Verbal Abuse." In *New Directions in the Study of Language,* edited by Eric H. Lenneberg, 123–56. Cambridge: Cambridge University Press.

Levy, Robert I. 1973. *Tahitians: Mind and Experience in the Society Islands.* Chicago: University of Chicago Press.

Linton, R. 1936. *The Study of Man.* New York: Appleton, Century, and Crofts.

Little, Walter E. 2000. "Home as a Place of Exhibition and Performance: Mayan Household Transformations in Guatemala." *Ethnology* 39: 166–67.

Little, Walter E. 2004. "Performing Tourism: Maya Women's Strategies." *Signs* 29: 527–28.

Lockhart, J. 1992. *The Nahuas after the Conquest.* Stanford, CA: Stanford University Press.

Lucy, J. A. 1992. *Grammatical Categories and Cognition.* Cambridge: Cambridge University Press.

Lucy, J. A. 1993. "Reflexive Language and the Human Disciplines." In *Reflexive Language: Reported Speech and Metapragmatics,* edited by J. A. Lucy, 1–33. Cambridge: Cambridge University Press.

MacCannell, D. 1976. *The Tourist.* New York: Schocken Books.

Maine, H. S. [1866] 2002. *Ancient Law.* New Brunswick, NJ: Transaction.

Malinowski, B. [1922] 1984. *Argonauts of the Western Pacific.* Prospect Heights, IL: Waveland.

Manning, Paul. 2012. *The Semiotics of Drink and Drinking.* New York: Continuum.

Marx, Karl. 1967. *Capital.* Vol. 1. New York: International Publishers.

Marx, Karl. 2000. *Theories of Surplus Value*. Amherst, NY: Prometheus Books.

Maurer, Bill. 2005. *Mutual Life, Limited: Islamic Banking, Alternative Currencies, Lateral Reason*. Princeton, NJ: Princeton University Press.

Maurer, Bill. 2006. "The Anthropology of Money." *Annual Review of Anthropology* 35: 15–36.

Maurer, Bill. 2012a. "Late to the Party: Debt and Data." *Social Anthropology* 20 (4): 474–81.

Maurer, Bill. 2012b. "Mobile Money: Communication, Consumption and Change in the Payments Space." *Journal of Development Studies* 48 (5): 589–604.

Maurer, Bill, Taylor Nelms, and Stephen Rea. 2013. "Bridges to Cash: Channeling Agency in Mobile Money." *Journal of the Royal Anthropological Institute* 19 (1): 52–74.

Mauss, M. [1938] 1979. "A Category of the Human Mind: The Notion of Person, the Notion of 'Self.'" In *Sociology and Psychology: Essays by Marcel Mauss*, translated by B. Brewster, 57–94. London: Routledge and Kegan Paul.

Mauss, M. [1950] 1990. *The Gift*. Translated by W. D. Halls. New York: W. W. Norton.

Mead, George Herbert. 1934. *Mind, Self, and Society from the Standpoint of a Social Behavioralist*. Edited by Charles S. Morris. Chicago: University of Chicago Press.

Medin, Douglas L., and Scott Atran, eds. 1999. *Folkbiology*. Cambridge, MA: Bradford.

Meikle, S. 1995. *Aristotle's Economic Thought*. Oxford: Oxford University Press.

Miller, Kassandra Lynne. 2008. "Evaluating the Design and Management of Community-Based Eco-Tourism Projects in Guatemala." M.A. thesis, University of Montana.

Mondloch, J. L. 1980. "K'e?s: Quiche Naming." *Journal of Mayan Linguistics* 2: 9–25.

Mosaic. 2001. *Mosaic of Guatemala*. National magazine of ecotourism.

Munn, Nancy. 1992. *The Fame of Gawa*. Durham, NC: Duke University Press.

Nash, Dennison. 1989. "Tourism as a Form of Imperialism." In *Hosts and Guests: The Anthropology of Tourism*, edited by Valene L. Smith, 37–52. Philadelphia: University of Pennsylvania Press.

NFWF. 1999. *Progress Report on the National Fish and Wildlife Foundation of the Alta Verapaz Bird Habitat Conservation Project #98–196*. Submitted on July 16.

NFWF. 2000. *Progress Report on the National Fish and Wildlife Foundation of the Alta Verapaz Bird Habitat Conservation II, Project #99–222*. Submitted on January 16.

Orlove, Benjamin, and Stephen Brush. 1996. "Anthropology and the Conservation of Biodiversity." *Annual Review of Anthropology* 25: 329–52.

Parmentier, Richard J. 1994. "Peirce Divested for Nonintimates." In *Signs in Society: Studies in Semiotic Anthropology*, 3–22. Bloomington: Indiana University Press.

PC. 1997a. *Primer Informe de Turismo de Bajo Impacto.* Written by Carol Meyer and Carolina Russell, May 13.

PC. 1997b. *Segundo Informe de Turismo de Bajo Impacto.* Written by Carol Meyer and Carolina Russell, September 5.

PC. 1999. *Informe #3 de Turismo.* Written by Carol Meyer and Carolina Russell, February 1.

Pedroni, G. 1991. *Territorialidad Kekchi: Una Aproximación al Acceso a la Tierra; La Migración y la Titulación.* Debate 8. Guatemala City: FLASCO.

Peebles, Gustav. 2010. "The Anthropology of Credit and Debt." *Annual Review of Anthropology* 39: 225–40.

Peirce, C. S. 1934. *Collected Papers of Charles Sanders Peirce.* Vol. 5. Edited by Charles Hartshorne and Paul Weiss. Cambridge: Cambridge University Press.

Peirce, C. S. 1955a. "Logic as Semiotic: The Theory of Signs." In *Philosophical Writings of Peirce,* edited by Justus Buchler, 98–119. New York: Dover.

Peirce, C. S. 1955b. "Pragmatism in Retrospect: A Last Formulation." In *Philosophical Writings of Peirce,* edited by Justus Buchler, 269–89. New York: Dover.

Peirce, C. S. 1955c. "The Principles of Phenomenology." In *Philosophical Writings of Peirce,* edited by Justus Buchler, 74–97. New York: Dover.

Peirce, C. S. [1867] 1992. "On a New List of Categories." In *The Essential Peirce,* vol. 1, *1867–1893,* edited by Nathan Hauser and Christian Kloesel, 1. Bloomington: Indiana University Press.

Polanyi, K. 1957. *The Great Transformation.* Boston: Beacon.

Porter, Theodore M. 1995. *Trust in Numbers: The Pursuit of Objectivity in Science and Public Life.* Princeton, NJ: Princeton University Press.

Postone, Moishe. 1993. *Time, Labor, and Social Domination: A Reinterpretation of Marx's Critical Theory.* Cambridge: Cambridge University Press.

PQ. 1990. "Proyecto Quetzal." Undated manuscript found in the files of Project Eco-Quetzal. Written by David Unger, Nikolaus Döring, and Laura Scott.

Quine, Willard V. 1969a. "Natural Kinds." In *Ontological Relativity and Other Essays,* 114–38. New York: Columbia University Press.

Quine, Willard V. 1969b. "Ontological Relativity." In *Ontological Relativity and Other Essays,* 26–68. New York: Columbia University Press.

Reisinger, V. 1997. "Social Contact between Tourists and Hosts of Different Cultural Backgrounds." In *The Earthscan Reader in Sustainable Tourism,* edited by Leslie France, 129–34. London: Earthscan.

Romero, Sergio. 2008. "Historia, migraciones y cambio lingüístico en Q'eqchi': Homogenización dialectal o resignificación de las diferencias?" In *Memorias del VI Congreso de Estudios Mayas.* Guatemala City: Universidad Rafael Landívar.

Romero, Sergio. 2012. "'They Don't Speak Our Language Right': Language Standardization, Power and Migration among the Lowland Q'eqchi' Maya." *Journal of Linguistic Anthropology* 22 (2): 21–42.

Rosaldo, Michelle Z. 1980. *Knowledge and Passion: Ilongot Notions of Self and Social Life*. Cambridge: Cambridge University Press.

Rotman, Brian. 1993. *Signifying Nothing: The Semiotics of Zero*. Stanford, CA: Stanford University Press.

Ruz Lluillier, A. 1973. *El Templo de las Inscripciones, Palenque*. Mexico: INAH, Universidad Autonoma de Mexico.

Saa Vidal, R. 1979. *Mapa de cobertura y uso actual de la tierra* [Map of land cover and present use]. Guatemala City: Secretaría General del Consejo Nacional de Planificación Económica.

Sacks, Karen. 1974. "Engels Revisited: Women, the Organization of Production, and Private Property." In *Women, Culture, and Society*, edited by Michelle Zimbalist Rosaldo and Louise Lamphere, 207–22. Stanford, CA: Stanford University Press.

Sahlins, Marshall. 1972. *Stone Age Economics*. New York: Aldine de Gruyter.

Sam Juárez, Miguel, et al. 1997. *Diccionario Q'eqchi'*. Antigua, Guatemala: Proyecto Lingüístico Francisco Marroquín.

Sanday, Peggy R. 1974. "Female Status in the Public Domain." In *Women, Culture, and Society*, edited by Michelle Zimbalist Rosaldo and Louise Lamphere, 189–206. Stanford, CA: Stanford University Press.

Sapir, Edward. [1923] 1985. "The Grammarian and His Language." In *Selected Writings in Language, Culture, and Personality*, edited by David G. Mandelbaum, 150–59. Berkeley: University of California Press.

Sapir, Edward. [1927] 1985. "The Unconscious Patterning of Behavior in Society." In *Selected Writings in Language, Culture, and Personality*, edited by David G. Mandelbaum, 544–59. Berkeley: University of California Press.

Sapir, Edward. [1944] 1985. "Grading: A Study in Semantics." In *Selected Writings in Language, Culture, and Personality*, edited by David G. Mandelbaum, 122–49. Berkeley: University of California Press.

Sapper, Karl. 1985. *The Verapaz in the Sixteenth and Seventeenth Centuries: A Contribution to the Historical Geography and Ethnography of Northeastern Guatemala*. Translated by Theodore E. Gutman. Institute of Archaeology Occasional Paper 13. Los Angeles: University of California–Los Angeles.

Sassen, Saskia. 1996. *Losing Control? Sovereignty in an Age of Globalization*. New York: Columbia University Press.

Schaffer, S. 1997. "Metrology, Metrication, and Victorian Values." In *Victorian Science in Context*, edited by B. Lightman, 438–74. Chicago: University of Chicago Press.

Schwartz, Norman B. 1990. *Forest Society: A Social History of Peten, Guatemala*. Philadelphia: University of Pennsylvania Press.

Secaira, Estuardo. 1992. "Conservation among the Q'eqchi'-Maya: A Comparison of Highland and Lowland Agriculture." M.A. thesis, University of Wisconsin, Madison.

Serres, Michel. [1980] 2007. *The Parasite*. Minneapolis: University of Minnesota Press.

Shweder, Richard A. 1994. "'You're Not Sick, You're Just in Love': Emotion as an Interpretive System." In *The Nature of Emotion: Fundamental Questions*, edited by Paul Ekman and Richard J. Davidson, 127–30. New York: Oxford University Press.

Silverstein, Michael. 1976. "Shifters, Linguistic Categories, and Cultural Description." In *Language, Culture, and Society: A Book of Readings*, edited by Ben G. Blunt, 187–221. Prospect Heights, IL: Waveland.

Silverstein, Michael. 2006. "Old Wine, New Ethnographic Lexicography." *Annual Review of Anthropology* 35: 481–96.

Silverstein, Michael, and Greg Urban. 1996. *The Natural History of Discourse*. Chicago: University of Chicago Press.

Smith, Adam. [1776] 1976. *An Inquiry into the Nature and Causes of the Wealth of Nations*. Chicago: University of Chicago Press.

Stewart, S. O. 1980. *Gramática Kekchí*. Guatemala: Editorial Académica Centro Americana.

Stoll, Otto. 1896. *Die Maya-Sprachen der Pokom-Gruppe (Die Sprache der K'e'kchi-Indianer)*. Leipzig: K. F. Köhler's Antiquarium.

Strathern, Marilyn. 1988. *The Gender of the Gift*. Berkeley: University of California Press.

Stronza, Amanda. 2001. "Anthropology of Tourism: Forging New Ground for Ecotourism and Other Alternatives." *Annual Review of Anthropology* 30: 261–83.

Tambiah, Stanley J. 1969. "Animals Are Good to Think and Good to Prohibit." *Ethnology* 8: 423–59.

Taylor, Charles. 1989. *Sources of the Self: The Making of Modern Identity*. Cambridge: Cambridge University Press.

Trouillot, Michel-Rolph. 2001. "The Anthropology of the State in the Age of Globalization." *Current Anthropology* 42 (1): 125–38.

Turner, Ethel, and Victor Turner. 1978. *Image and Pilgrimage in Christian Culture: Anthropological Perspectives*. New York: Columbia University Press.

Turner, Terrence. 1984. "Value, Production and Exploitation in Simple Non-Capitalist Societies." Unpublished manuscript.

Veblen, Thorstein. 1991. *The Theory of the Leisure Class*. New Brunswick, NJ: Transaction Publishers.

Veblen, Thorstein. [1898] 1998. "The Beginnings of Ownership." In *Essays in Our Changing Order*, edited by Leon Ardzrooni, 32–49. New Brunswick, NJ: Transaction.

Verran, Helen. 2001. *Science and an African Logic*. Chicago: University of Chicago Press.

Virno, Paolo, and Michael Hardt, eds. 1996. *Radical Thought in Italy*. Minneapolis: University of Minnesota Press.

von Schnitzler, Antina. 2008. "Citizenship Prepaid: Water, Calculability, and Techno-politics in South Africa." *Journal of Southern African Studies* 34 (4): 899–917.

von Schnitzler, Antina. 2013. "Traveling Technologies: Infrastructure, Ethical Regimes, and the Materiality of Politics in South Africa." *Cultural Anthropology* 28 (4): 670–93.

Wagner, R. 1996. *Los Alemanes en Guatemala, 1828–1944.* Guatemala City: Afanes.

Warren, K. B. 1989. *The Symbols of Subordination: Indian Identity in a Guatemalan Town.* Austin: University of Texas Press.

Weber, M. 1968. *Economy and Society.* Vol. 1. Edited by Guenther Roth and Claus Wittich. Berkeley: University of California Press.

Weber, M. [1930] 1992. *The Protestant Ethic and the Spirit of Capitalism.* Translated by T. Parsons. New York: Routledge.

West, Paige. 2006. *Conservation Is Our Government Now: The Politics of Ecology in Papua New Guinea.* Durham, NC: Duke University Press.

Whorf, Benjamin Lee. 1956. "The Relation of Habitual Thought and Behavior to Language." In *Language, Thought and Reality: John B. Carroll,* edited by John B. Carroll, 134–59. Cambridge, MA: MIT Press.

Wilce, James M. 2009. *Language and Emotion.* Cambridge: Cambridge University Press.

Wilk, Richard R. 1991. *Household Ecology: Economic Change and Domestic Life among the Kekchi Maya in Belize.* Tucson: University of Arizona Press.

Williams, Brent. 2001. "The Lanquin Cave and Semuc Champey." *Revue.*

Wilson, Michael R. 1972. "A Highland Maya People and Their Habitat: The Natural History, Demography and Economy of the K'ekchi'." PhD diss., University of Oregon.

Wilson, Richard. 1995. *Maya Resurgence in Guatemala.* Norman: University of Oklahoma Press.

Wolf, Erik R. 1954. "Closed Corporate Peasant Communities in Mesoamerica and Central Java." *Southwestern Journal of Anthropology* 13 (1): 1–18.

Yanagisako, Sylvia Junko. 1987. "Mixed Metaphors: Native and Anthropological Models of Gender and Kinship Domains." In *Gender and Kinship: Essays toward a Unified Analysis,* edited by Jane Fishburne Collier and Sylvia Junko Yanagisako, 86–118. Stanford, CA: Stanford University Press.

Zupko, R. 1990. *Revolution in Measurement: Western European Weights and Measures since the Age of Science.* Philadelphia: American Philosophical Association.

INDEX